SPIDER-WOMAN

KING IN BLACK

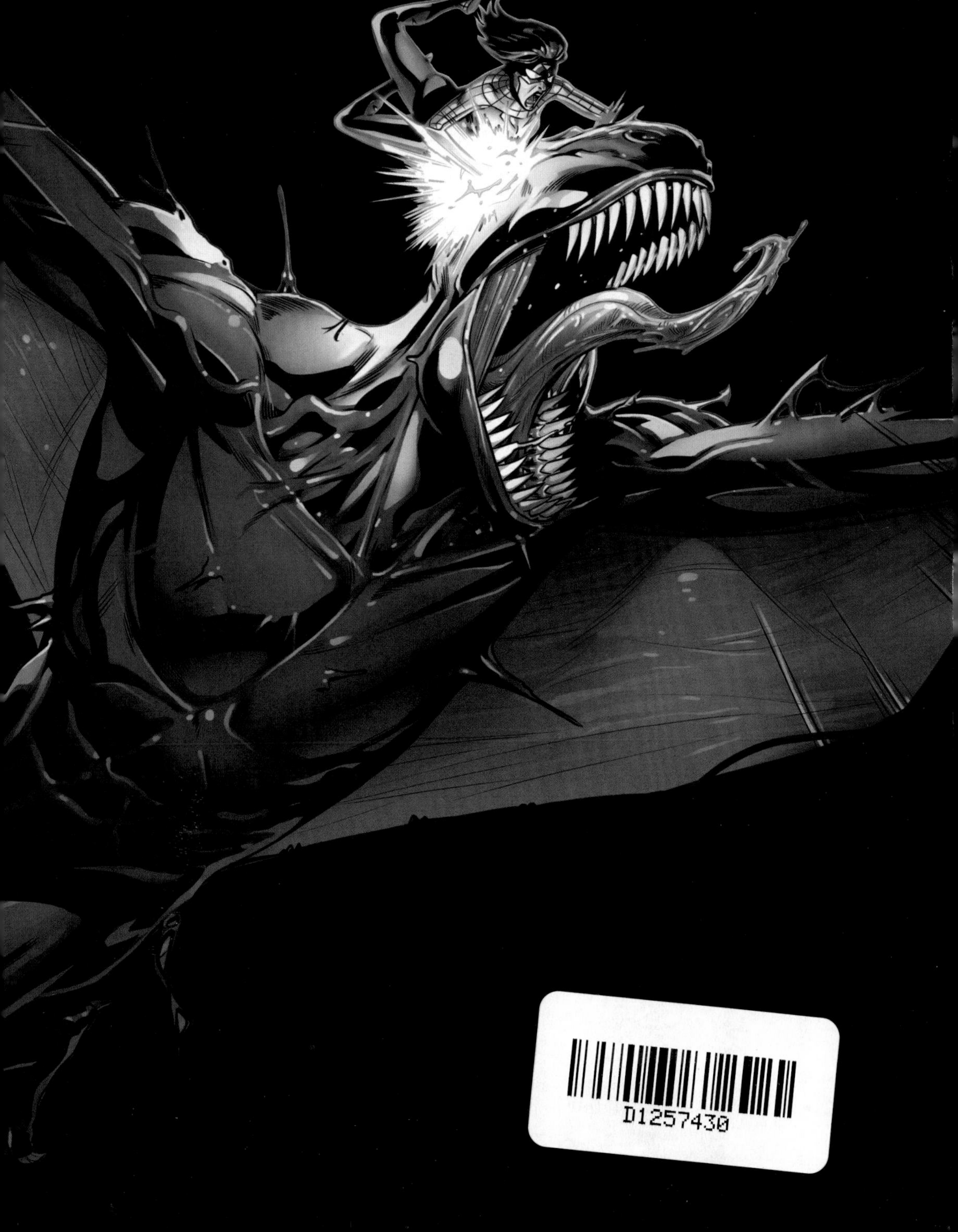

SPIDER-WOMAN

KING IN BLACK

WRITER
KARLA PACHECO

ARTIST
PERE PÉREZ

COLOR ARTIST
FRANK D'ARMATA

LETTERER *VC's TRAVIS LANHAM*
COVER ART *JUNGGEUN YOON*

ASSISTANT EDITOR *LINDSEY COHICK* & *SHANNON ANDREWS BALLESTEROS*
EDITOR *JAKE THOMAS*

COLLECTION EDITOR *JENNIFER GRÜNWALD*   VP PRODUCTION & SPECIAL PROJECTS *JEFF YOUNGQUIST*
ASSISTANT EDITOR: *DANIEL KIRCHHOFFER*   BOOK DESIGNER *STACIE ZUCKER* & *ADAM DEL RE*
ASSISTANT MANAGING EDITOR *MAIA LOY*   SVP PRINT, SALES & MARKETING *DAVID GABRIEL*
ASSISTANT MANAGING EDITOR *LISA MONTALBANO*   EDITOR IN CHIEF *C.B. CEBULSKI*

SPIDER-WOMAN VOL. 2: KING IN BLACK. Contains material originally published in magazine form as SPIDER-WOMAN (2020) #6-10. First printing 2021. ISBN 978-1-302-92752-3. Published by MARVEL WORLDWIDE, INC., a subsidiary of MARVEL ENTERTAINMENT, LLC. OFFICE OF PUBLICATION: 1290 Avenue of the Americas, New York, NY 10104. © 2021 MARVEL No similarity between any of the names, characters, persons, and/or institutions in this magazine with those of any living or dead person or institution is intended, and any such similarity which may exist is purely coincidental. **Printed in Canada.** KEVIN FEIGE, Chief Creative Officer; DAN BUCKLEY, President, Marvel Entertainment; JOE QUESADA, EVP & Creative Director; DAVID BOGART, Associate Publisher & SVP of Talent Affairs; TOM BREVOORT, VP, Executive Editor; NICK LOWE, Executive Editor, VP of Content, Digital Publishing; DAVID GABRIEL, VP of Print & Digital Publishing; JEFF YOUNGQUIST, VP of Production & Special Projects; ALEX MORALES, Director of Publishing Operations; DAN EDINGTON, Managing Editor; RICKEY PURDIN, Director of Talent Relations; JENNIFER GRUNWALD, Senior Editor, Special Projects; SUSAN CRESPI, Production Manager; STAN LEE, Chairman Emeritus. For information regarding advertising in Marvel Comics or on Marvel.com, please contact Vit DeBellis, Custom Solutions & Integrated Advertising Manager, at vdebellis@marvel.com. For Marvel subscription inquiries, please call 888-511-5480. **Manufactured between 4/9/2021 and 5/11/2021 by SOLISCO PRINTERS, SCOTT, QC, CANADA.**

10 9 8 7 6 5 4 3 2 1

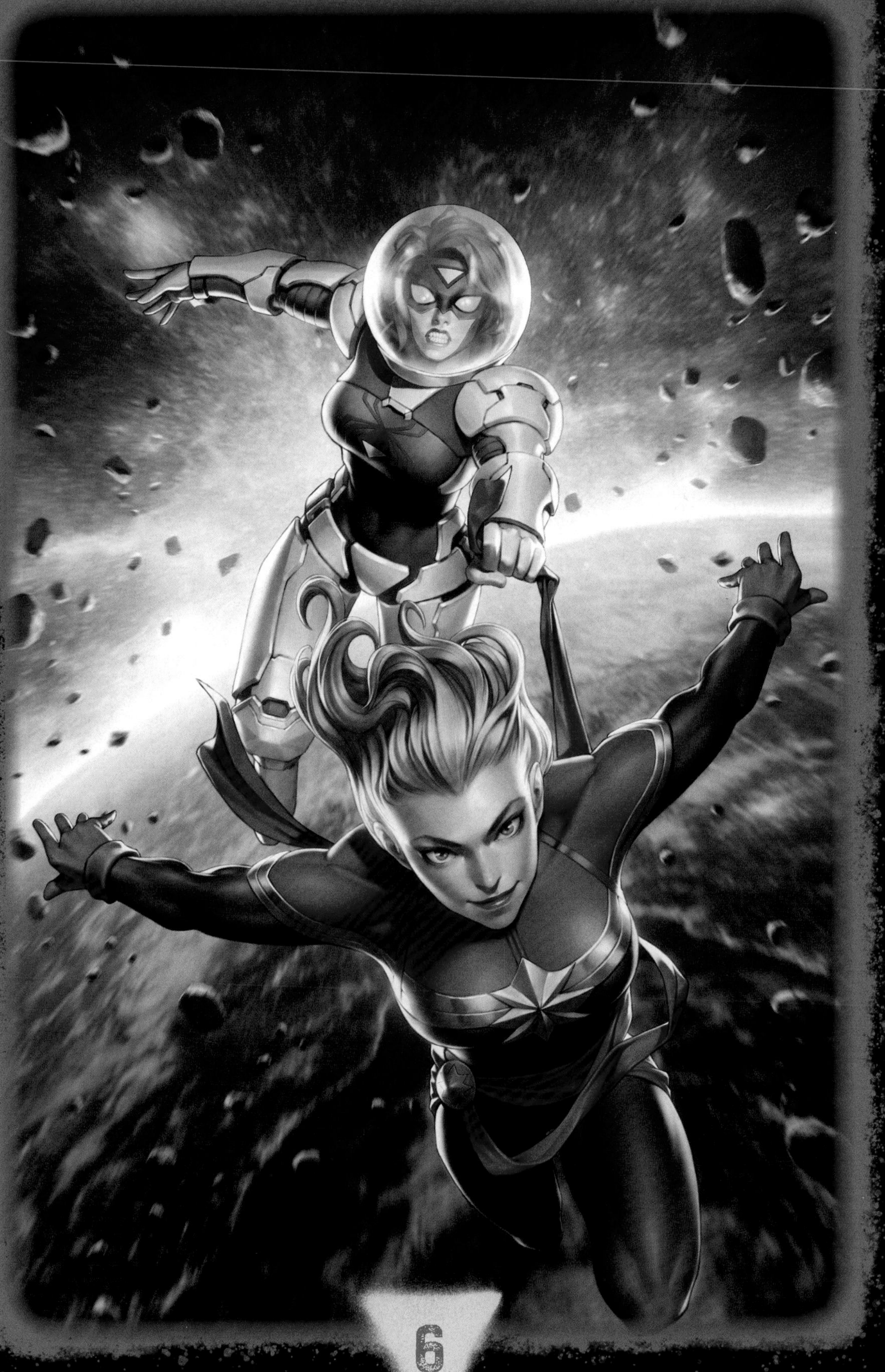

6

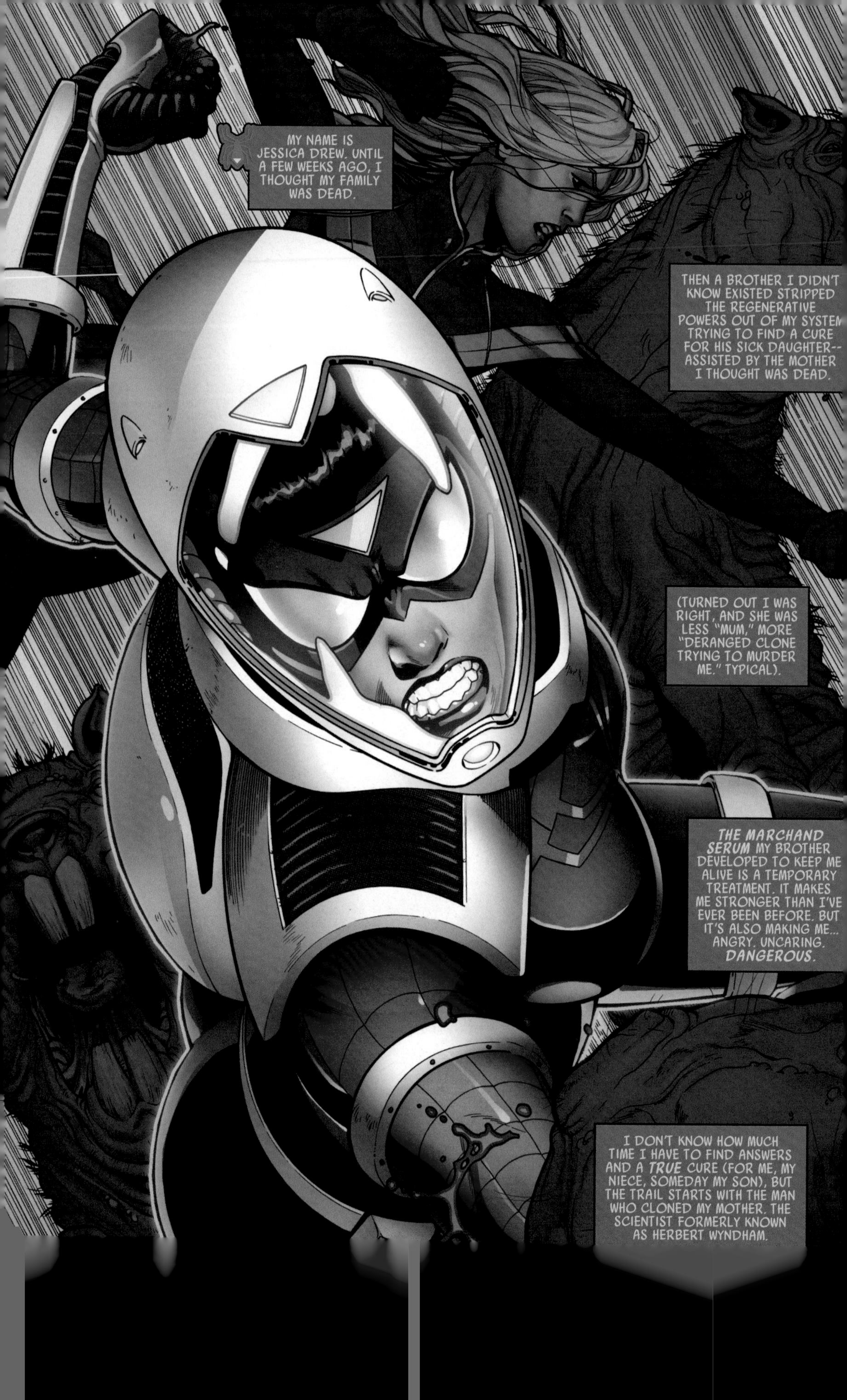
MY NAME IS JESSICA DREW. UNTIL A FEW WEEKS AGO, I THOUGHT MY FAMILY WAS DEAD.
THEN A BROTHER I DIDN'T KNOW EXISTED STRIPPED THE REGENERATIVE POWERS OUT OF MY SYSTEM TRYING TO FIND A CURE FOR HIS SICK DAUGHTER-- ASSISTED BY THE MOTHER I THOUGHT WAS DEAD.
(TURNED OUT I WAS RIGHT, AND SHE WAS LESS "MUM," MORE "DERANGED CLONE TRYING TO MURDER ME." TYPICAL).
THE MARCHAND SERUM MY BROTHER DEVELOPED TO KEEP ME ALIVE IS A TEMPORARY TREATMENT. IT MAKES ME STRONGER THAN I'VE EVER BEEN BEFORE. BUT IT'S ALSO MAKING ME... ANGRY. UNCARING. *DANGEROUS.*
I DON'T KNOW HOW MUCH TIME I HAVE TO FIND ANSWERS AND A *TRUE* CURE (FOR ME, MY NIECE, SOMEDAY MY SON), BUT THE TRAIL STARTS WITH THE MAN WHO CLONED MY MOTHER. THE SCIENTIST FORMERLY KNOWN AS HERBERT WYNDHAM.

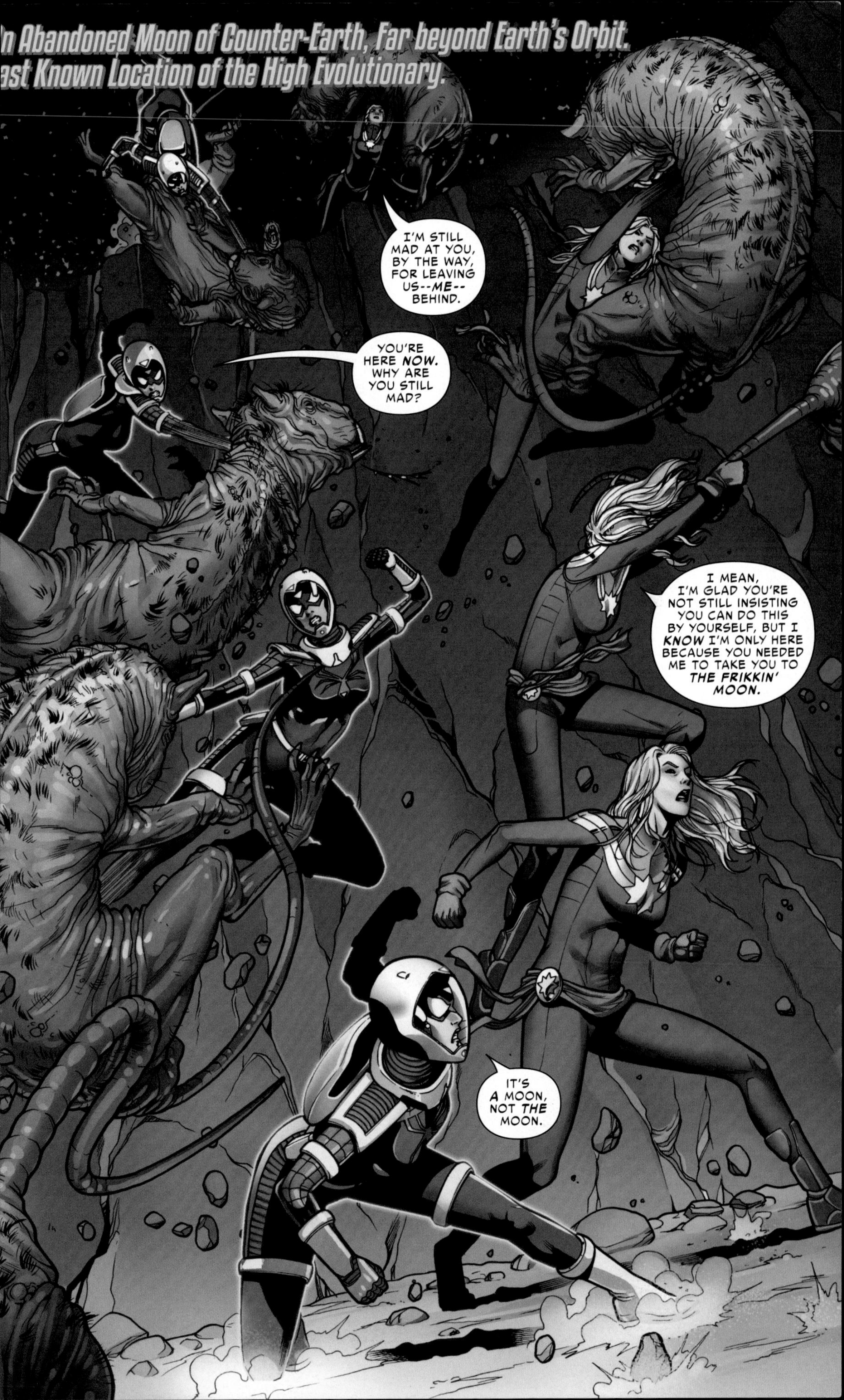
n Abandoned Moon of Counter-Earth, Far beyond Earth's Orbit.
ast Known Location of the High Evolutionary.
I'M STILL MAD AT YOU, BY THE WAY, FOR LEAVING US--ME--BEHIND.
YOU'RE HERE NOW. WHY ARE YOU STILL MAD?
I MEAN, I'M GLAD YOU'RE NOT STILL INSISTING YOU CAN DO THIS BY YOURSELF, BUT I KNOW I'M ONLY HERE BECAUSE YOU NEEDED ME TO TAKE YOU TO THE FRIKKIN' MOON.
IT'S A MOON, NOT THE MOON.

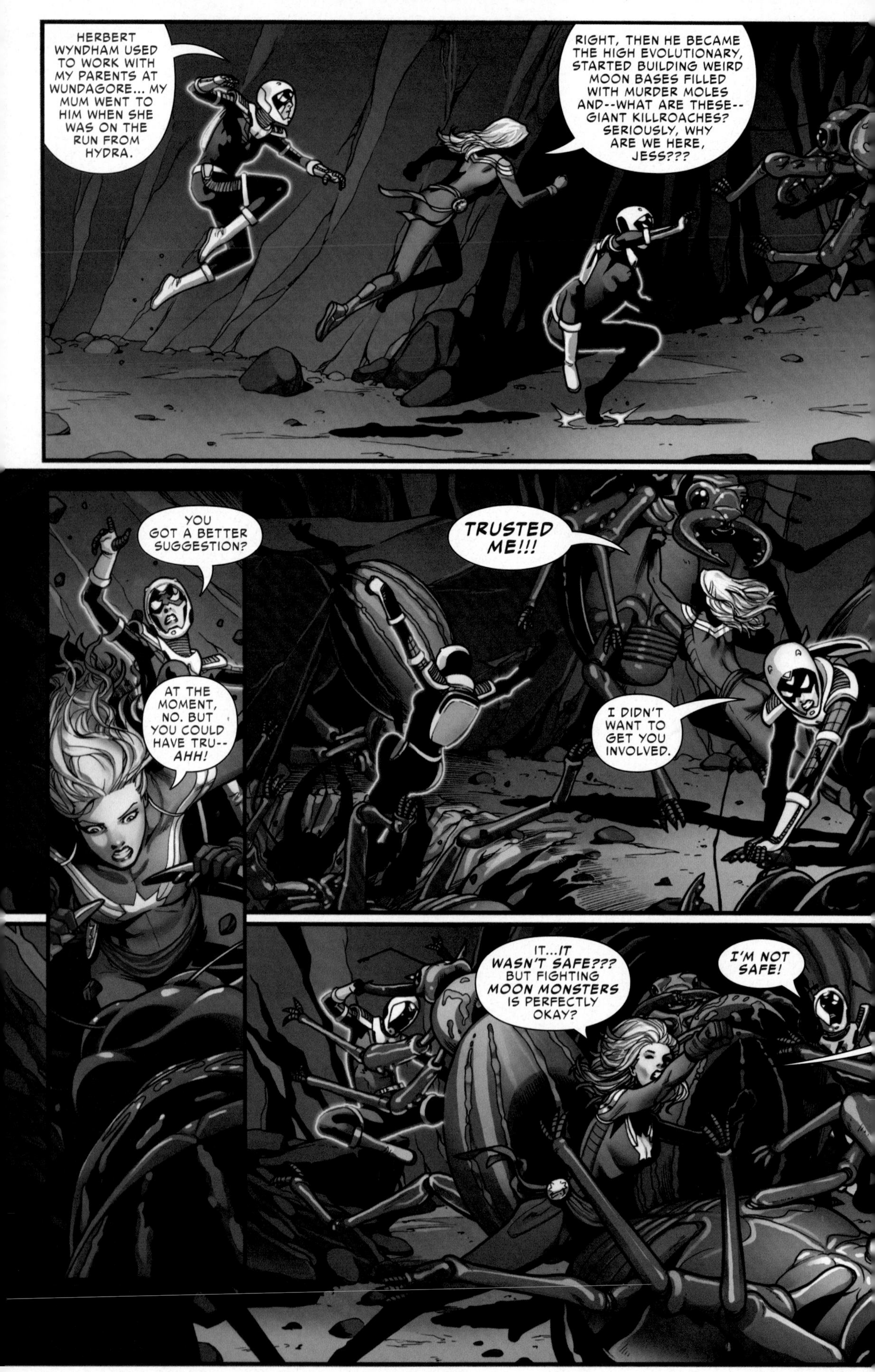
HERBERT WYNDHAM USED TO WORK WITH MY PARENTS AT WUNDAGORE... MY MUM WENT TO HIM WHEN SHE WAS ON THE RUN FROM HYDRA.
RIGHT, THEN HE BECAME THE HIGH EVOLUTIONARY, STARTED BUILDING WEIRD MOON BASES FILLED WITH MURDER MOLES AND--WHAT ARE THESE--GIANT KILLROACHES? SERIOUSLY, WHY ARE WE HERE, JESS???
YOU GOT A BETTER SUGGESTION?
AT THE MOMENT, NO. BUT YOU COULD HAVE TRU--*AHH!*
TRUSTED ME!!!
I DIDN'T WANT TO GET YOU INVOLVED.
IT...*IT* ***WASN'T SAFE???*** BUT FIGHTING ***MOON MONSTERS*** IS PERFECTLY OKAY?
I'M NOT SAFE!

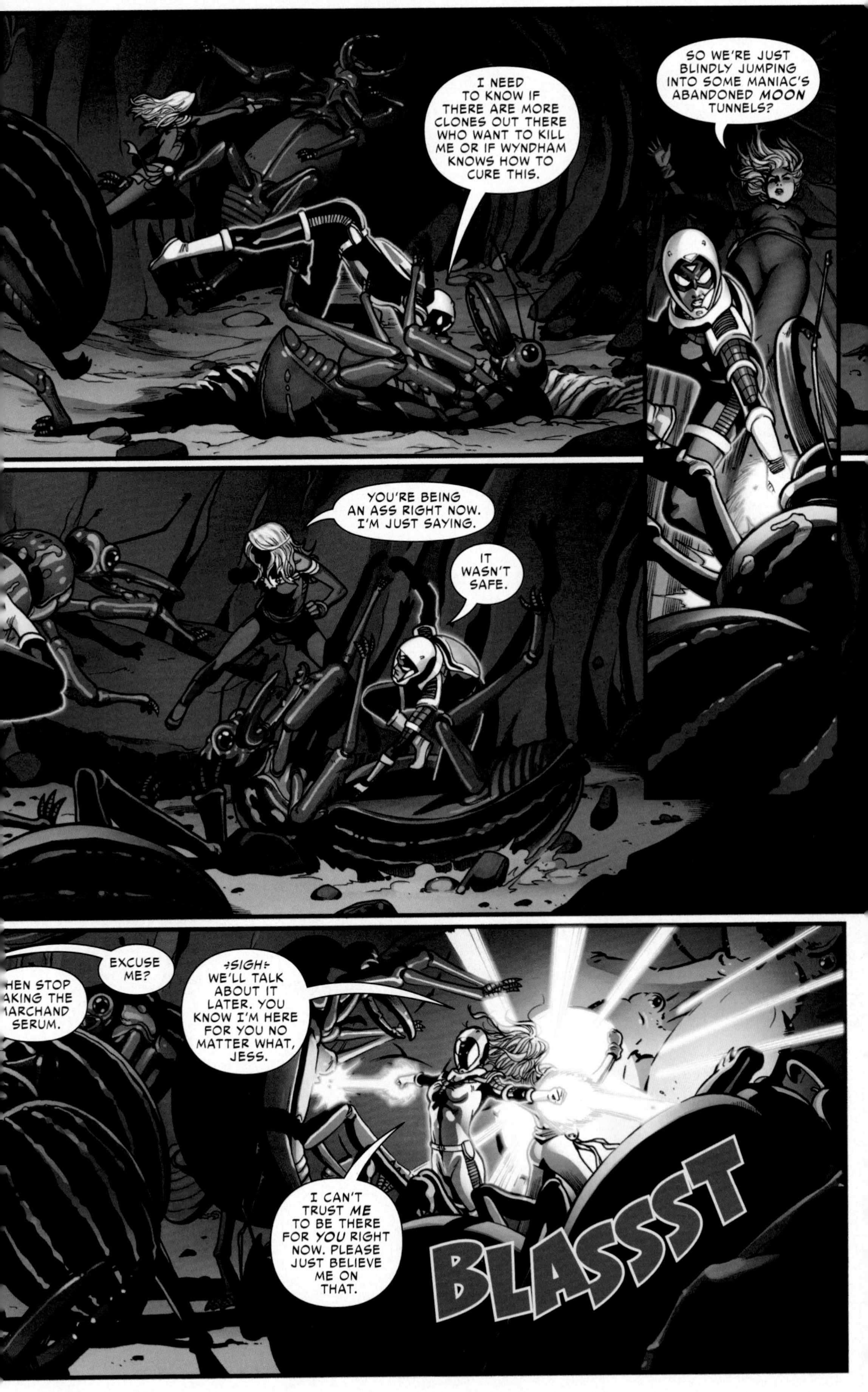
I NEED TO KNOW IF THERE ARE MORE CLONES OUT THERE WHO WANT TO KILL ME OR IF WYNDHAM KNOWS HOW TO CURE THIS.
SO WE'RE JUST BLINDLY JUMPING INTO SOME MANIAC'S ABANDONED *MOON* TUNNELS?
YOU'RE BEING AN ASS RIGHT NOW. I'M JUST SAYING.
IT WASN'T SAFE.
HEN STOP AKING THE ARCHAND SERUM.
EXCUSE ME?
SIGH WE'LL TALK ABOUT IT LATER. YOU KNOW I'M HERE FOR YOU NO MATTER WHAT, JESS.
I CAN'T TRUST *ME* TO BE THERE FOR *YOU* RIGHT NOW. PLEASE JUST BELIEVE ME ON THAT.
BLASSST

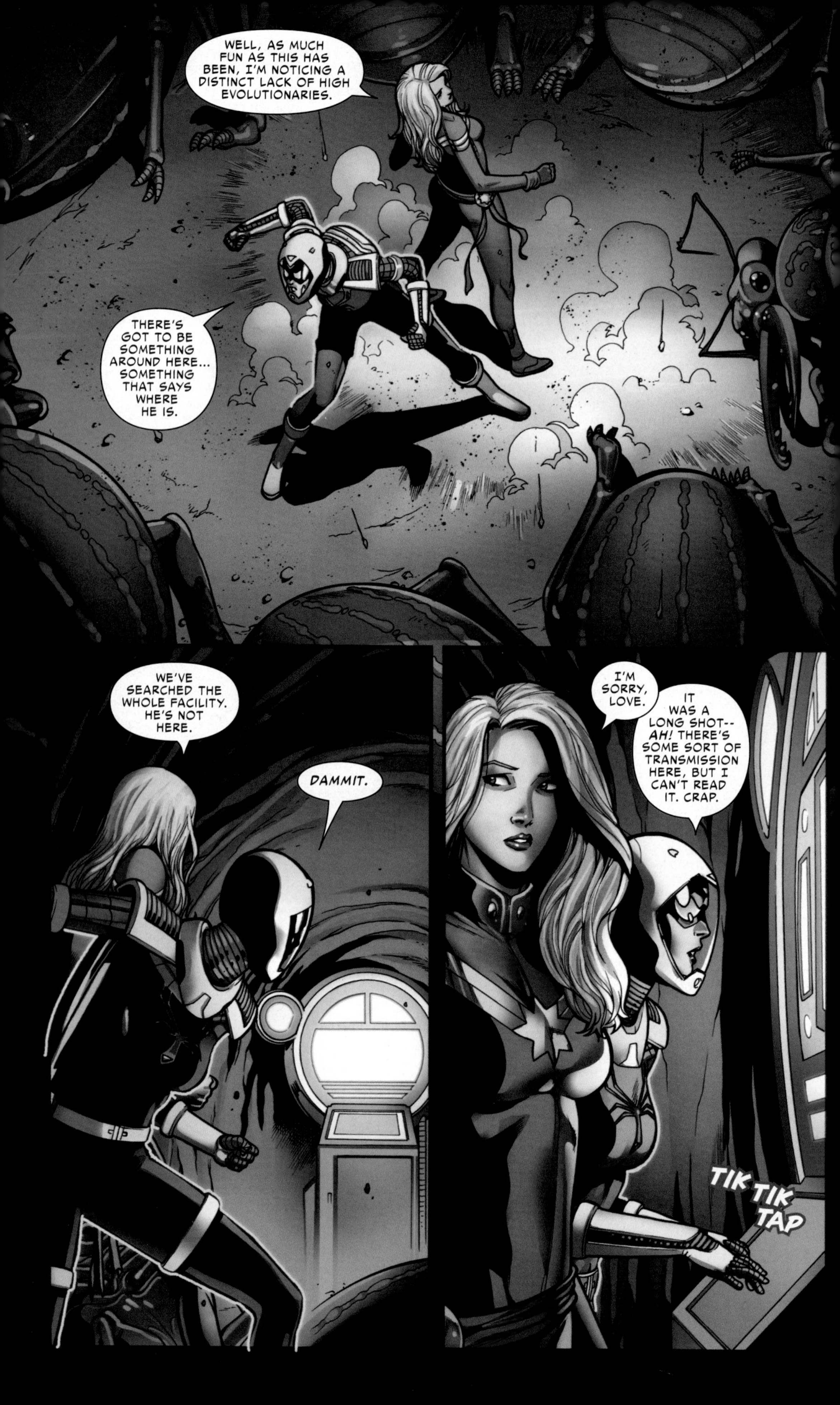

WELL, AS MUCH FUN AS THIS HAS BEEN, I'M NOTICING A DISTINCT LACK OF HIGH EVOLUTIONARIES.
THERE'S GOT TO BE SOMETHING AROUND HERE... SOMETHING THAT SAYS WHERE HE IS.
WE'VE SEARCHED THE WHOLE FACILITY. HE'S NOT HERE.
DAMMIT.
I'M SORRY, LOVE.
IT WAS A LONG SHOT-- AH! THERE'S SOME SORT OF TRANSMISSION HERE, BUT I CAN'T READ IT. CRAP.
TIK TIK TAP

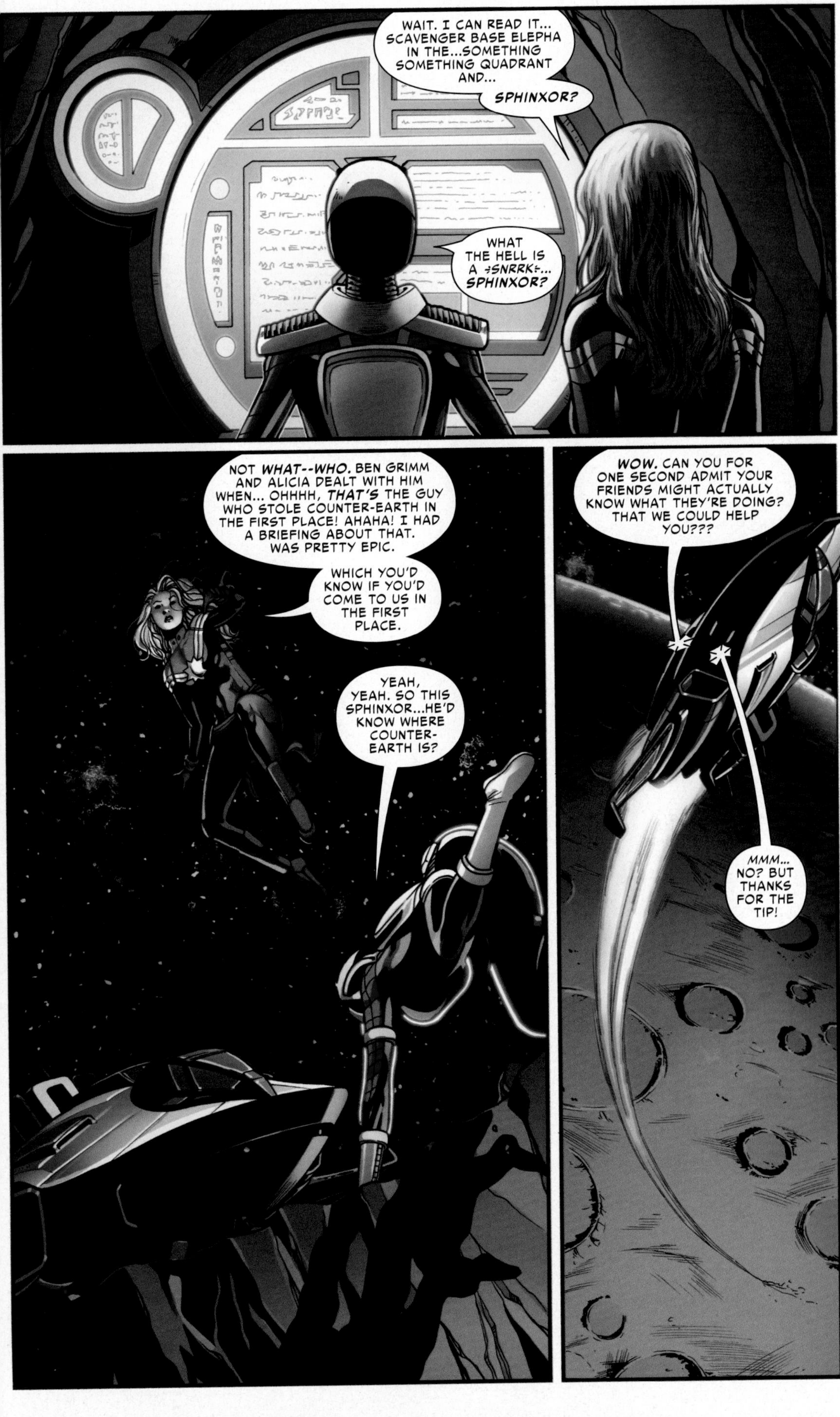

WAIT. I CAN READ IT... SCAVENGER BASE ELEPHA IN THE...SOMETHING SOMETHING QUADRANT AND...
SPHINXOR?
WHAT THE HELL IS A ÷SNRRK÷... SPHINXOR?
NOT WHAT--WHO. BEN GRIMM AND ALICIA DEALT WITH HIM WHEN... OHHHH, THAT'S THE GUY WHO STOLE COUNTER-EARTH IN THE FIRST PLACE! AHAHA! I HAD A BRIEFING ABOUT THAT. WAS PRETTY EPIC.
WHICH YOU'D KNOW IF YOU'D COME TO US IN THE FIRST PLACE.
YEAH, YEAH. SO THIS SPHINXOR...HE'D KNOW WHERE COUNTER-EARTH IS?
WOW. CAN YOU FOR ONE SECOND ADMIT YOUR FRIENDS MIGHT ACTUALLY KNOW WHAT THEY'RE DOING? THAT WE COULD HELP YOU???
MMM... NO? BUT THANKS FOR THE TIP!

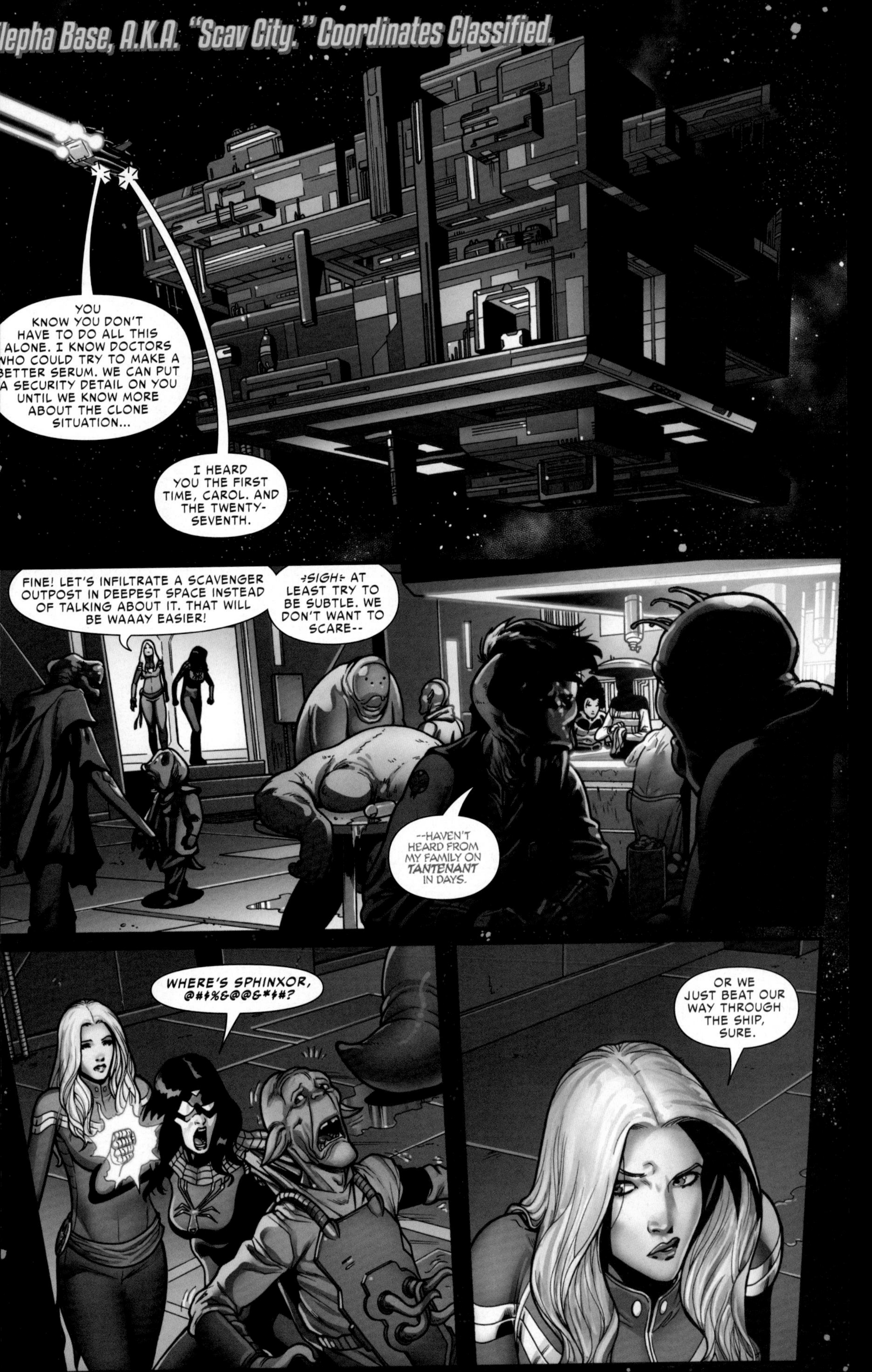

lepha Base, A.K.A. "Scav City." Coordinates Classified.
YOU KNOW YOU DON'T HAVE TO DO ALL THIS ALONE. I KNOW DOCTORS WHO COULD TRY TO MAKE A BETTER SERUM. WE CAN PUT A SECURITY DETAIL ON YOU UNTIL WE KNOW MORE ABOUT THE CLONE SITUATION...
I HEARD YOU THE FIRST TIME, CAROL. AND THE TWENTY-SEVENTH.
FINE! LET'S INFILTRATE A SCAVENGER OUTPOST IN DEEPEST SPACE INSTEAD OF TALKING ABOUT IT. THAT WILL BE WAAAY EASIER!
SIGH AT LEAST TRY TO BE SUBTLE. WE DON'T WANT TO SCARE--
--HAVEN'T HEARD FROM MY FAMILY ON TANTENANT IN DAYS.
WHERE'S SPHINXOR, @#$%&@@&*$#?
OR WE JUST BEAT OUR WAY THROUGH THE SHIP, SURE.

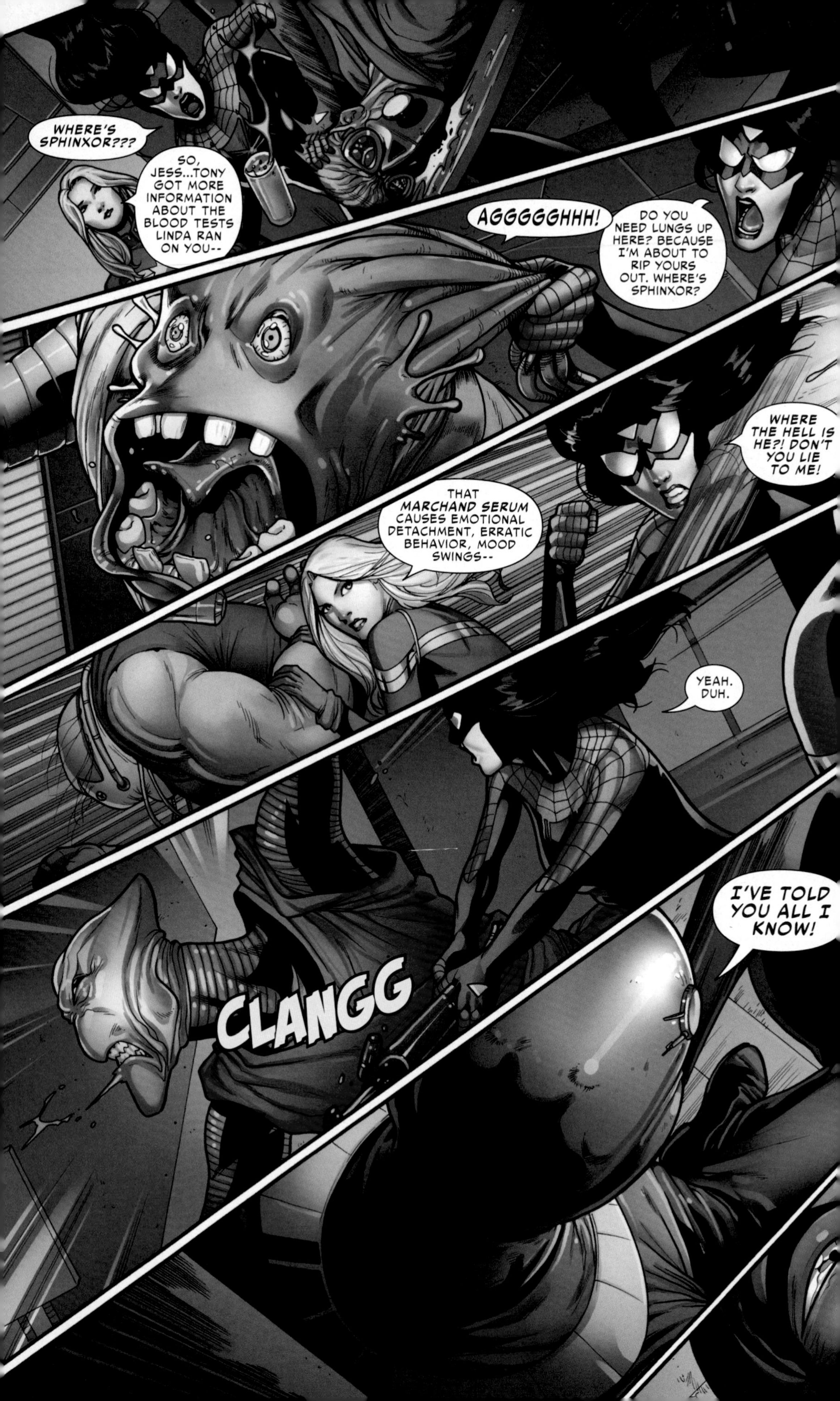
WHERE'S SPHINXOR???
SO, JESS...TONY GOT MORE INFORMATION ABOUT THE BLOOD TESTS LINDA RAN ON YOU--
AGGGGGHHH!
DO YOU NEED LUNGS UP HERE? BECAUSE I'M ABOUT TO RIP YOURS OUT. WHERE'S SPHINXOR?
WHERE THE HELL IS HE?! DON'T YOU LIE TO ME!
THAT MARCHAND SERUM CAUSES EMOTIONAL DETACHMENT, ERRATIC BEHAVIOR, MOOD SWINGS--
YEAH. DUH.
I'VE TOLD YOU ALL I KNOW!
CLANGG

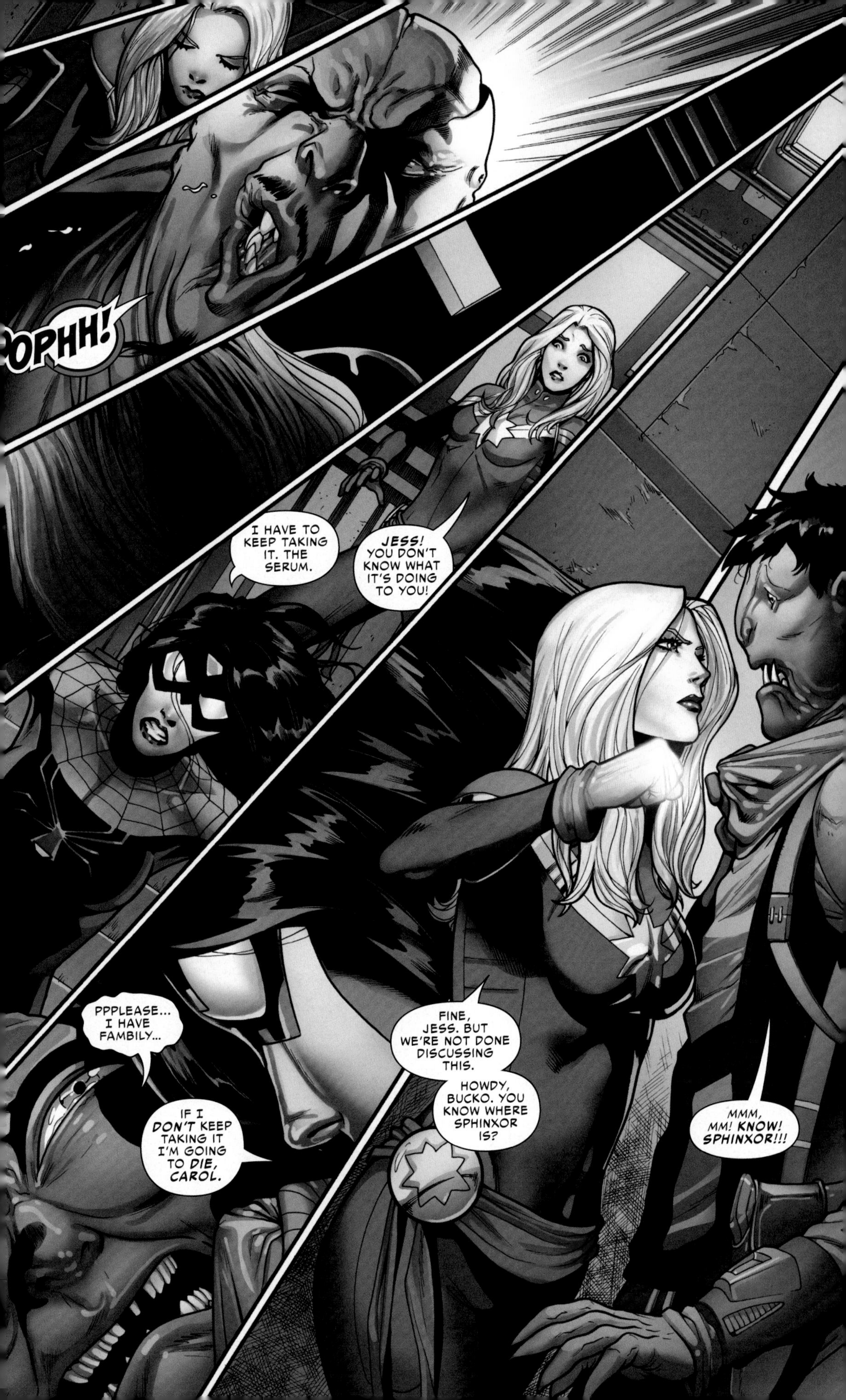
OPHH!
I HAVE TO KEEP TAKING IT. THE SERUM.
JESS! YOU DON'T KNOW WHAT IT'S DOING TO YOU!
PPPLEASE... I HAVE FAMBILY...
IF I DON'T KEEP TAKING IT I'M GOING TO DIE, CAROL.
FINE, JESS. BUT WE'RE NOT DONE DISCUSSING THIS.
HOWDY, BUCKO. YOU KNOW WHERE SPHINXOR IS?
MMM, MM! KNOW! SPHINXOR!!!

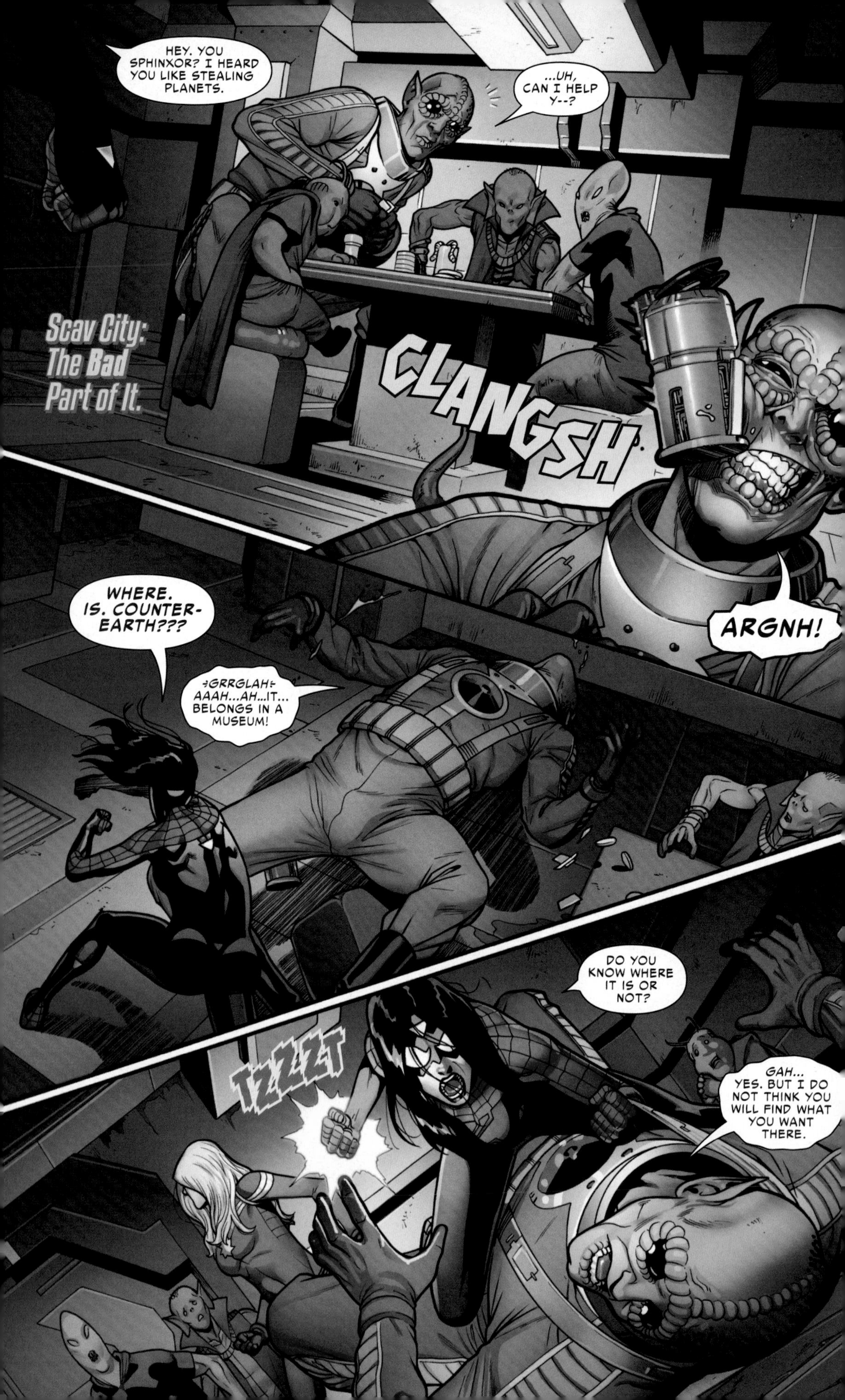
Scav City: The Bad Part of It.
HEY. YOU SPHINXOR? I HEARD YOU LIKE STEALING PLANETS.
...UH, CAN I HELP Y--?
CLANGSH
ARGNH!
WHERE. IS. COUNTER-EARTH???
GRRGLAH AAAH...AH...IT... BELONGS IN A MUSEUM!
DO YOU KNOW WHERE IT IS OR NOT?
TZZZT
GAH... YES. BUT I DO NOT THINK YOU WILL FIND WHAT YOU WANT THERE.

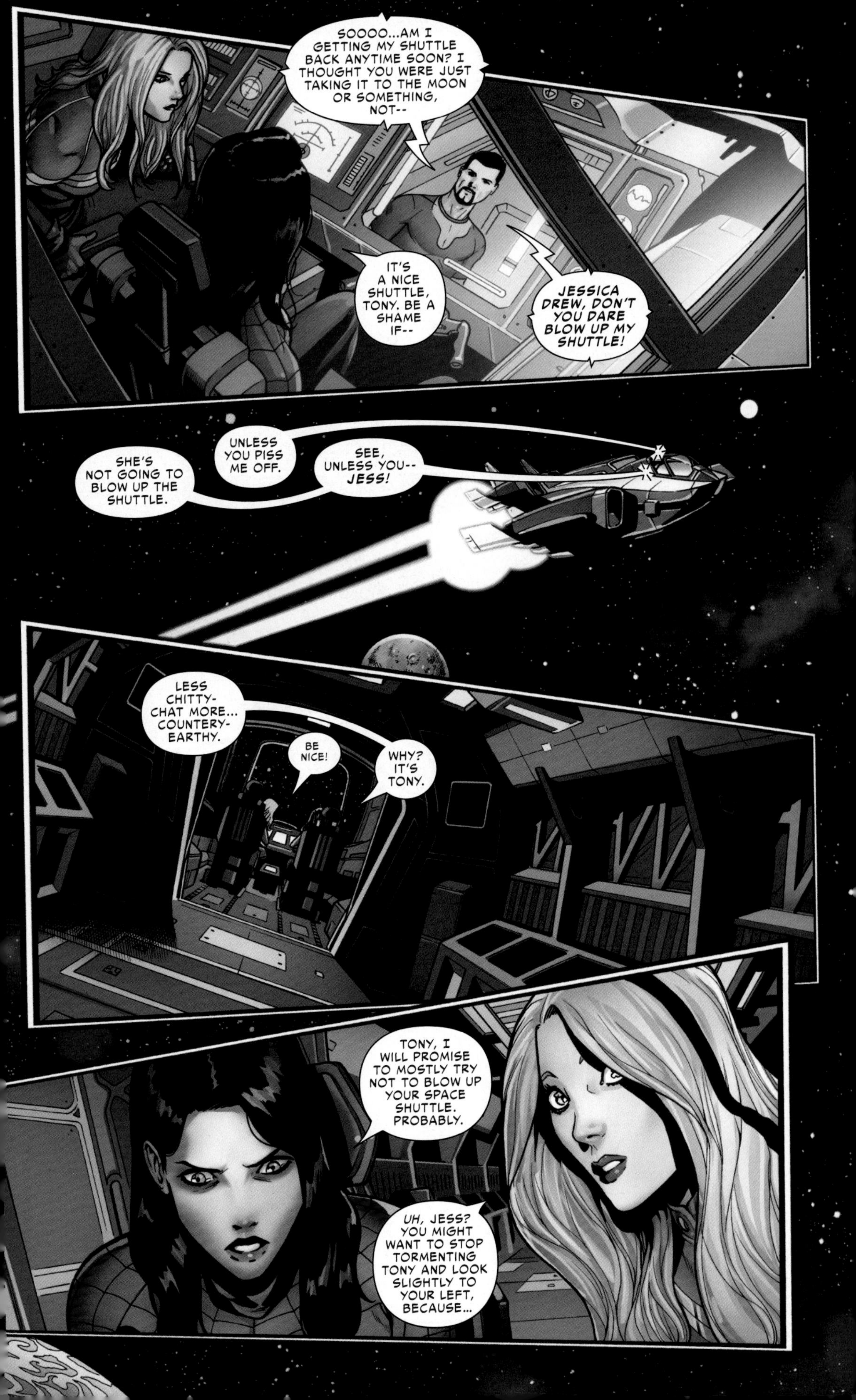

SOOOO...AM I GETTING MY SHUTTLE BACK ANYTIME SOON? I THOUGHT YOU WERE JUST TAKING IT TO THE MOON OR SOMETHING, NOT--
IT'S A NICE SHUTTLE, TONY. BE A SHAME IF--
JESSICA DREW, DON'T YOU DARE BLOW UP MY SHUTTLE!
SHE'S NOT GOING TO BLOW UP THE SHUTTLE.
UNLESS YOU PISS ME OFF.
SEE, UNLESS YOU-- JESS!
LESS CHITTY-CHAT MORE... COUNTERY-EARTHY.
BE NICE!
WHY? IT'S TONY.
TONY, I WILL PROMISE TO MOSTLY TRY NOT TO BLOW UP YOUR SPACE SHUTTLE. PROBABLY.
UH, JESS? YOU MIGHT WANT TO STOP TORMENTING TONY AND LOOK SLIGHTLY TO YOUR LEFT, BECAUSE...

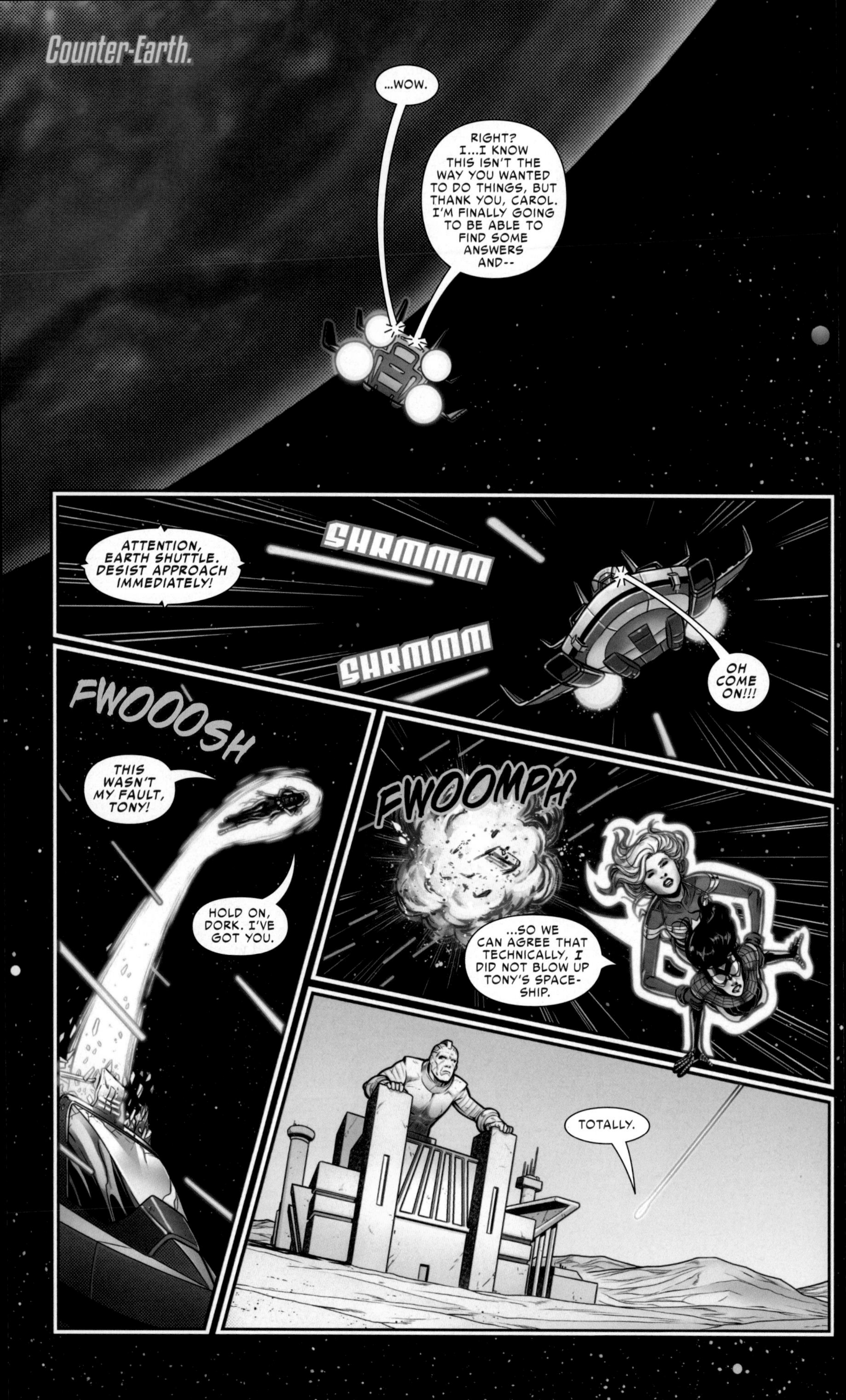
Counter-Earth.
...WOW.
RIGHT? I...I KNOW THIS ISN'T THE WAY YOU WANTED TO DO THINGS, BUT THANK YOU, CAROL. I'M FINALLY GOING TO BE ABLE TO FIND SOME ANSWERS AND--
ATTENTION, EARTH SHUTTLE. DESIST APPROACH IMMEDIATELY!
SHRMMM
SHRMMM
OH COME ON!!!
FWOOOSH
THIS WASN'T MY FAULT, TONY!
HOLD ON, DORK. I'VE GOT YOU.
FWOOMPH
...SO WE CAN AGREE THAT TECHNICALLY, I DID NOT BLOW UP TONY'S SPACE-SHIP.
TOTALLY.

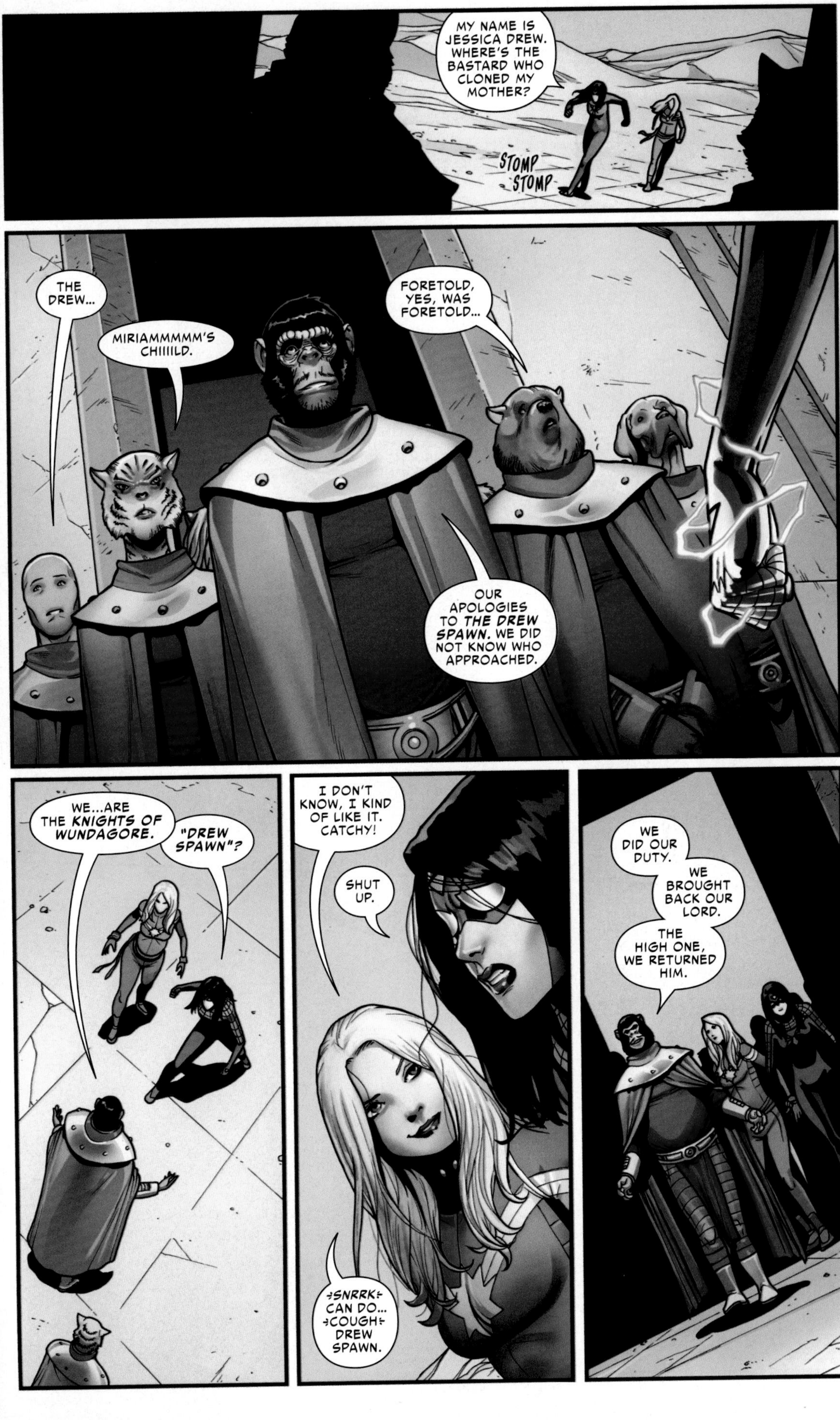
MY NAME IS JESSICA DREW. WHERE'S THE BASTARD WHO CLONED MY MOTHER?
STOMP STOMP
THE DREW...
MIRIAMMMMM'S CHIIIILD.
FORETOLD, YES, WAS FORETOLD...
OUR APOLOGIES TO THE DREW SPAWN. WE DID NOT KNOW WHO APPROACHED.
WE...ARE THE KNIGHTS OF WUNDAGORE.
"DREW SPAWN"?
I DON'T KNOW, I KIND OF LIKE IT. CATCHY!
SHUT UP.
SNRRK CAN DO... COUGH DREW SPAWN.
WE DID OUR DUTY.
WE BROUGHT BACK OUR LORD.
THE HIGH ONE, WE RETURNED HIM.

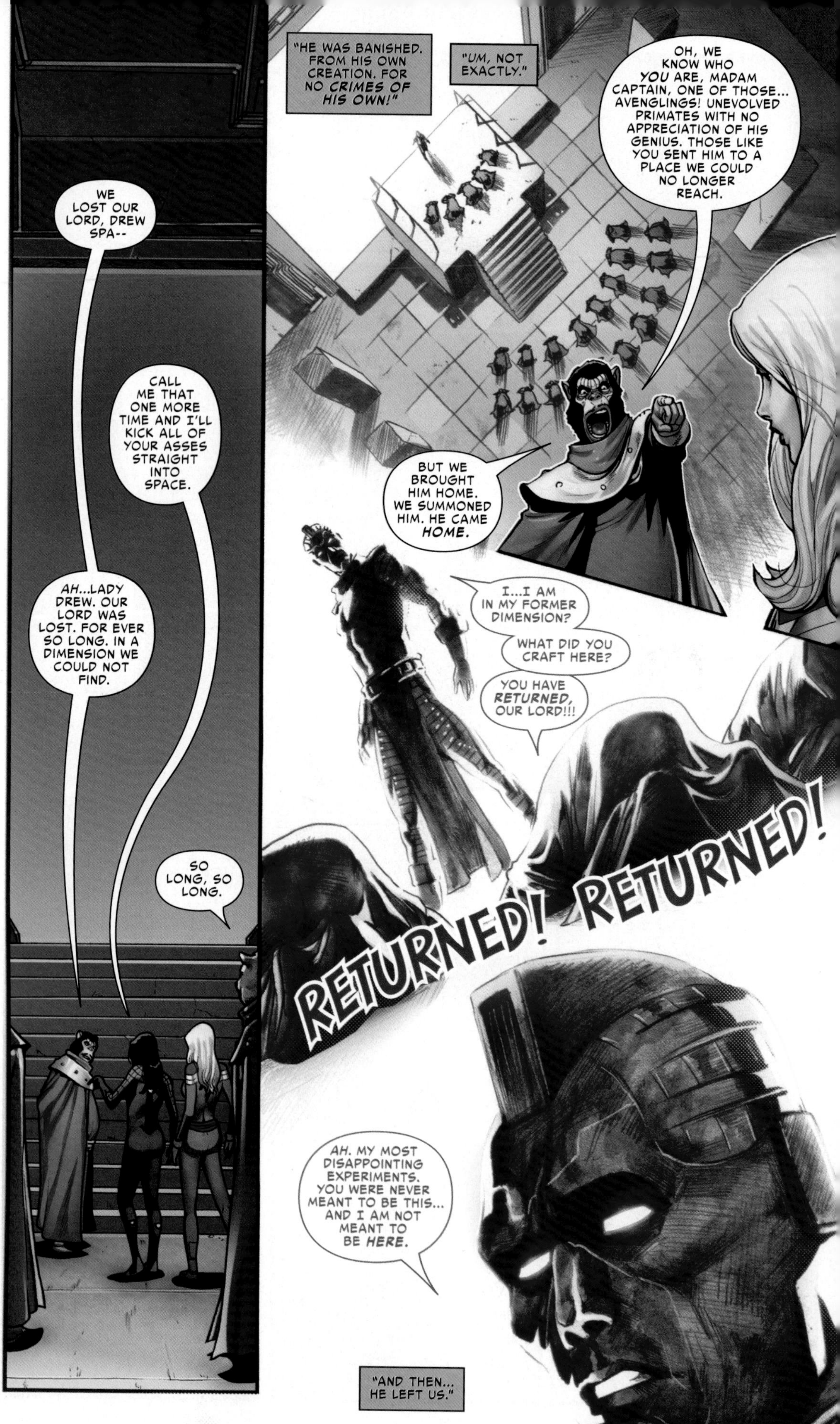
WE LOST OUR LORD, DREW SPA--
CALL ME THAT ONE MORE TIME AND I'LL KICK ALL OF YOUR ASSES STRAIGHT INTO SPACE.
AH...LADY DREW. OUR LORD WAS LOST. FOR EVER SO LONG. IN A DIMENSION WE COULD NOT FIND.
SO LONG, SO LONG.
"HE WAS BANISHED. FROM HIS OWN CREATION. FOR NO CRIMES OF HIS OWN!"
"UM, NOT EXACTLY."
OH, WE KNOW WHO YOU ARE, MADAM CAPTAIN, ONE OF THOSE... AVENGLINGS! UNEVOLVED PRIMATES WITH NO APPRECIATION OF HIS GENIUS. THOSE LIKE YOU SENT HIM TO A PLACE WE COULD NO LONGER REACH.
BUT WE BROUGHT HIM HOME. WE SUMMONED HIM. HE CAME HOME.
I...I AM IN MY FORMER DIMENSION?
WHAT DID YOU CRAFT HERE?
YOU HAVE RETURNED, OUR LORD!!!
RETURNED! RETURNED! RETURNED!
AH. MY MOST DISAPPOINTING EXPERIMENTS. YOU WERE NEVER MEANT TO BE THIS... AND I AM NOT MEANT TO BE HERE.
"AND THEN... HE LEFT US."

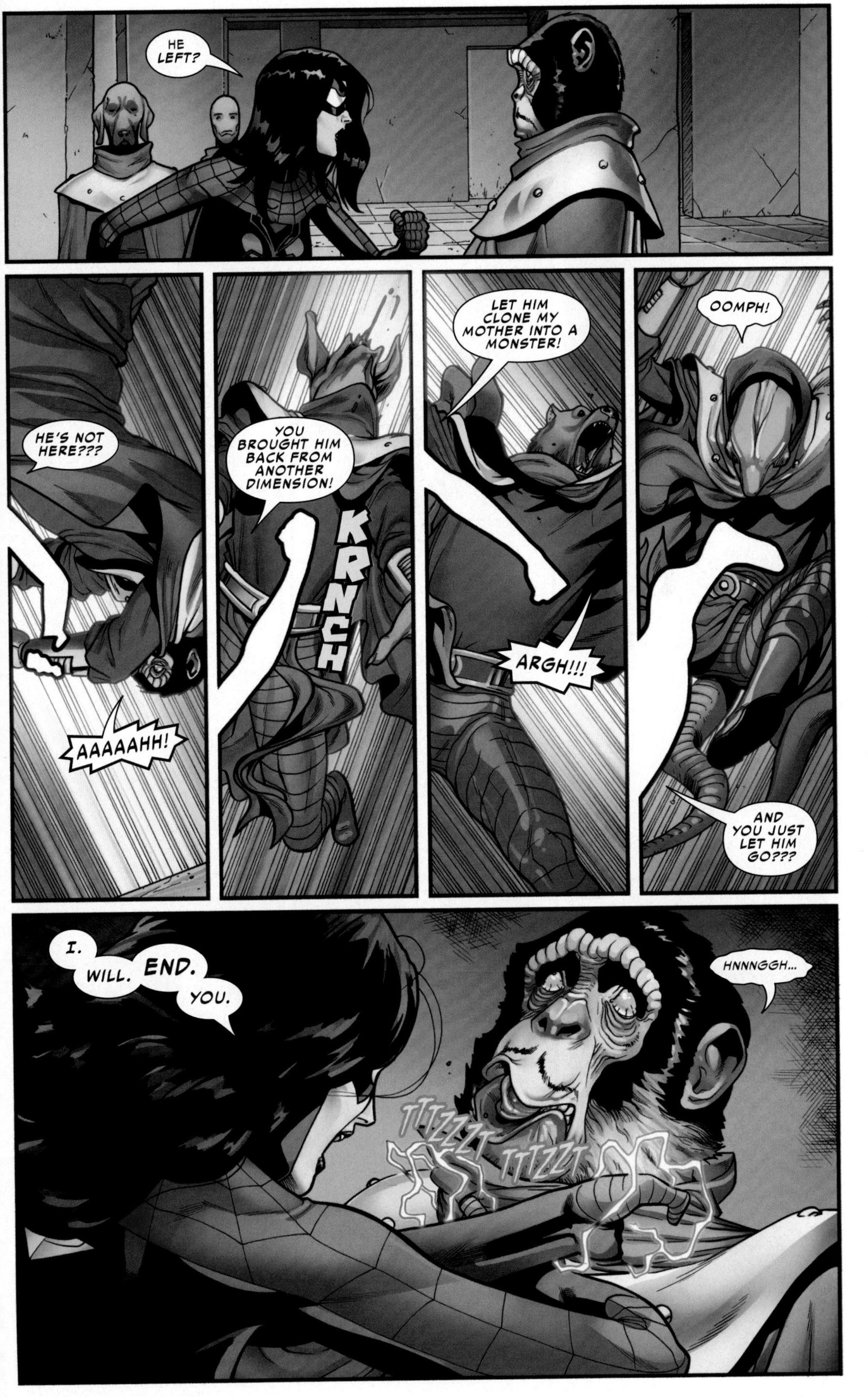
HE LEFT?
HE'S NOT HERE???
AAAAAHH!
YOU BROUGHT HIM BACK FROM ANOTHER DIMENSION!
KRNCH
LET HIM CLONE MY MOTHER INTO A MONSTER!
ARGH!!!
OOMPH!
AND YOU JUST LET HIM GO???
I. WILL. END. YOU.
HNNNGGH...
TTTZZZT
TTTZZZT

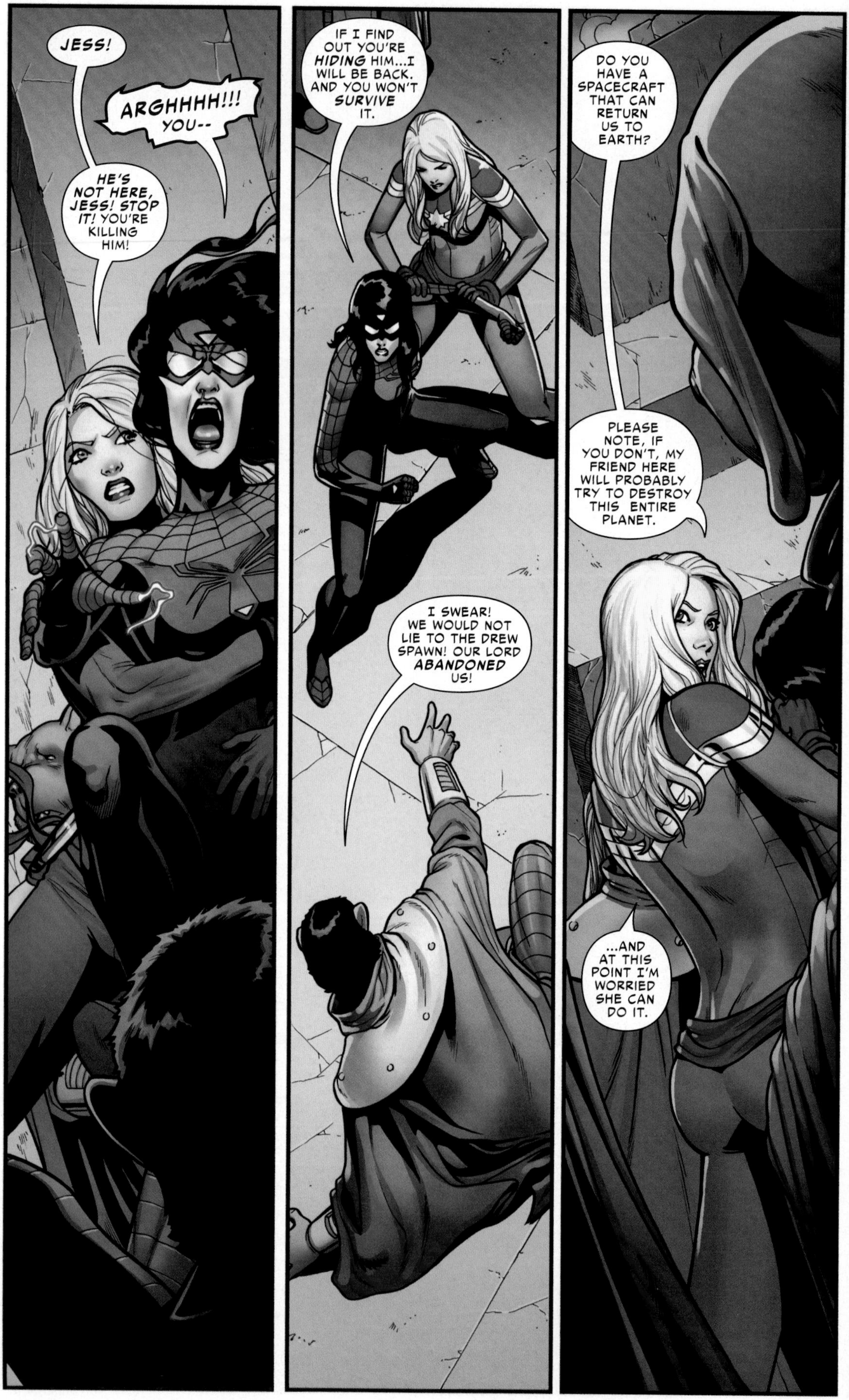
JESS!
ARGHHHH!!! YOU--
HE'S NOT HERE, JESS! STOP IT! YOU'RE KILLING HIM!
IF I FIND OUT YOU'RE HIDING HIM...I WILL BE BACK. AND YOU WON'T SURVIVE IT.
I SWEAR! WE WOULD NOT LIE TO THE DREW SPAWN! OUR LORD ABANDONED US!
DO YOU HAVE A SPACECRAFT THAT CAN RETURN US TO EARTH?
PLEASE NOTE, IF YOU DON'T, MY FRIEND HERE WILL PROBABLY TRY TO DESTROY THIS ENTIRE PLANET.
...AND AT THIS POINT I'M WORRIED SHE CAN DO IT.

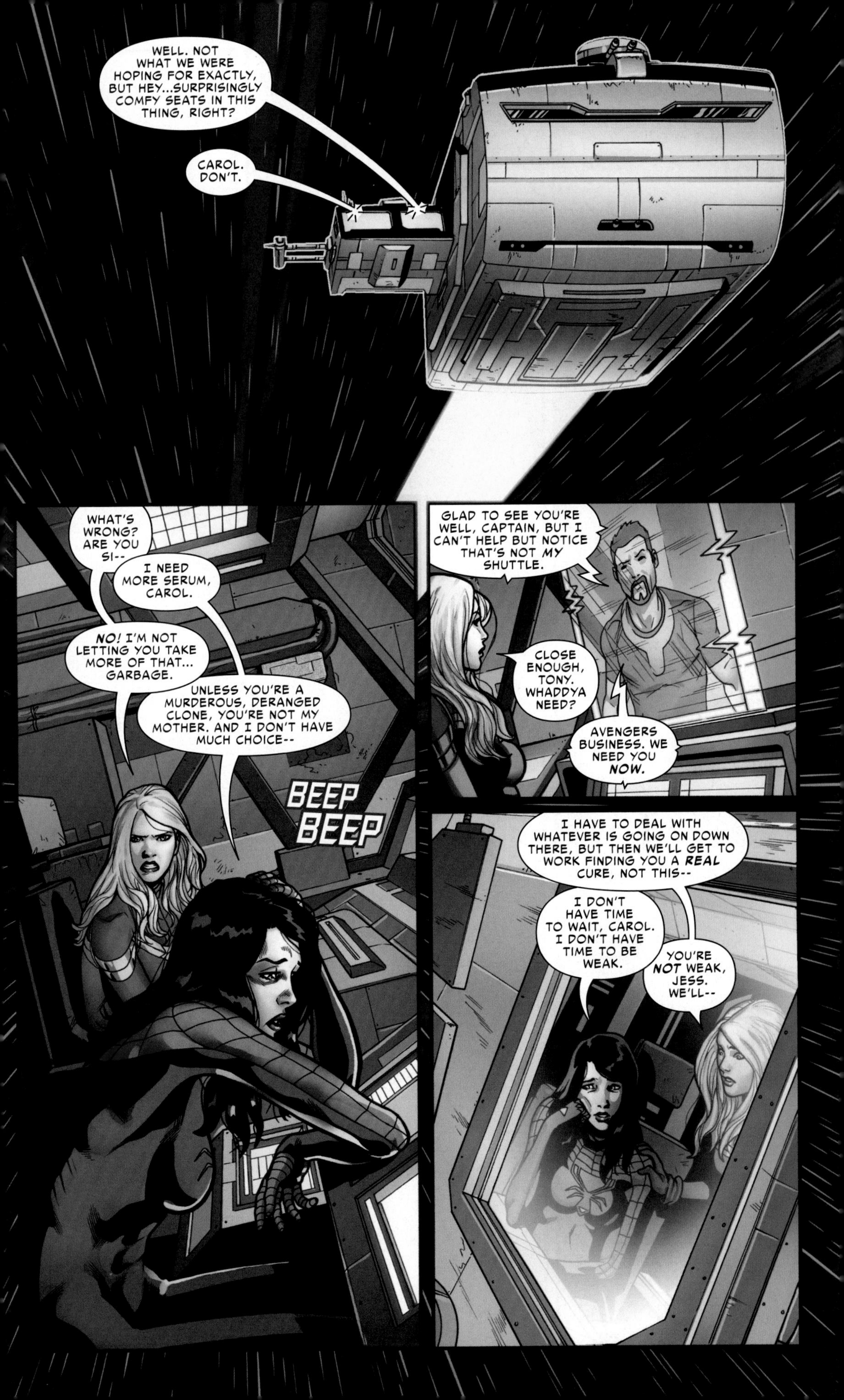
WELL. NOT WHAT WE WERE HOPING FOR EXACTLY, BUT HEY...SURPRISINGLY COMFY SEATS IN THIS THING, RIGHT?
CAROL. DON'T.
WHAT'S WRONG? ARE YOU SI--
I NEED MORE SERUM, CAROL.
NO! I'M NOT LETTING YOU TAKE MORE OF THAT... GARBAGE.
UNLESS YOU'RE A MURDEROUS, DERANGED CLONE, YOU'RE NOT MY MOTHER. AND I DON'T HAVE MUCH CHOICE--
BEEP BEEP
GLAD TO SEE YOU'RE WELL, CAPTAIN, BUT I CAN'T HELP BUT NOTICE THAT'S NOT MY SHUTTLE.
CLOSE ENOUGH, TONY. WHADDYA NEED?
AVENGERS BUSINESS. WE NEED YOU NOW.
I HAVE TO DEAL WITH WHATEVER IS GOING ON DOWN THERE, BUT THEN WE'LL GET TO WORK FINDING YOU A REAL CURE, NOT THIS--
I DON'T HAVE TIME TO WAIT, CAROL. I DON'T HAVE TIME TO BE WEAK.
YOU'RE NOT WEAK, JESS. WE'LL--

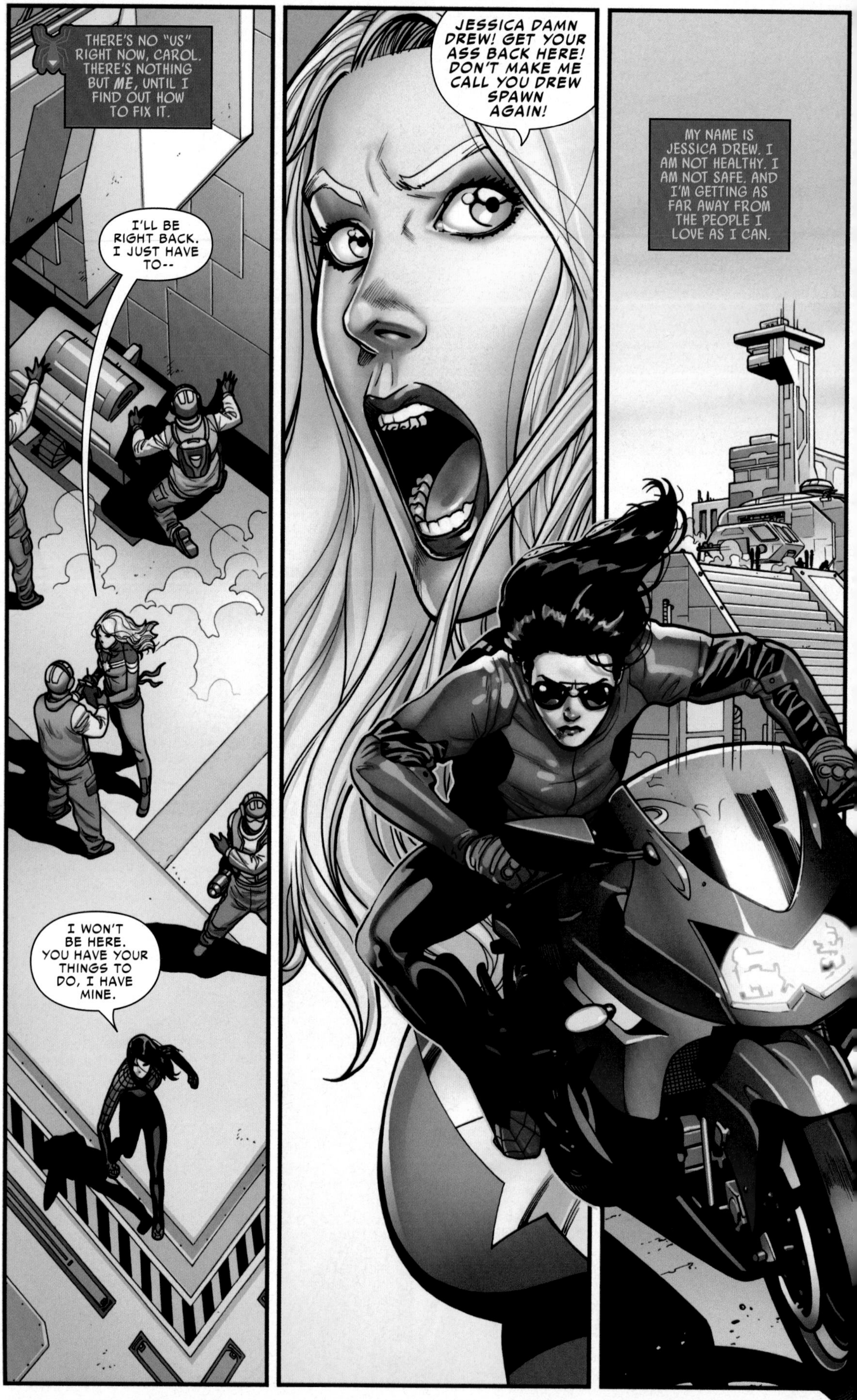
THERE'S NO "US" RIGHT NOW, CAROL. THERE'S NOTHING BUT ME, UNTIL I FIND OUT HOW TO FIX IT.
I'LL BE RIGHT BACK. I JUST HAVE TO--
I WON'T BE HERE. YOU HAVE YOUR THINGS TO DO, I HAVE MINE.
JESSICA DAMN DREW! GET YOUR ASS BACK HERE! DON'T MAKE ME CALL YOU DREW SPAWN AGAIN!
MY NAME IS JESSICA DREW. I AM NOT HEALTHY. I AM NOT SAFE. AND I'M GETTING AS FAR AWAY FROM THE PEOPLE I LOVE AS I CAN.

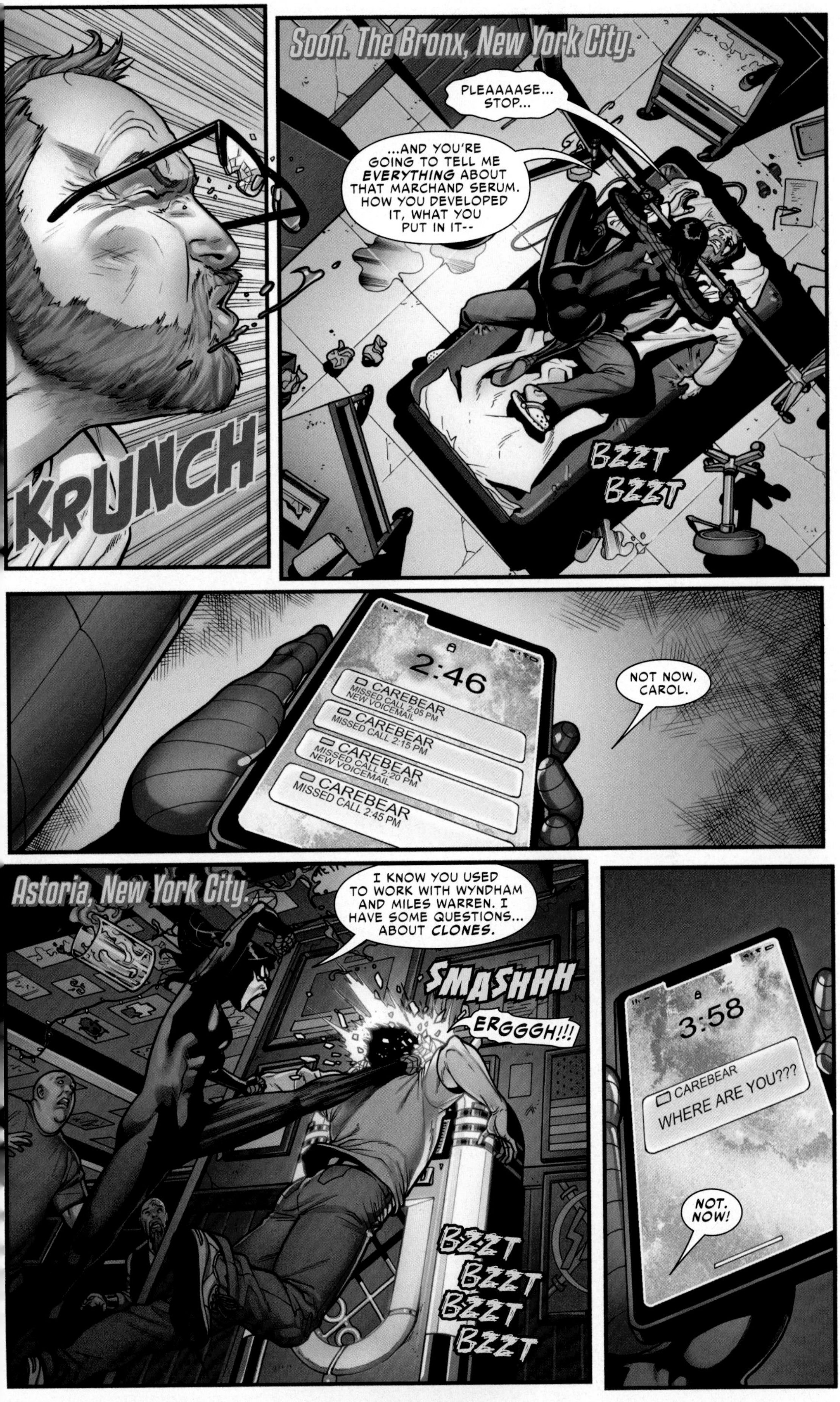
KRUNCH
Soon. The Bronx, New York City.
PLEAAAASE... STOP...
...AND YOU'RE GOING TO TELL ME EVERYTHING ABOUT THAT MARCHAND SERUM. HOW YOU DEVELOPED IT, WHAT YOU PUT IN IT--
BZZT BZZT
2:46
CAREBEAR
MISSED CALL 2:05 PM
NEW VOICEMAIL
CAREBEAR
MISSED CALL 2:15 PM
CAREBEAR
MISSED CALL 2:20 PM
NEW VOICEMAIL
CAREBEAR
MISSED CALL 2:45 PM
NOT NOW, CAROL.
Astoria, New York City.
I KNOW YOU USED TO WORK WITH WYNDHAM AND MILES WARREN. I HAVE SOME QUESTIONS... ABOUT CLONES.
SMASHHH
ERGGGH!!!
BZZT BZZT BZZT BZZT
3:58
CAREBEAR
WHERE ARE YOU???
NOT. NOW!

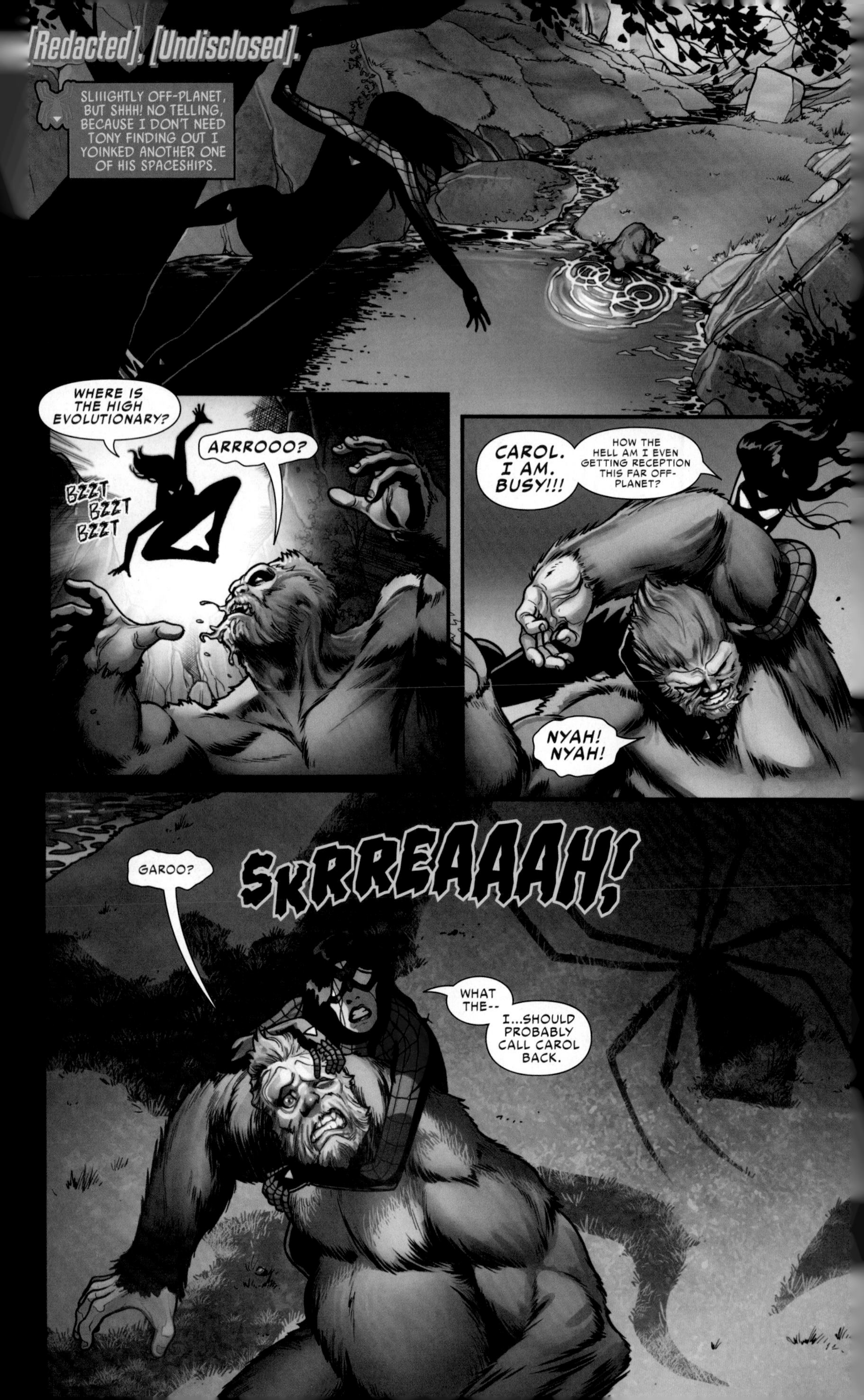
[Redacted], [Undisclosed].
SLIIIGHTLY OFF-PLANET, BUT SHHH! NO TELLING, BECAUSE I DON'T NEED TONY FINDING OUT I YOINKED ANOTHER ONE OF HIS SPACESHIPS.
WHERE IS THE HIGH EVOLUTIONARY?
ARRROOO?
BZZT BZZT BZZT
CAROL. I AM. BUSY!!!
HOW THE HELL AM I EVEN GETTING RECEPTION THIS FAR OFF-PLANET?
NYAH! NYAH!
GAROO?
SKRREAAAAH!
WHAT THE--
I...SHOULD PROBABLY CALL CAROL BACK.

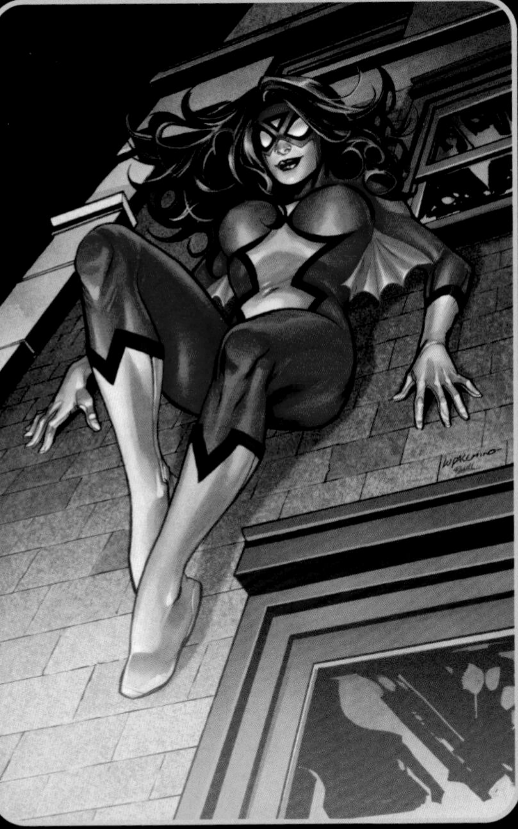

#6 VARIANT BY
EMA LUPACCHINO & RACHELLE ROSENBERG

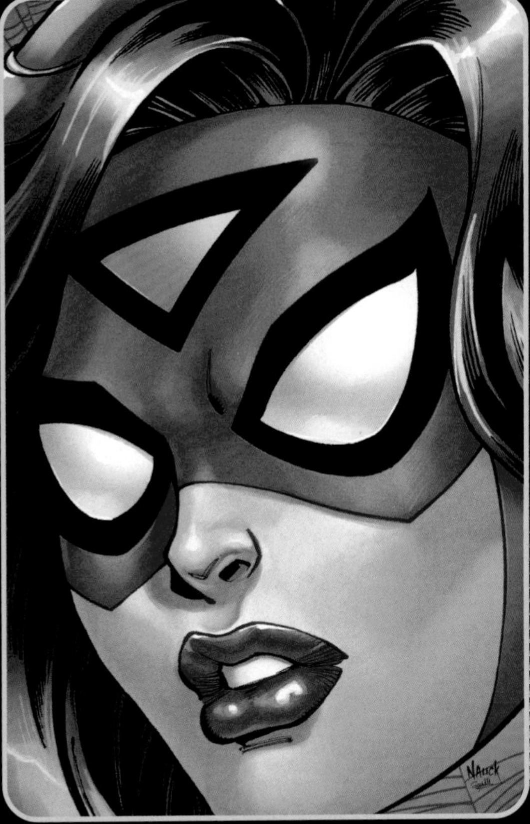

#6 VARIANT BY
TODD NAUCK & RACHELLE ROSENBERG

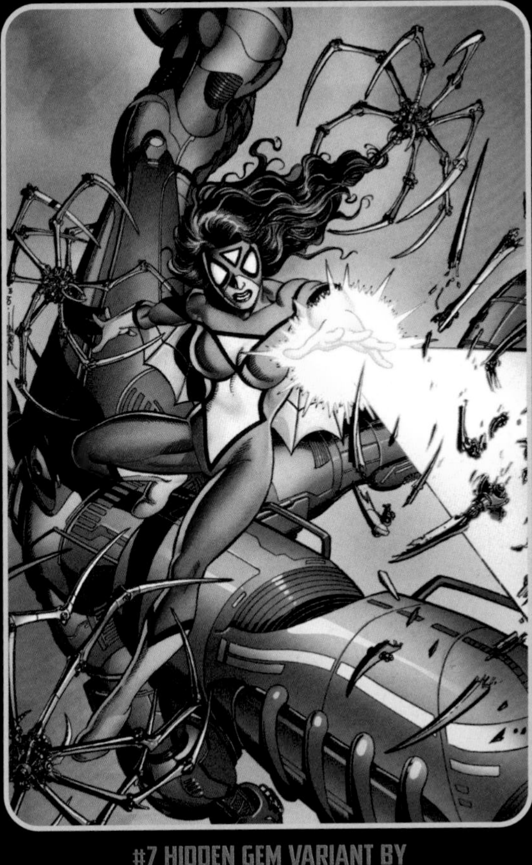

#7 HIDDEN GEM VARIANT BY
GEORGE PÉREZ & FRANK D'ARMATA

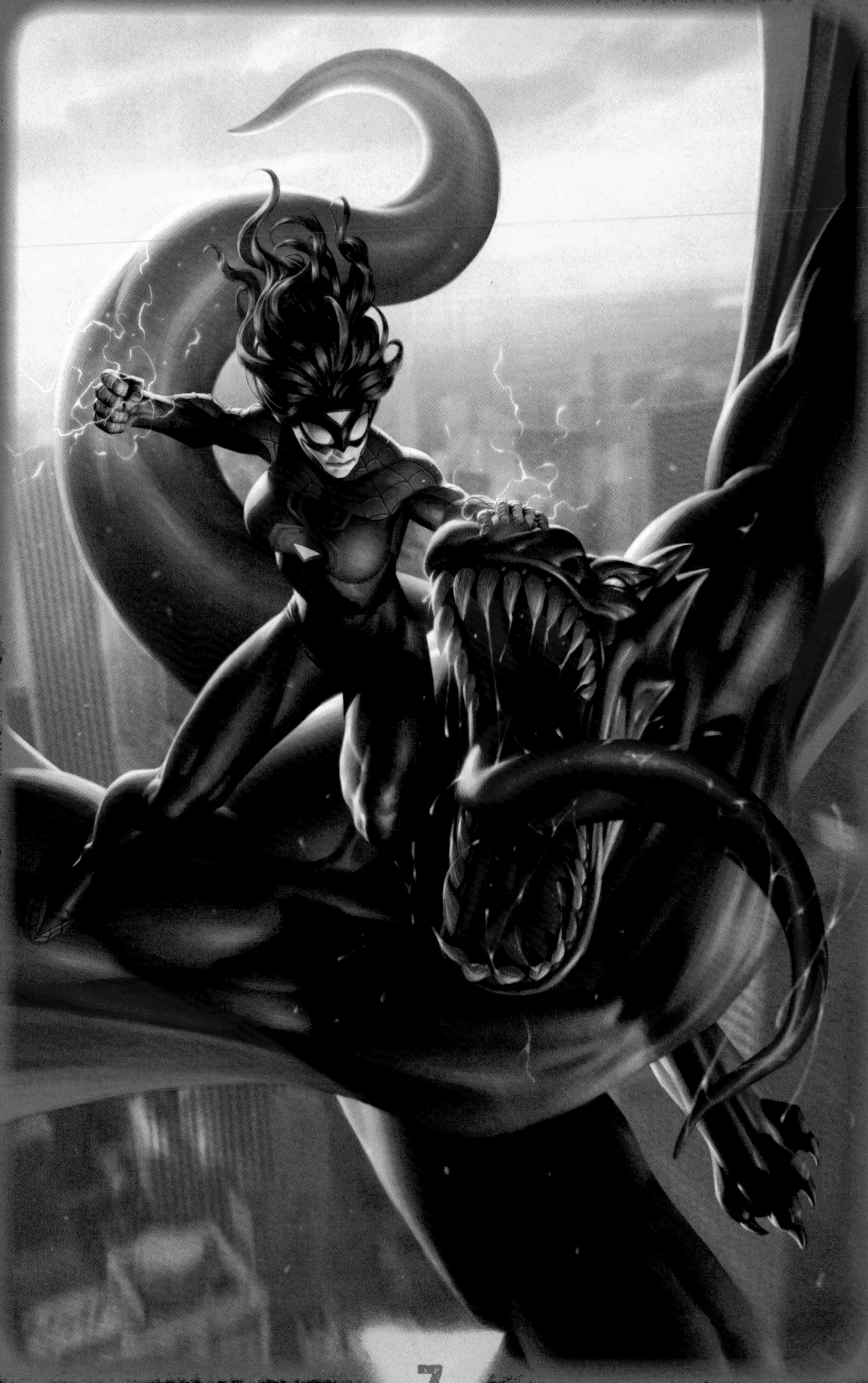

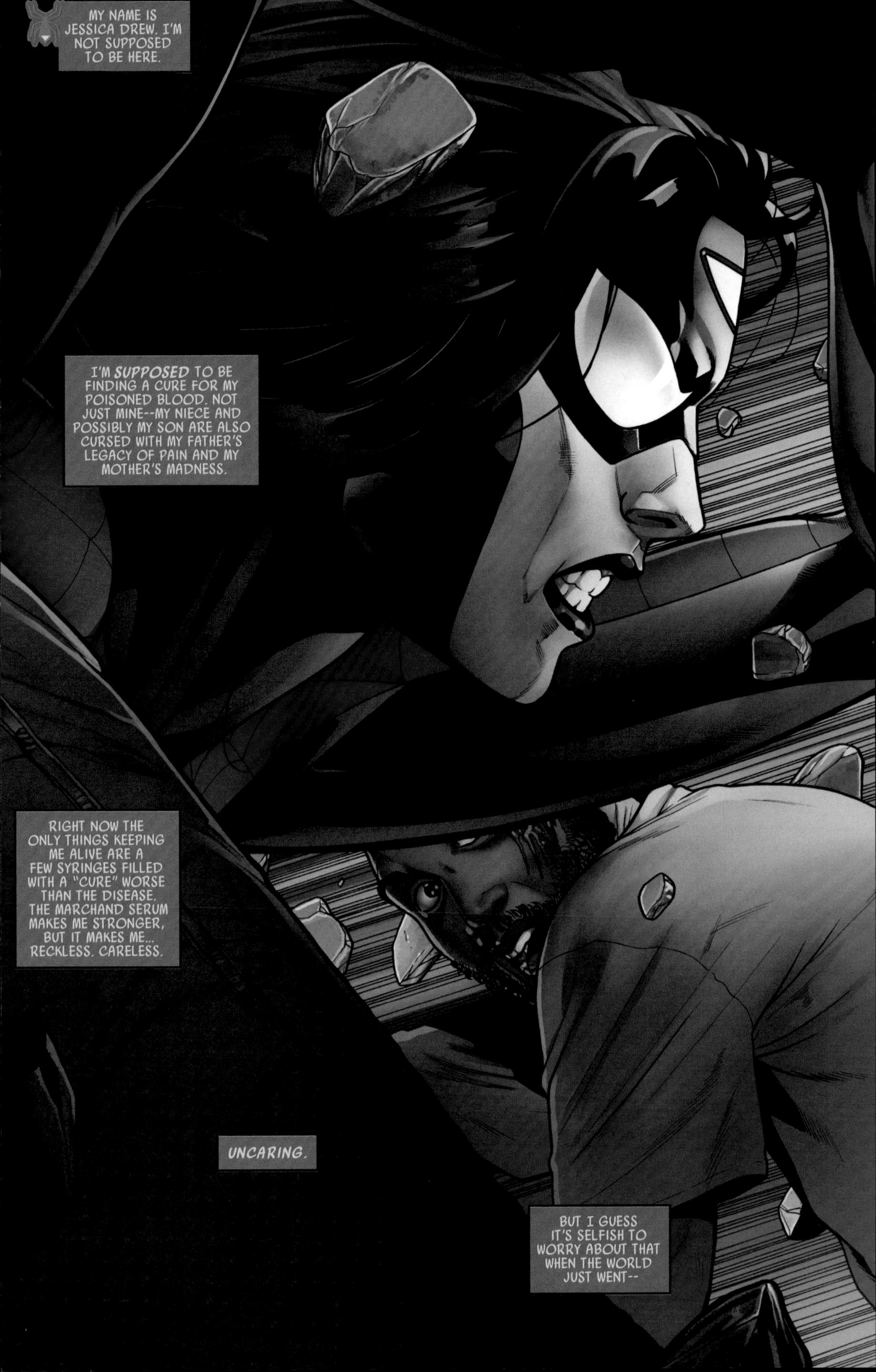
MY NAME IS JESSICA DREW. I'M NOT SUPPOSED TO BE HERE.
I'M *SUPPOSED* TO BE FINDING A CURE FOR MY POISONED BLOOD. NOT JUST MINE--MY NIECE AND POSSIBLY MY SON ARE ALSO CURSED WITH MY FATHER'S LEGACY OF PAIN AND MY MOTHER'S MADNESS.
RIGHT NOW THE ONLY THINGS KEEPING ME ALIVE ARE A FEW SYRINGES FILLED WITH A "CURE" WORSE THAN THE DISEASE. THE MARCHAND SERUM MAKES ME STRONGER, BUT IT MAKES ME... RECKLESS. CARELESS.
UNCARING.
BUT I GUESS IT'S SELFISH TO WORRY ABOUT THAT WHEN THE WORLD JUST WENT--

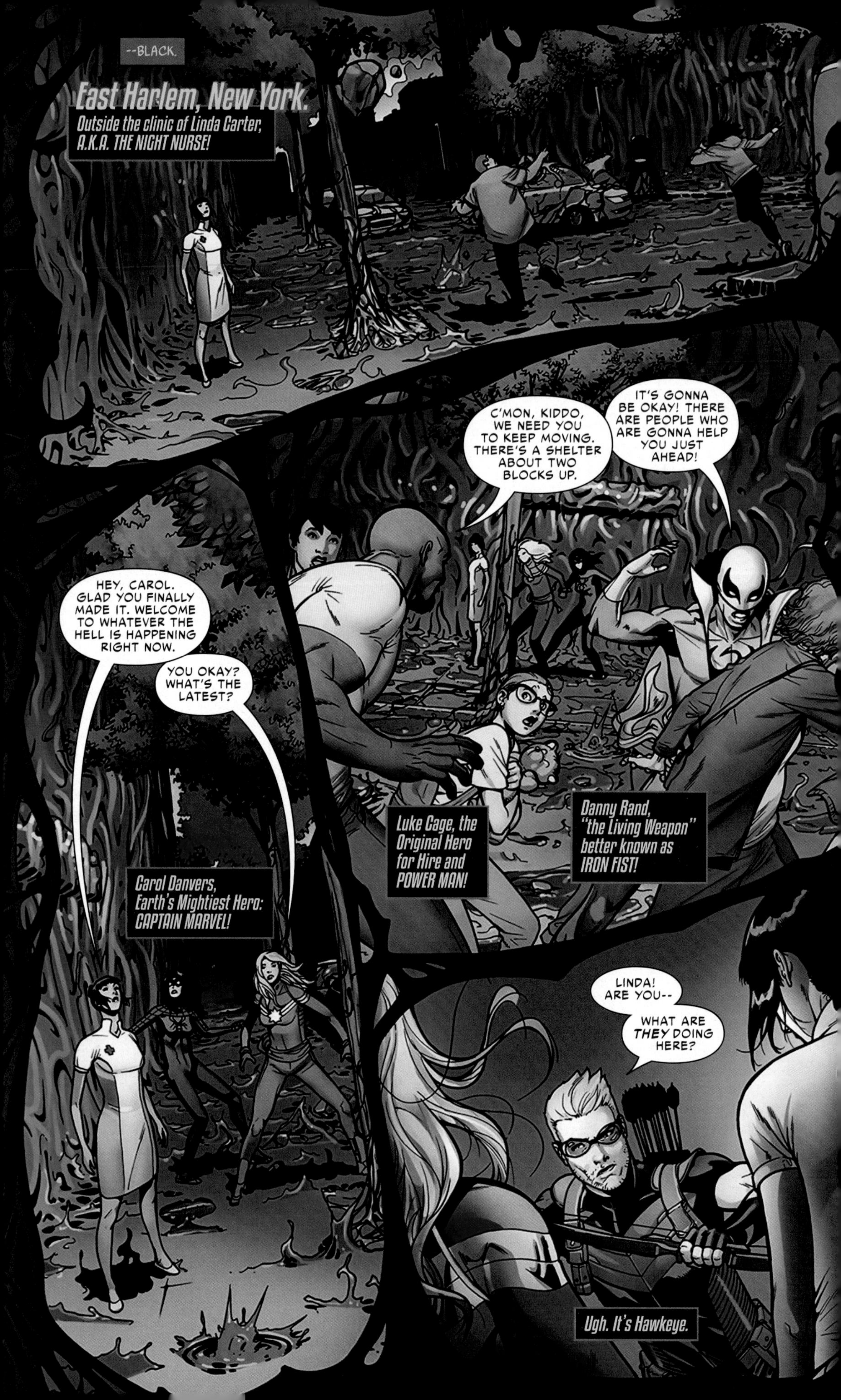

--BLACK.
East Harlem, New York.
Outside the clinic of Linda Carter, A.K.A. THE NIGHT NURSE!
C'MON, KIDDO, WE NEED YOU TO KEEP MOVING. THERE'S A SHELTER ABOUT TWO BLOCKS UP.
IT'S GONNA BE OKAY! THERE ARE PEOPLE WHO ARE GONNA HELP YOU JUST AHEAD!
HEY, CAROL. GLAD YOU FINALLY MADE IT. WELCOME TO WHATEVER THE HELL IS HAPPENING RIGHT NOW.
YOU OKAY? WHAT'S THE LATEST?
Luke Cage, the Original Hero for Hire and POWER MAN!
Danny Rand, "the Living Weapon" better known as IRON FIST!
Carol Danvers, Earth's Mightiest Hero: CAPTAIN MARVEL!
LINDA! ARE YOU--
WHAT ARE THEY DOING HERE?
Ugh. It's Hawkeye.

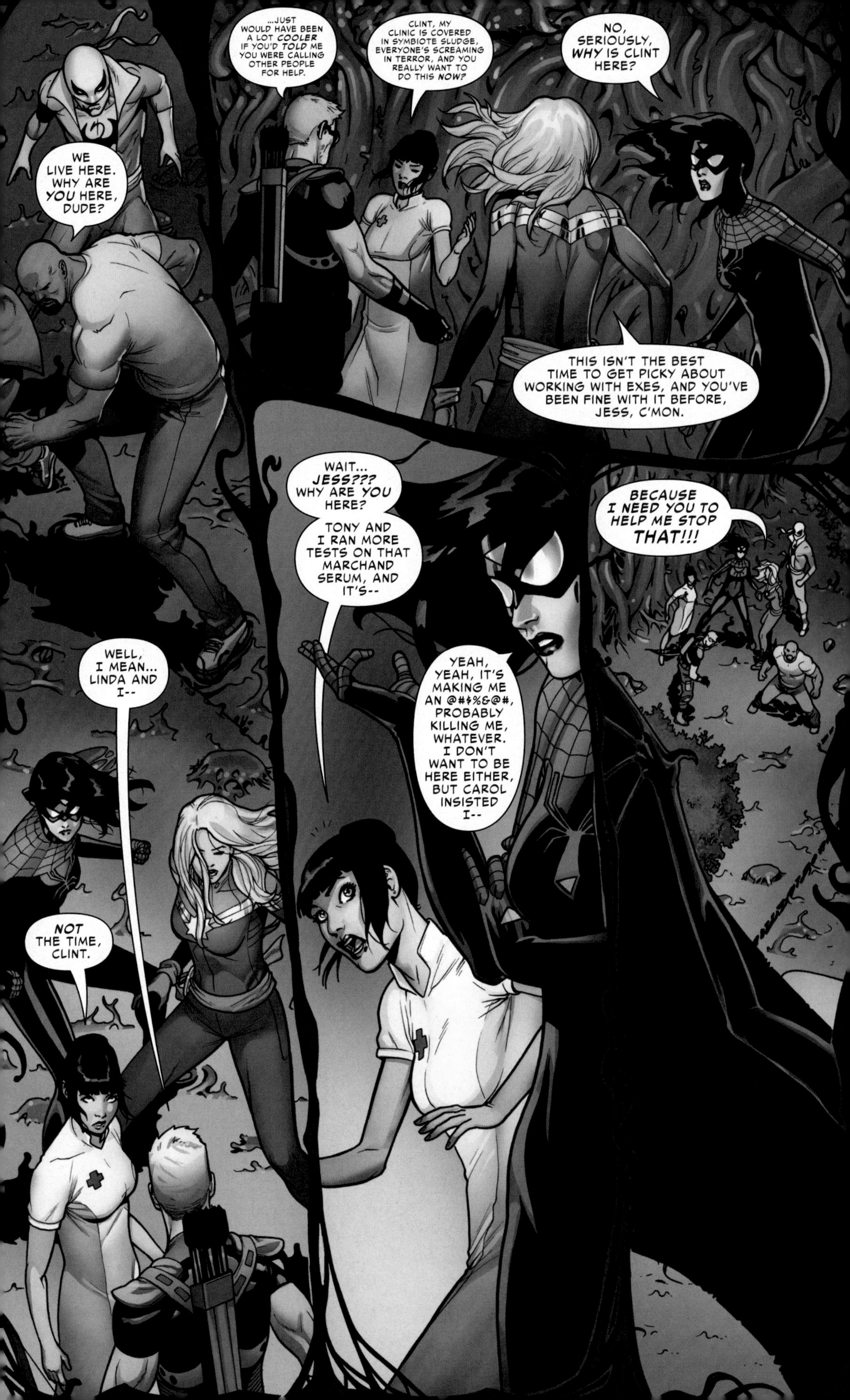

...JUST WOULD HAVE BEEN A LOT COOLER IF YOU'D TOLD ME YOU WERE CALLING OTHER PEOPLE FOR HELP.
WE LIVE HERE. WHY ARE YOU HERE, DUDE?
CLINT, MY CLINIC IS COVERED IN SYMBIOTE SLUDGE, EVERYONE'S SCREAMING IN TERROR, AND YOU REALLY WANT TO DO THIS NOW?
NO, SERIOUSLY, WHY IS CLINT HERE?
THIS ISN'T THE BEST TIME TO GET PICKY ABOUT WORKING WITH EXES, AND YOU'VE BEEN FINE WITH IT BEFORE, JESS, C'MON.
WELL, I MEAN... LINDA AND I--
NOT THE TIME, CLINT.
WAIT... JESS??? WHY ARE YOU HERE?
TONY AND I RAN MORE TESTS ON THAT MARCHAND SERUM, AND IT'S--
YEAH, YEAH, IT'S MAKING ME AN @#$%&@#, PROBABLY KILLING ME, WHATEVER. I DON'T WANT TO BE HERE EITHER, BUT CAROL INSISTED I--
BECAUSE I NEED YOU TO HELP ME STOP THAT!!!

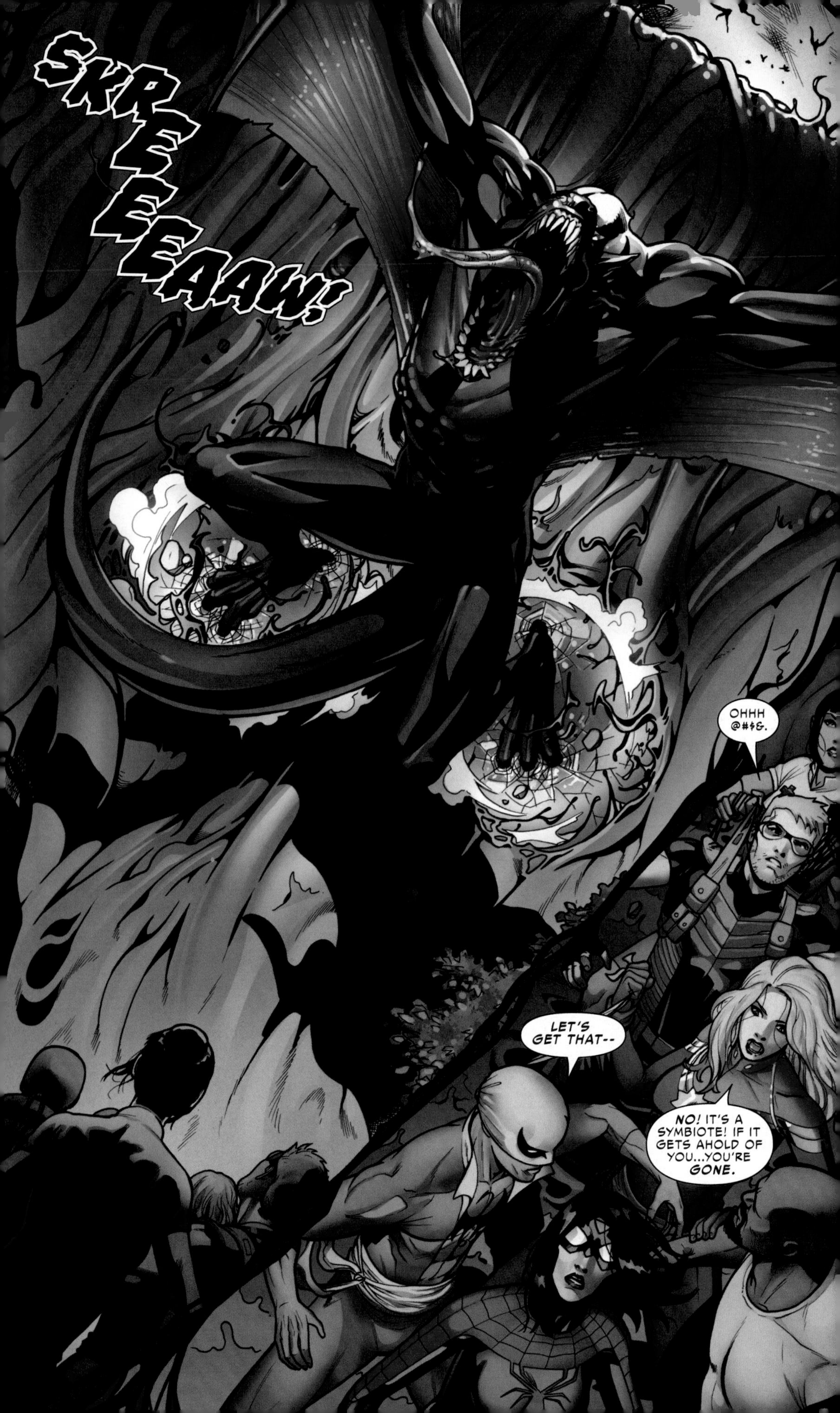
SKREEEEAAW!
OHHH @#$&.
LET'S GET THAT--
NO! IT'S A SYMBIOTE! IF IT GETS AHOLD OF YOU...YOU'RE GONE.

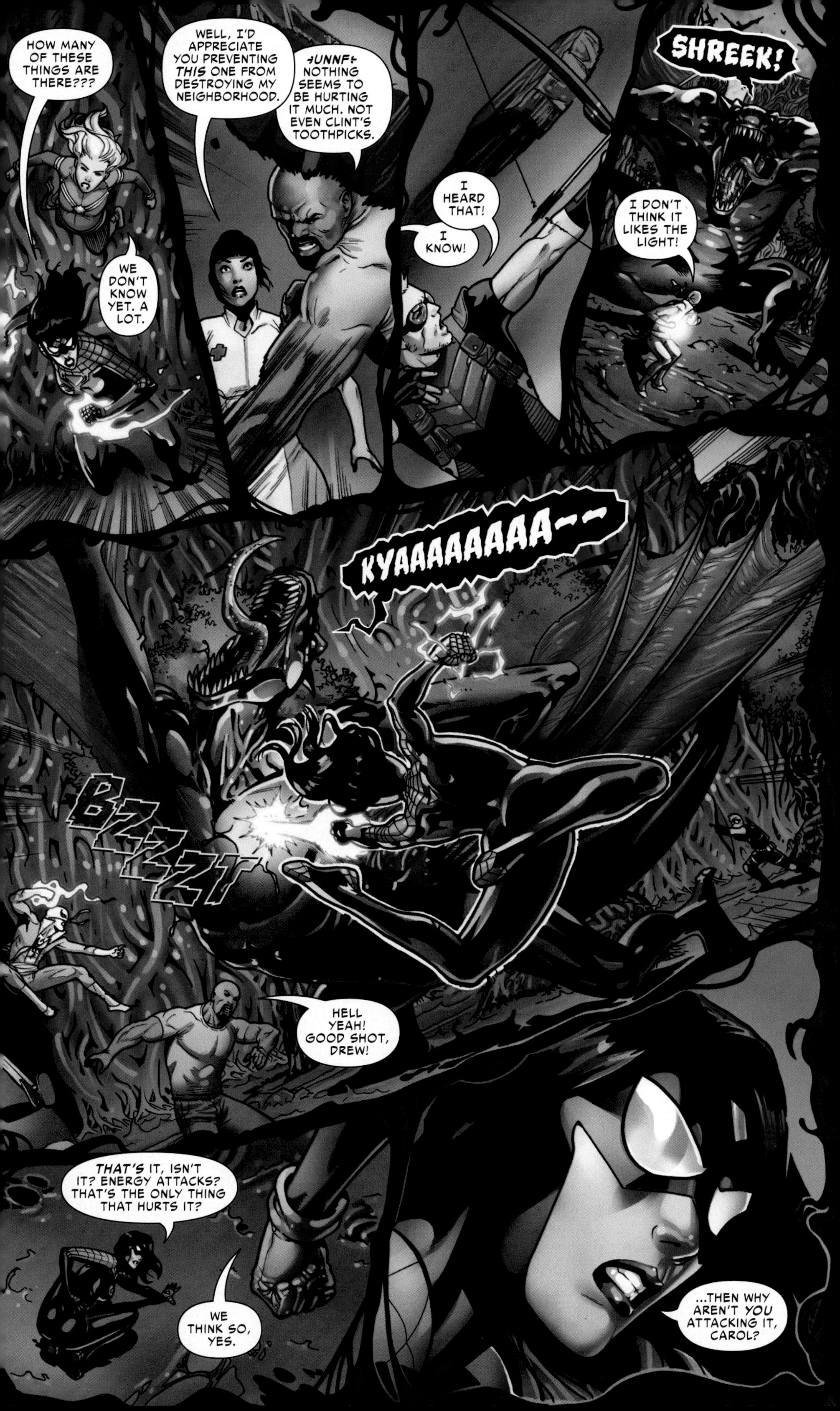

HOW MANY OF THESE THINGS ARE THERE???
WELL, I'D APPRECIATE YOU PREVENTING *THIS* ONE FROM DESTROYING MY NEIGHBORHOOD.
-UNNF- NOTHING SEEMS TO BE HURTING IT MUCH. NOT EVEN CLINT'S TOOTHPICKS.
SHREEK!
WE DON'T KNOW YET. A LOT.
I HEARD THAT!
I KNOW!
I DON'T THINK IT LIKES THE LIGHT!
KYAAAAAAAA--
BZZZZT
HELL YEAH! GOOD SHOT, DREW!
THAT'S IT, ISN'T IT? ENERGY ATTACKS? THAT'S THE ONLY THING THAT HURTS IT?
WE THINK SO, YES.
...THEN WHY AREN'T *YOU* ATTACKING IT, CAROL?

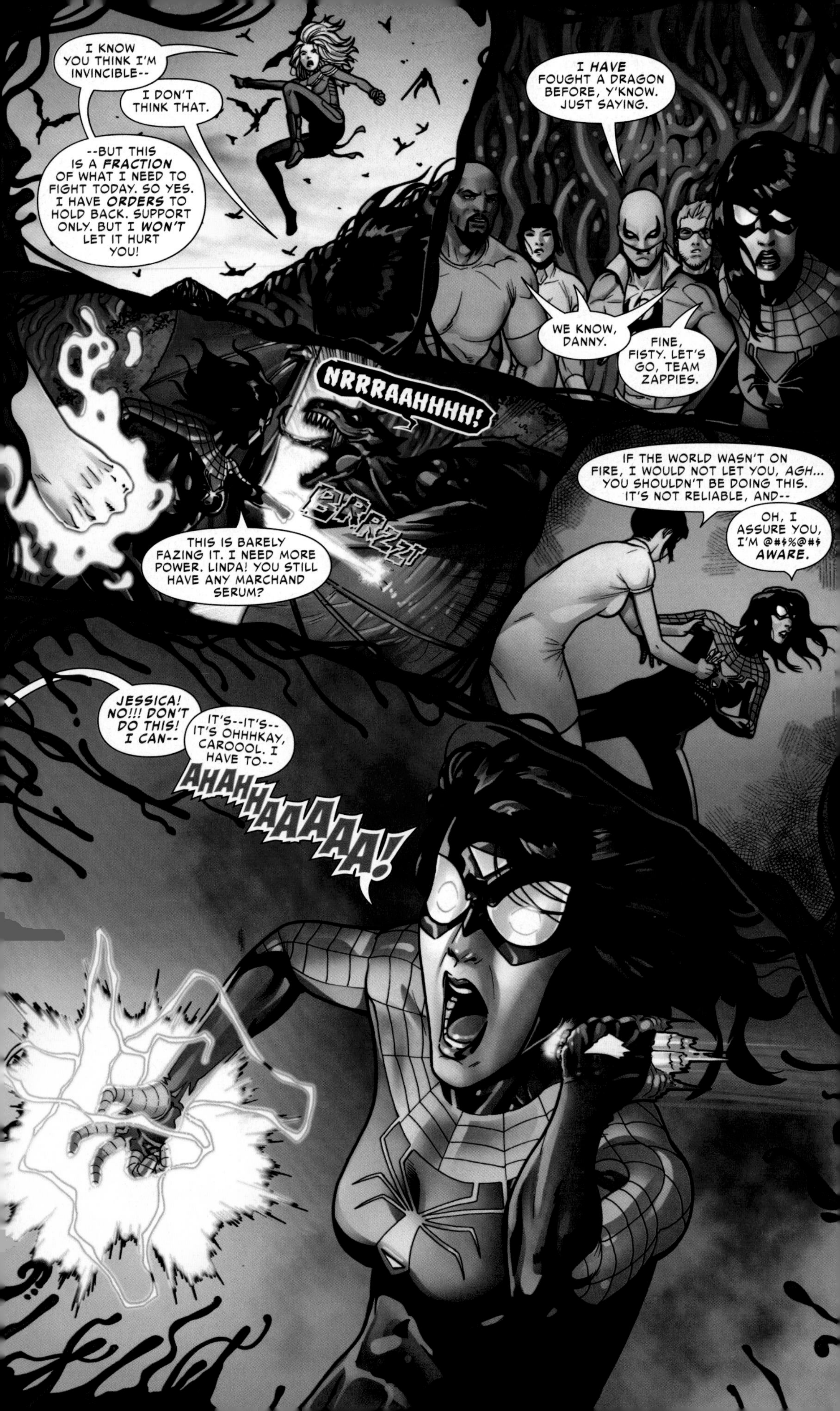

I KNOW YOU THINK I'M INVINCIBLE--
I DON'T THINK THAT.
--BUT THIS IS A FRACTION OF WHAT I NEED TO FIGHT TODAY. SO YES. I HAVE ORDERS TO HOLD BACK. SUPPORT ONLY. BUT I WON'T LET IT HURT YOU!
I HAVE FOUGHT A DRAGON BEFORE, Y'KNOW. JUST SAYING.
WE KNOW, DANNY.
FINE, FISTY. LET'S GO, TEAM ZAPPIES.
NRRRAAHHHH!
BRRZZT
THIS IS BARELY FAZING IT. I NEED MORE POWER. LINDA! YOU STILL HAVE ANY MARCHAND SERUM?
IF THE WORLD WASN'T ON FIRE, I WOULD NOT LET YOU, AGH... YOU SHOULDN'T BE DOING THIS. IT'S NOT RELIABLE, AND--
OH, I ASSURE YOU, I'M @#$%@#$ AWARE.
JESSICA! NO!!! DON'T DO THIS! I CAN--
IT'S--IT'S-- IT'S OHHHKAY, CAROOOL. I HAVE TO--
AHAHHAAAAAA!

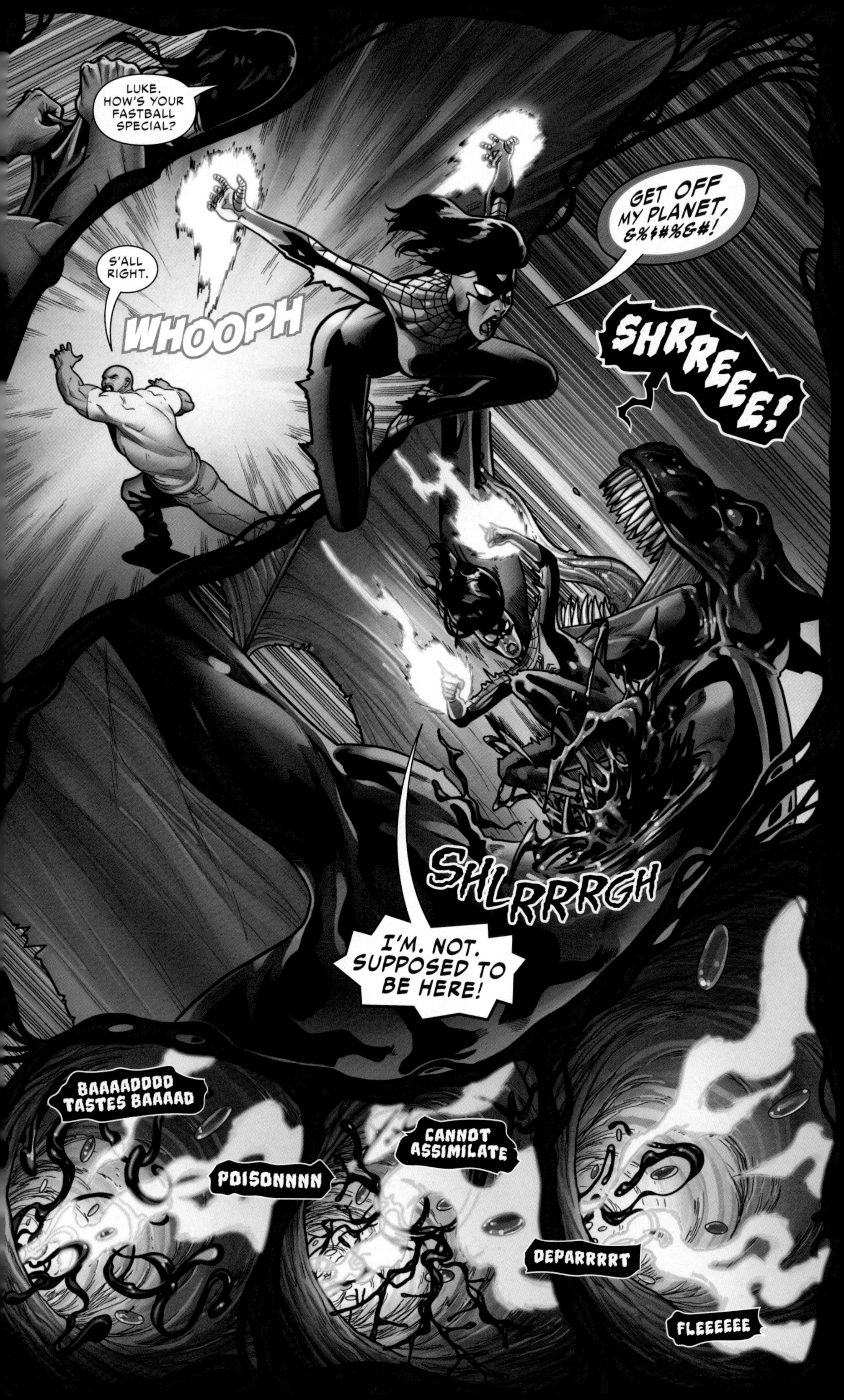
LUKE. HOW'S YOUR FASTBALL SPECIAL?
S'ALL RIGHT.
WHOOPH
GET OFF MY PLANET, &%$#%&#!
SHRREEE!
SHLRRRRGH
I'M. NOT. SUPPOSED TO BE HERE!
BAAAADDDD TASTES BAAAAD
POISONNNN
CANNOT ASSIMILATE
DEPARRRRRT
FLEEEEEE

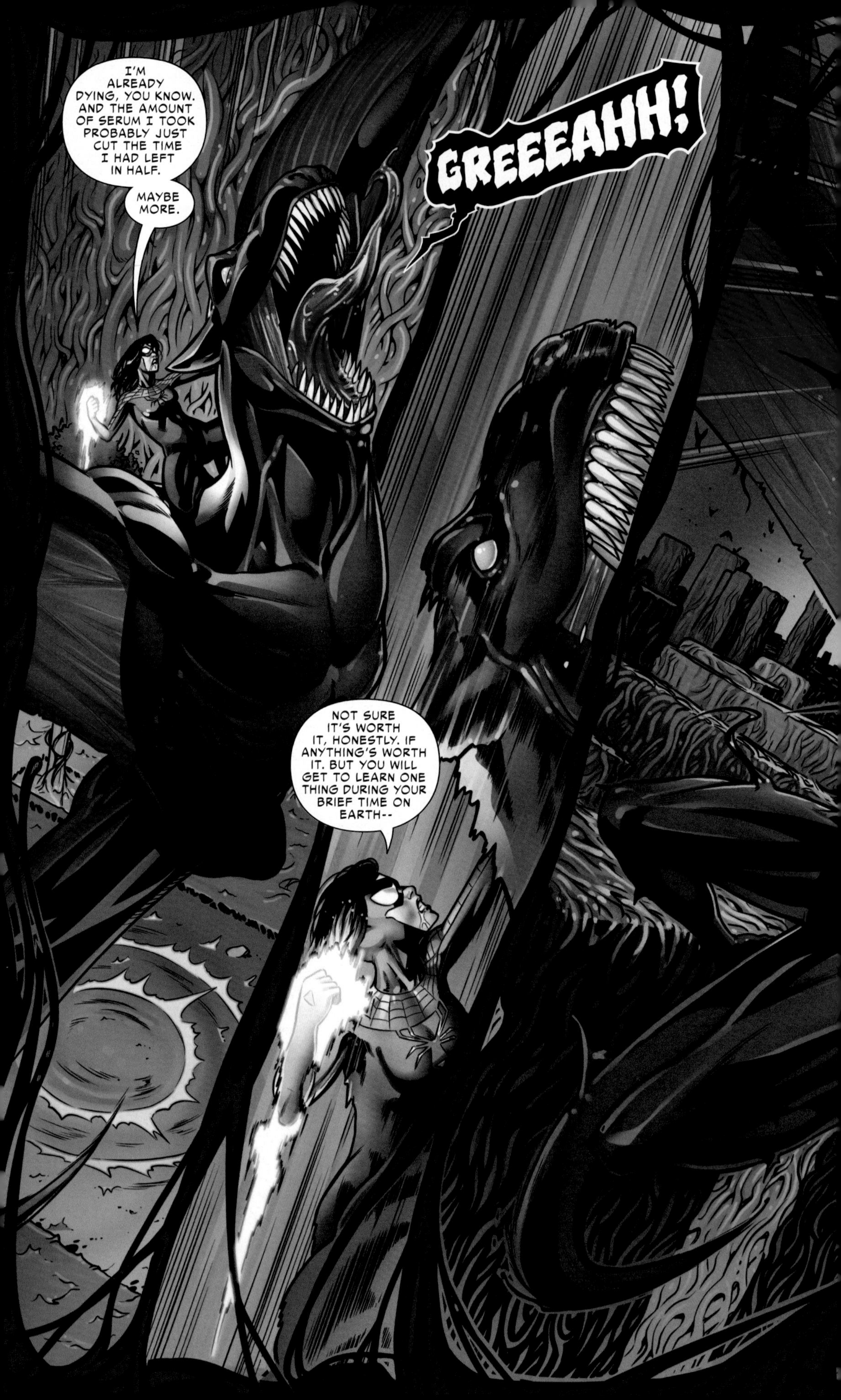
I'M ALREADY DYING, YOU KNOW. AND THE AMOUNT OF SERUM I TOOK PROBABLY JUST CUT THE TIME I HAD LEFT IN HALF.
MAYBE MORE.
GREEEAHH!
NOT SURE IT'S WORTH IT, HONESTLY. IF ANYTHING'S WORTH IT. BUT YOU WILL GET TO LEARN ONE THING DURING YOUR BRIEF TIME ON EARTH--

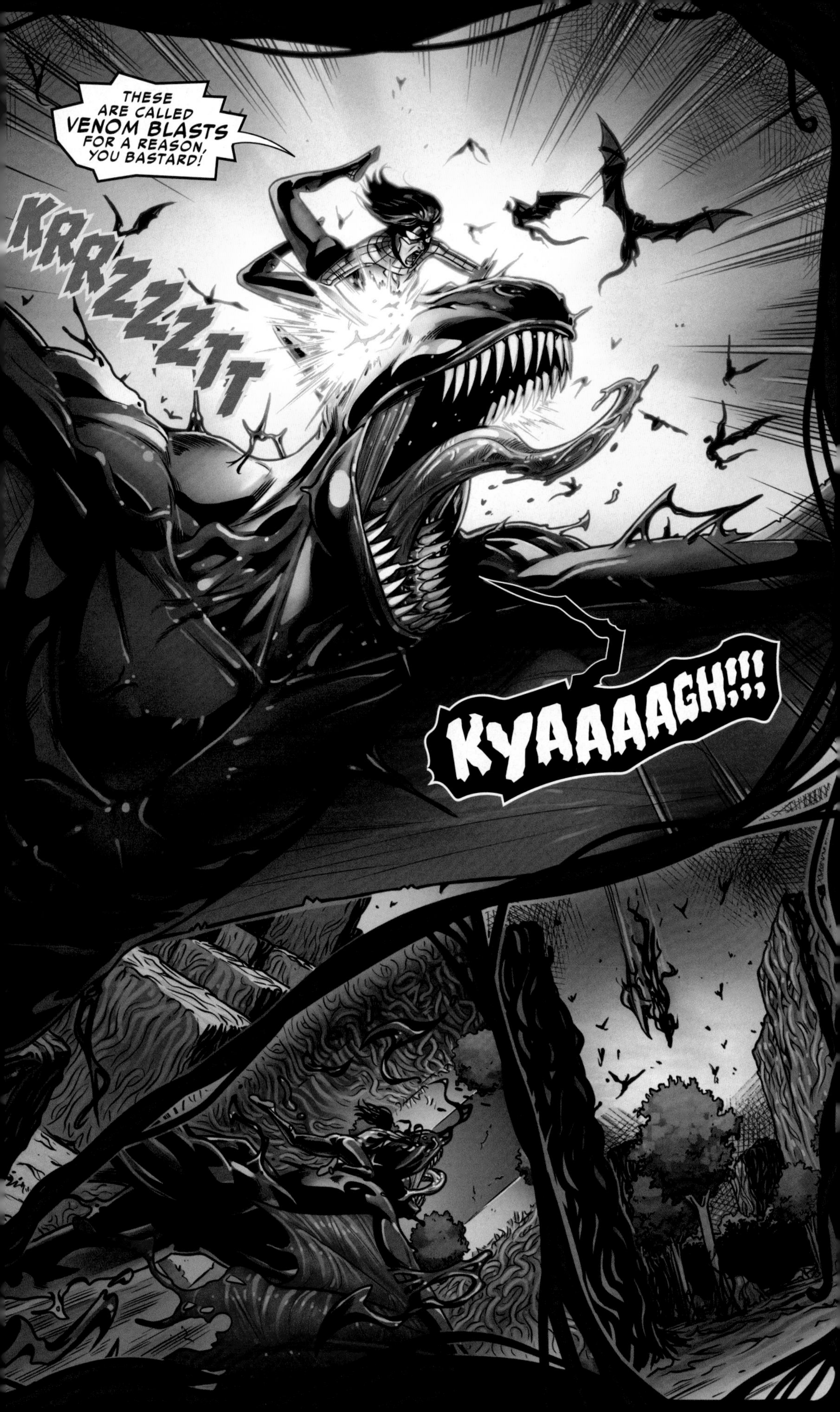
THESE ARE CALLED VENOM BLASTS FOR A REASON, YOU BASTARD!
KRRZZZZTT
KYAAAAGH!!!

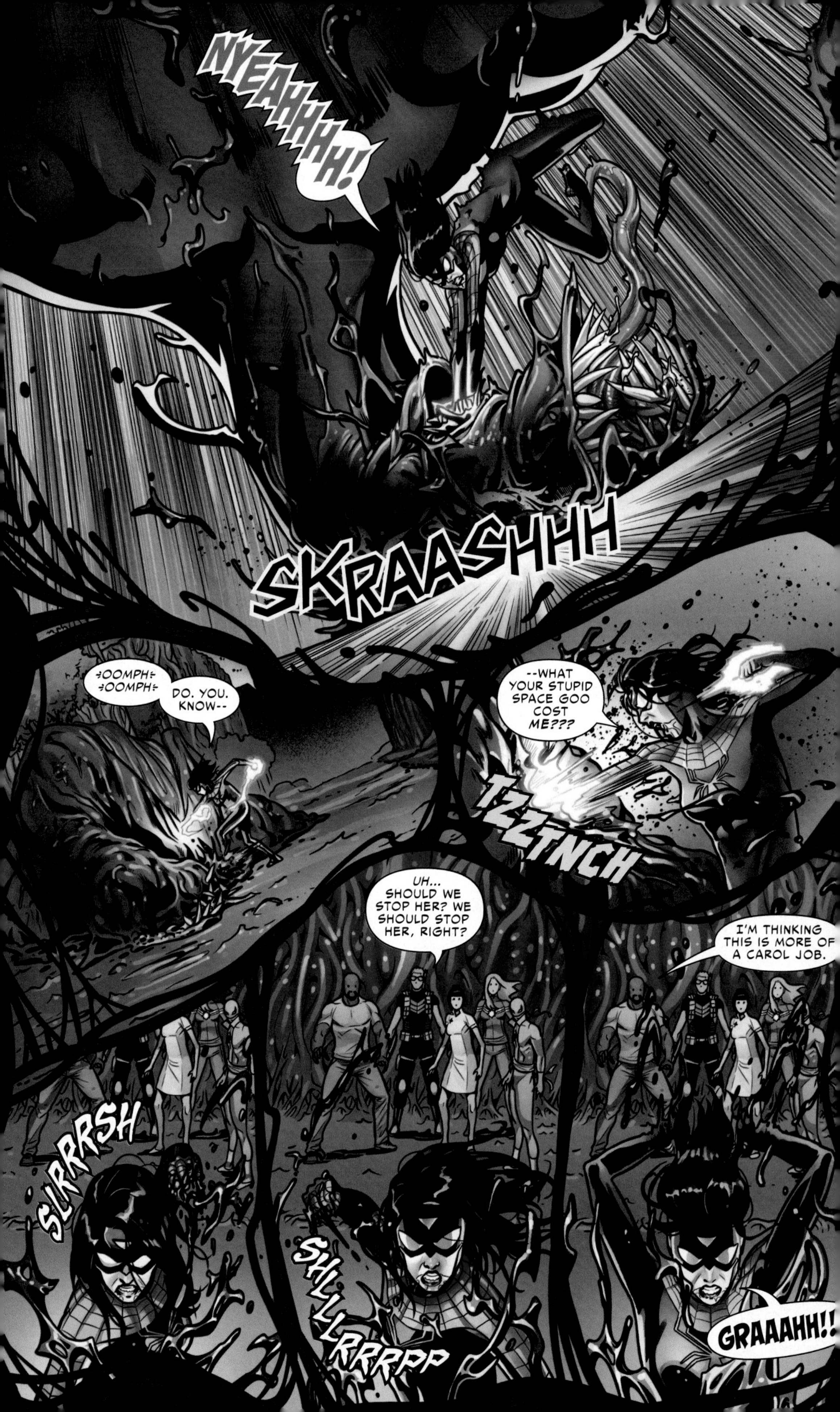
NYEAHHHH!
SKRAASHHH
OOMPH
OOMPH
DO. YOU. KNOW--
--WHAT YOUR STUPID SPACE GOO COST ME???
TZZTNCH
UH... SHOULD WE STOP HER? WE SHOULD STOP HER, RIGHT?
I'M THINKING THIS IS MORE OF A CAROL JOB.
SLRRRSH
SHLLLRRRPP
GRAAAHH!!

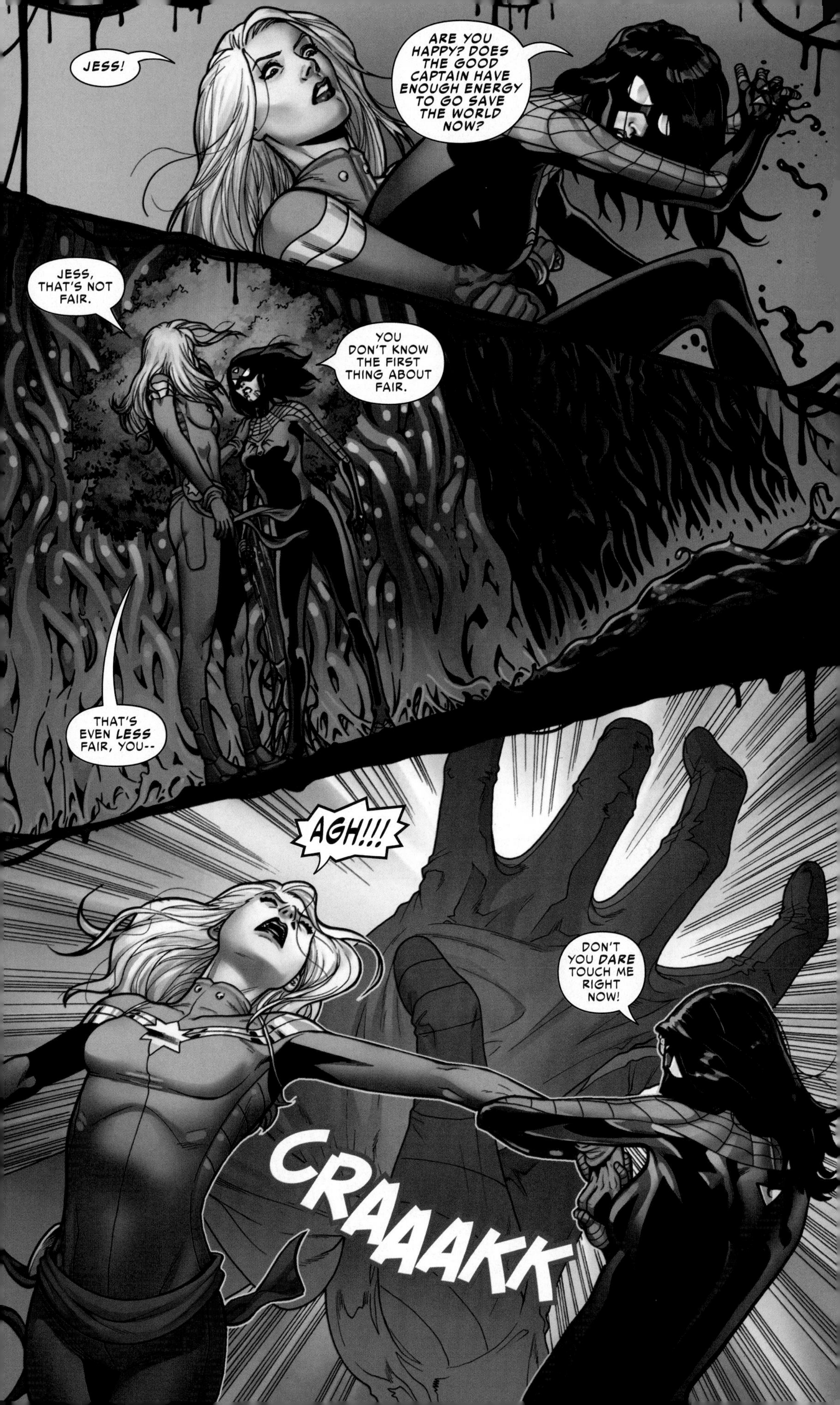
JESS!
ARE YOU HAPPY? DOES THE GOOD CAPTAIN HAVE ENOUGH ENERGY TO GO SAVE THE WORLD NOW?
JESS, THAT'S NOT FAIR.
YOU DON'T KNOW THE FIRST THING ABOUT FAIR.
THAT'S EVEN LESS FAIR, YOU--
AGH!!!
DON'T YOU DARE TOUCH ME RIGHT NOW!
CRAAAKK

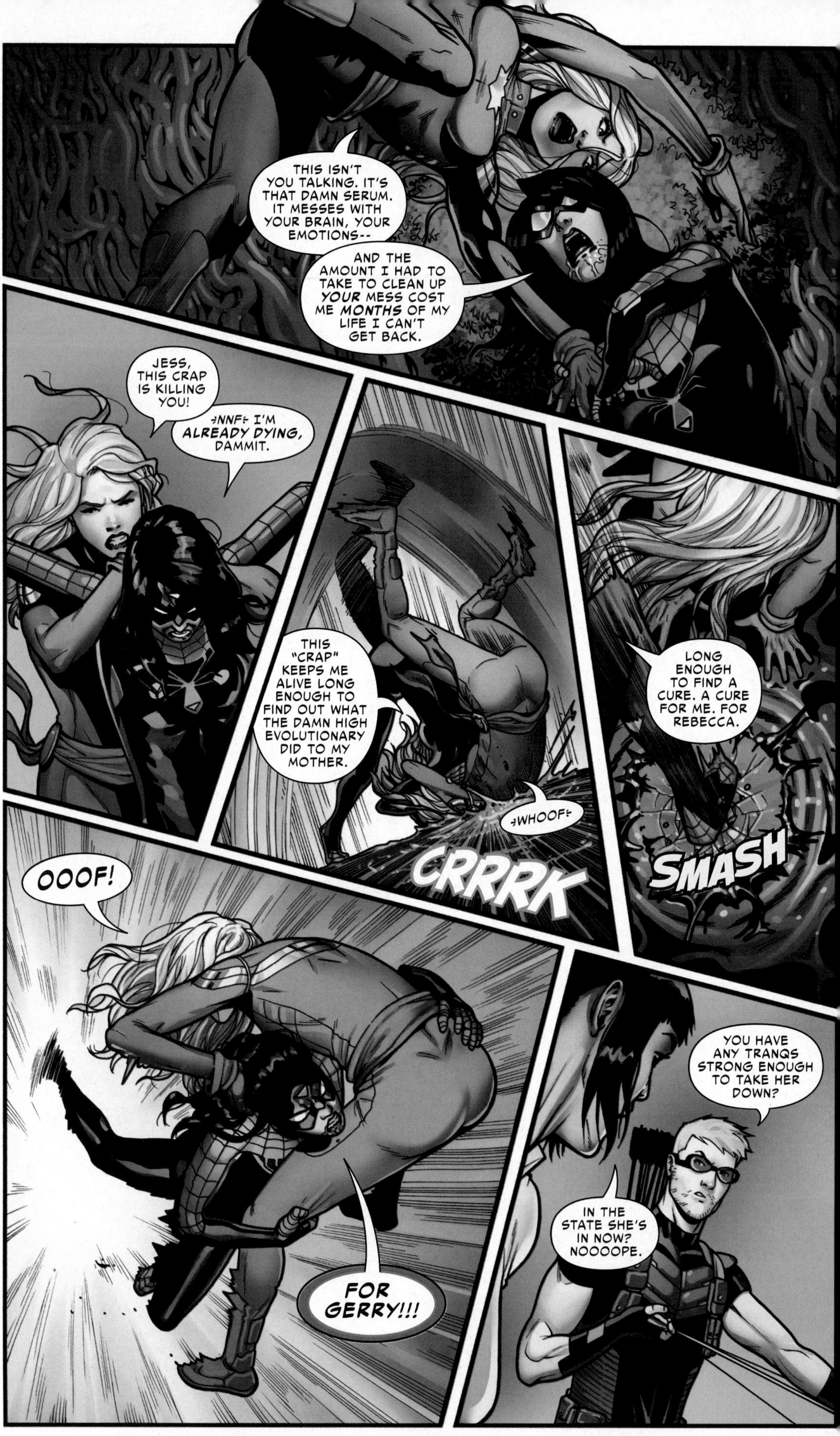

THIS ISN'T YOU TALKING. IT'S THAT DAMN SERUM. IT MESSES WITH YOUR BRAIN, YOUR EMOTIONS--
AND THE AMOUNT I HAD TO TAKE TO CLEAN UP YOUR MESS COST ME MONTHS OF MY LIFE I CAN'T GET BACK.
JESS, THIS CRAP IS KILLING YOU!
NNF I'M ALREADY DYING, DAMMIT.
THIS "CRAP" KEEPS ME ALIVE LONG ENOUGH TO FIND OUT WHAT THE DAMN HIGH EVOLUTIONARY DID TO MY MOTHER.
WHOOF
CRRRK
LONG ENOUGH TO FIND A CURE. A CURE FOR ME. FOR REBECCA.
SMASH
OOOF!
FOR GERRY!!!
YOU HAVE ANY TRANQS STRONG ENOUGH TO TAKE HER DOWN?
IN THE STATE SHE'S IN NOW? NOOOOPE.

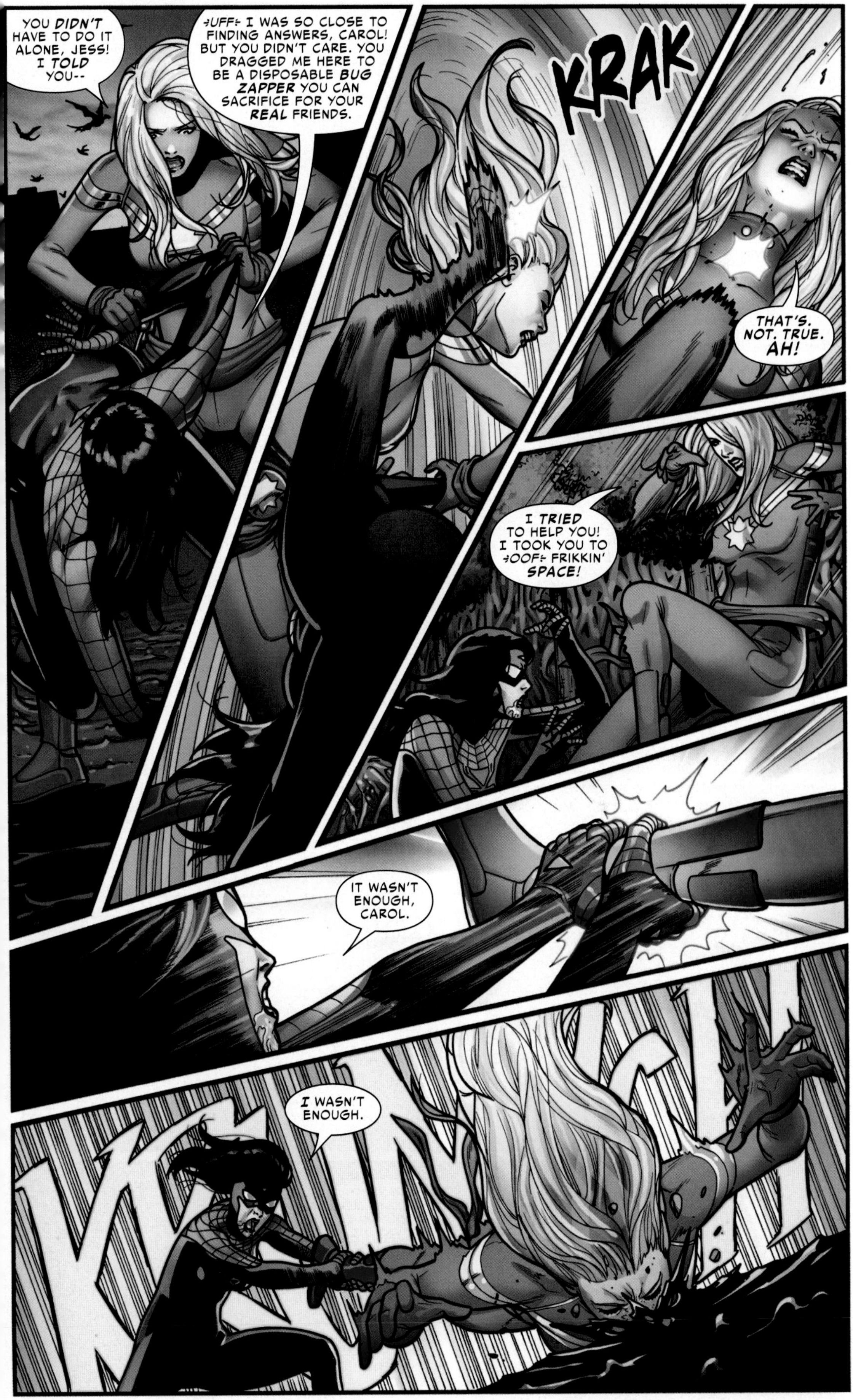

YOU DIDN'T HAVE TO DO IT ALONE, JESS! I TOLD YOU--
UFF I WAS SO CLOSE TO FINDING ANSWERS, CAROL! BUT YOU DIDN'T CARE. YOU DRAGGED ME HERE TO BE A DISPOSABLE BUG ZAPPER YOU CAN SACRIFICE FOR YOUR REAL FRIENDS.
KRAK
THAT'S. NOT. TRUE. AH!
I TRIED TO HELP YOU! I TOOK YOU TO OOF FRIKKIN' SPACE!
IT WASN'T ENOUGH, CAROL.
I WASN'T ENOUGH.

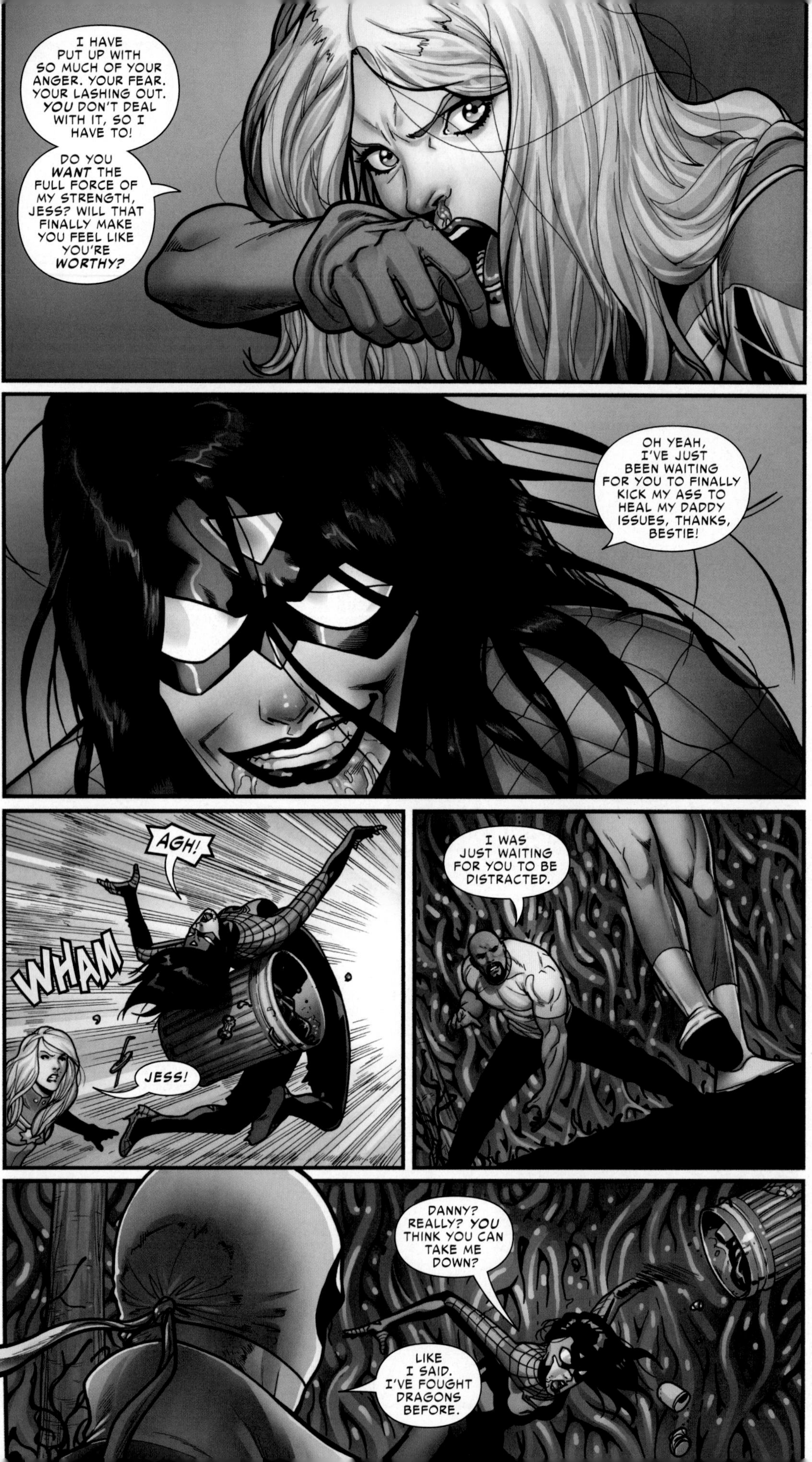

I HAVE PUT UP WITH SO MUCH OF YOUR ANGER. YOUR FEAR. YOUR LASHING OUT. YOU DON'T DEAL WITH IT, SO I HAVE TO!
DO YOU WANT THE FULL FORCE OF MY STRENGTH, JESS? WILL THAT FINALLY MAKE YOU FEEL LIKE YOU'RE WORTHY?
OH YEAH, I'VE JUST BEEN WAITING FOR YOU TO FINALLY KICK MY ASS TO HEAL MY DADDY ISSUES, THANKS, BESTIE!
AGH!
WHAM
JESS!
I WAS JUST WAITING FOR YOU TO BE DISTRACTED.
DANNY? REALLY? YOU THINK YOU CAN TAKE ME DOWN?
LIKE I SAID. I'VE FOUGHT DRAGONS BEFORE.

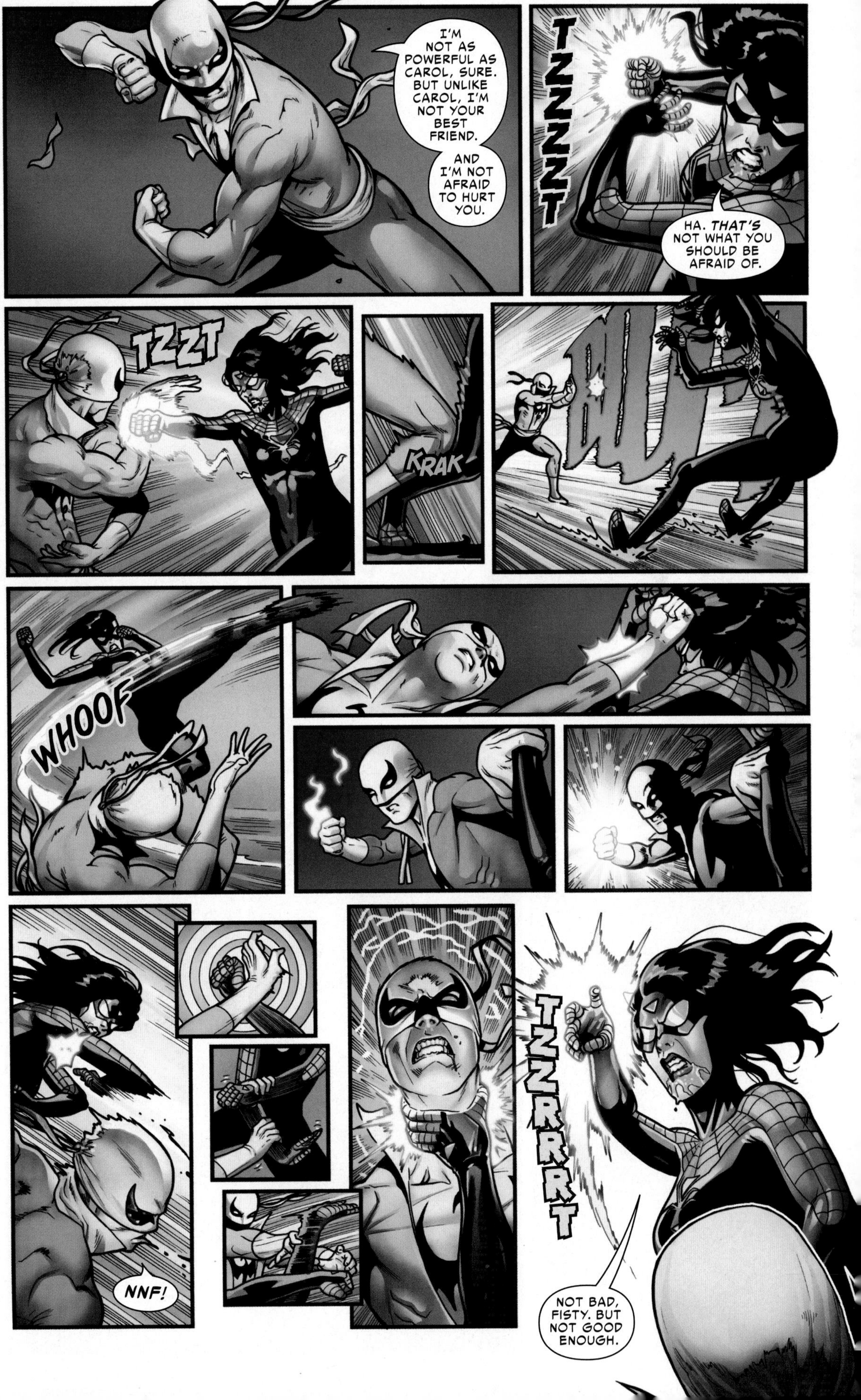
I'M NOT AS POWERFUL AS CAROL, SURE. BUT UNLIKE CAROL, I'M NOT YOUR BEST FRIEND.
AND I'M NOT AFRAID TO HURT YOU.
TZZZZT
HA. *THAT'S* NOT WHAT YOU SHOULD BE AFRAID OF.
TZZT
KRAK
WHOOF
NNF!
TZZRRRT
NOT BAD, FISTY. BUT NOT GOOD ENOUGH.

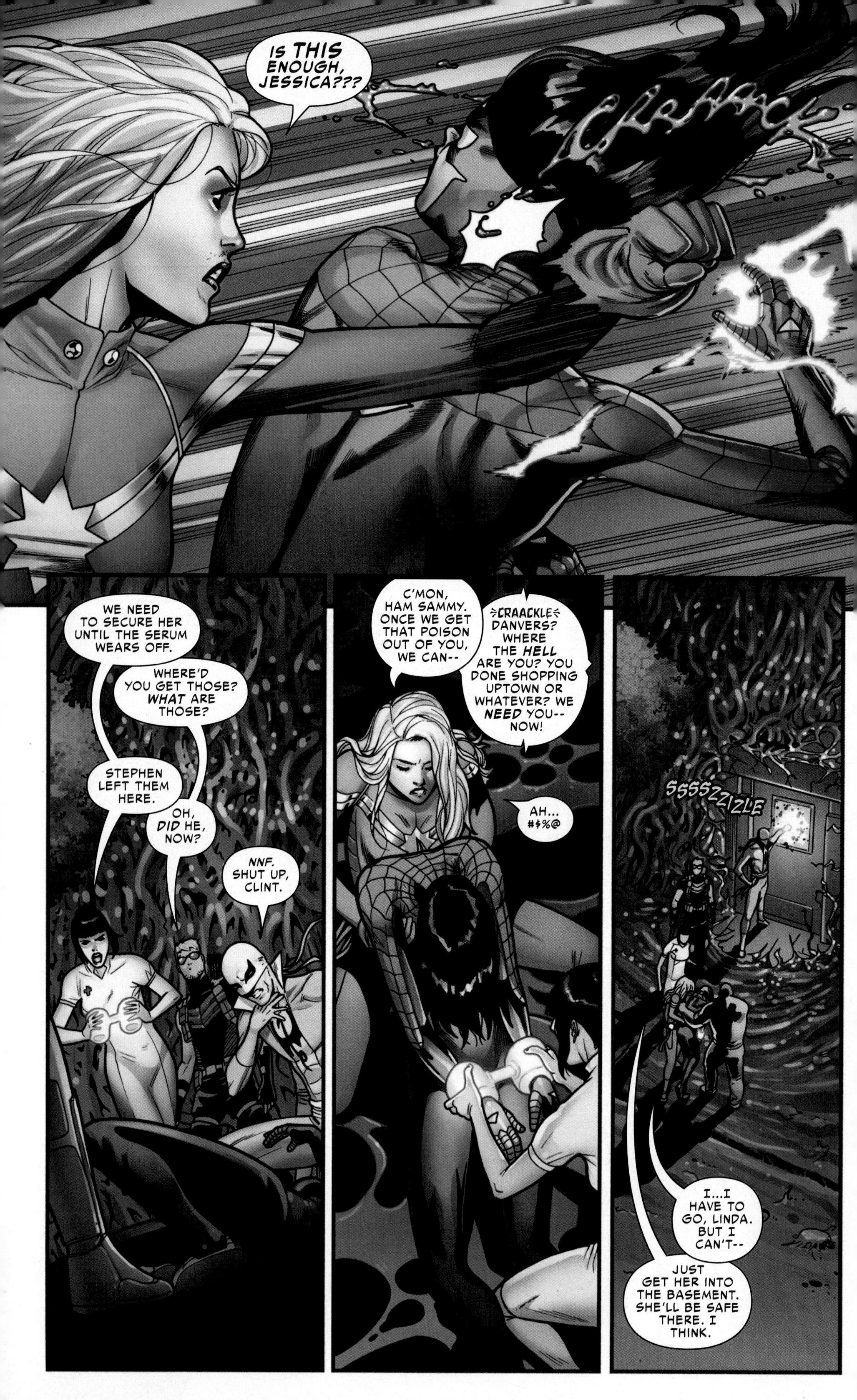
IS THIS ENOUGH, JESSICA???
CRAAACK
WE NEED TO SECURE HER UNTIL THE SERUM WEARS OFF.
WHERE'D YOU GET THOSE? WHAT ARE THOSE?
STEPHEN LEFT THEM HERE.
OH, DID HE, NOW?
NNF. SHUT UP, CLINT.
C'MON, HAM SAMMY. ONCE WE GET THAT POISON OUT OF YOU, WE CAN--
CRAACKLE DANVERS? WHERE THE HELL ARE YOU? YOU DONE SHOPPING UPTOWN OR WHATEVER? WE NEED YOU-- NOW!
AH... #$%@
SSSSZZIZLE
I...I HAVE TO GO, LINDA. BUT I CAN'T--
JUST GET HER INTO THE BASEMENT. SHE'LL BE SAFE THERE. I THINK.

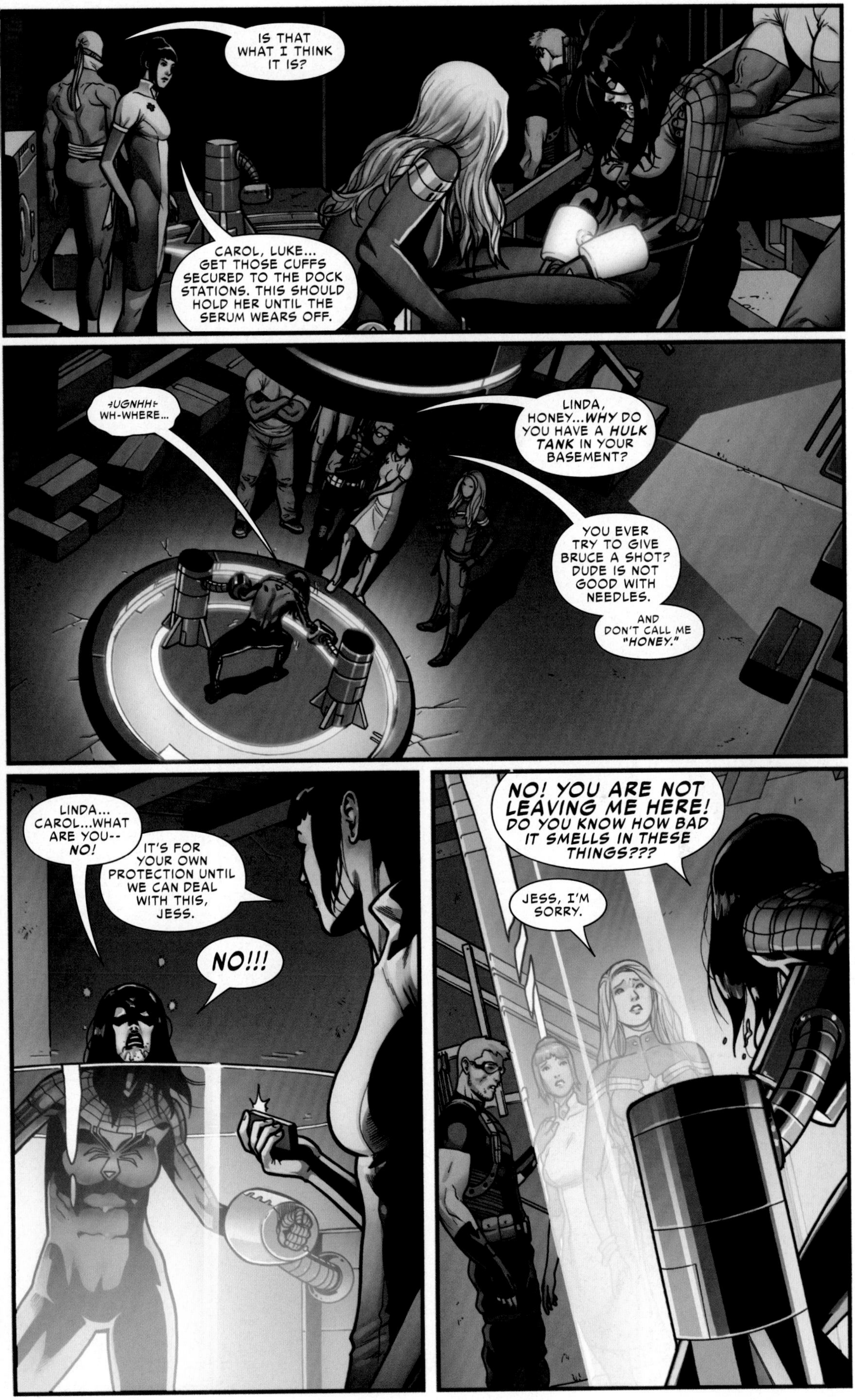

IS THAT WHAT I THINK IT IS?
CAROL, LUKE... GET THOSE CUFFS SECURED TO THE DOCK STATIONS. THIS SHOULD HOLD HER UNTIL THE SERUM WEARS OFF.
UGNHH WH-WHERE...
LINDA, HONEY...WHY DO YOU HAVE A HULK TANK IN YOUR BASEMENT?
YOU EVER TRY TO GIVE BRUCE A SHOT? DUDE IS NOT GOOD WITH NEEDLES.
AND DON'T CALL ME "HONEY."
LINDA... CAROL...WHAT ARE YOU-- NO!
IT'S FOR YOUR OWN PROTECTION UNTIL WE CAN DEAL WITH THIS, JESS.
NO!!!
NO! YOU ARE NOT LEAVING ME HERE! DO YOU KNOW HOW BAD IT SMELLS IN THESE THINGS???
JESS, I'M SORRY.

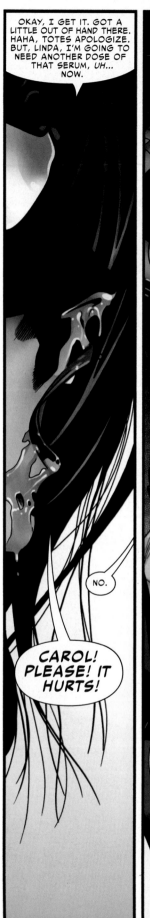

OKAY, I GET IT. GOT A LITTLE OUT OF HAND THERE. HAHA, TOTES APOLOGIZE. BUT, LINDA, I'M GOING TO NEED ANOTHER DOSE OF THAT SERUM, UH... NOW.

NO.

CAROL! PLEASE! IT HURTS!

RYAAHHH!!!

CAN THIS THING ACTUALLY HOLD HER?

I'M... NOT SURE. IN HINDSIGHT, I SHOULD HAVE WONDERED WHY IT WAS SO CHEAP.

...AND WHY TONY STARK WAS HAVING A GARAGE SALE IN THE FIRST PLACE.

CAROL!!!! GIVE ME THE SERUM!

YOU DON'T NEED IT, JESS! I'LL COME BACK AND WE'LL FIND SOMETHING THAT DOESN'T DO THIS TO YOU. THAT DOESN'T DESTROY YOU LIKE IT DID YOUR MOTHER ON WUNDAGORE!

KRSHH

THAT ABOMINATION WASN'T MY MOTHER!

GRRRNCH

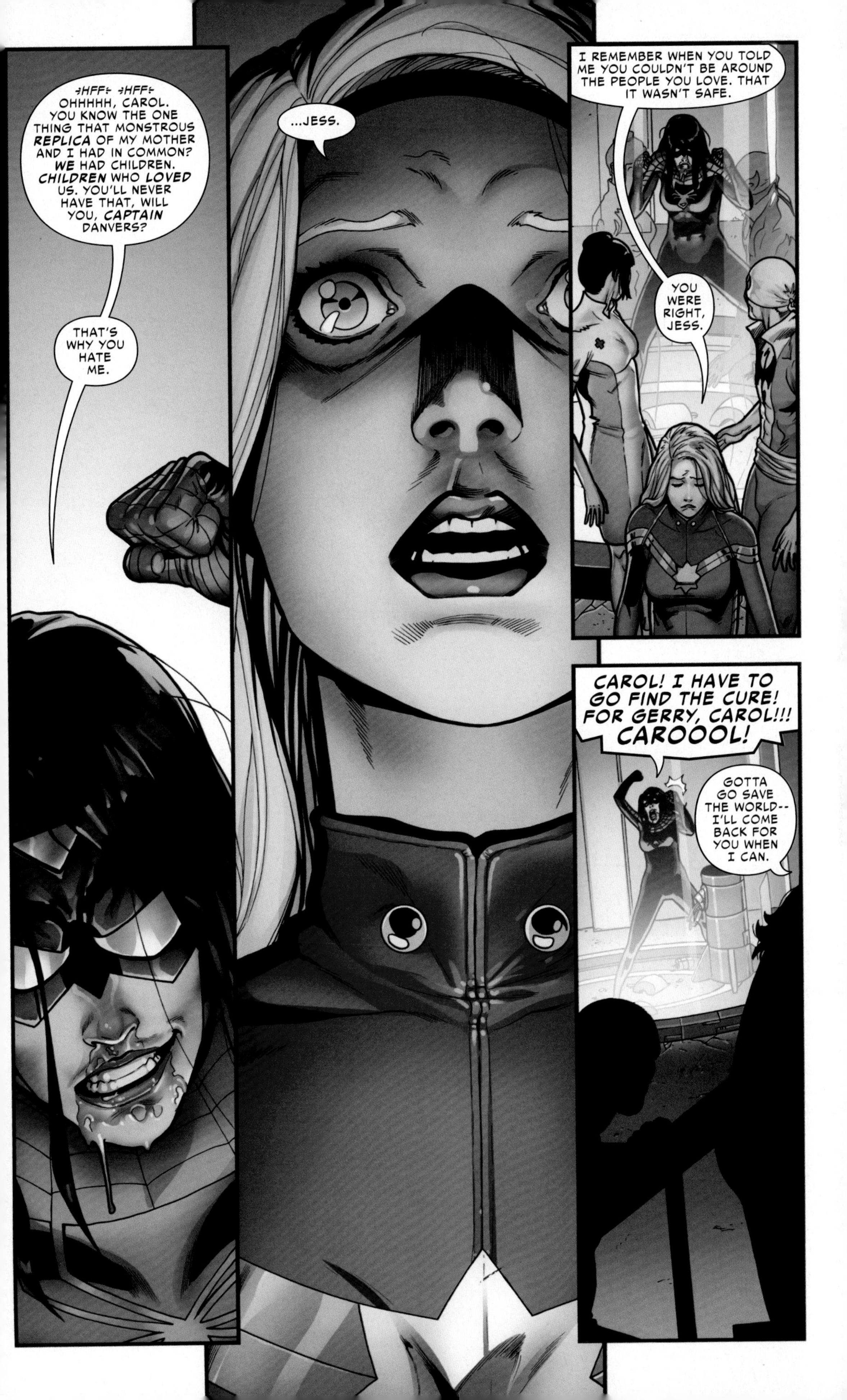

HFF HFF OHHHHH, CAROL. YOU KNOW THE ONE THING THAT MONSTROUS REPLICA OF MY MOTHER AND I HAD IN COMMON? WE HAD CHILDREN. CHILDREN WHO LOVED US. YOU'LL NEVER HAVE THAT, WILL YOU, CAPTAIN DANVERS?
THAT'S WHY YOU HATE ME.
...JESS.
I REMEMBER WHEN YOU TOLD ME YOU COULDN'T BE AROUND THE PEOPLE YOU LOVE. THAT IT WASN'T SAFE.
YOU WERE RIGHT, JESS.
CAROL! I HAVE TO GO FIND THE CURE! FOR GERRY, CAROL!!! CAROOOL!
GOTTA GO SAVE THE WORLD-- I'LL COME BACK FOR YOU WHEN I CAN.

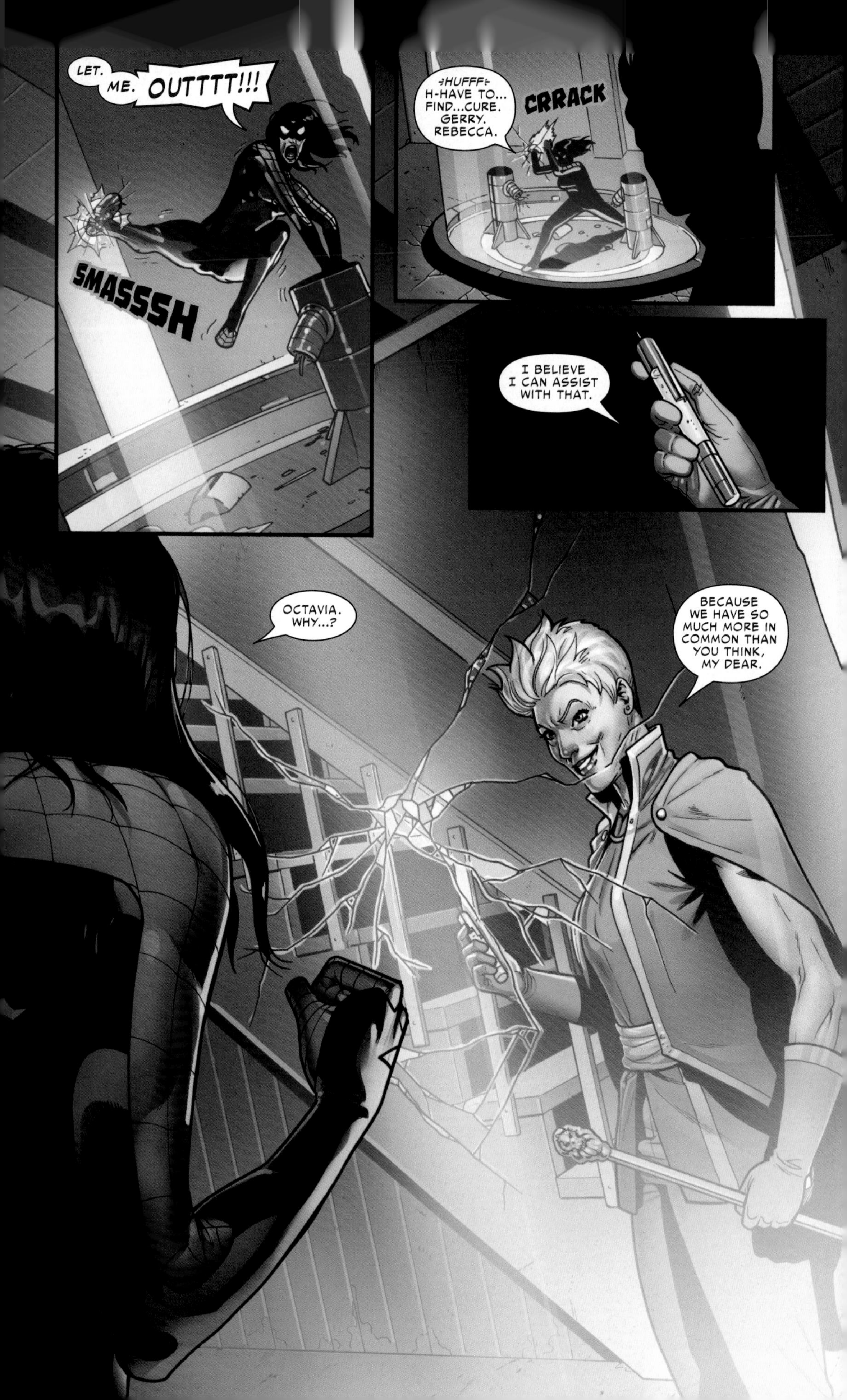

LET. ME. OUTTTT!!!
SMASSSH
⇌HUFFF⇌ H-HAVE TO... FIND...CURE. GERRY. REBECCA.
CRRACK
I BELIEVE I CAN ASSIST WITH THAT.
OCTAVIA. WHY...?
BECAUSE WE HAVE SO MUCH MORE IN COMMON THAN YOU THINK, MY DEAR.

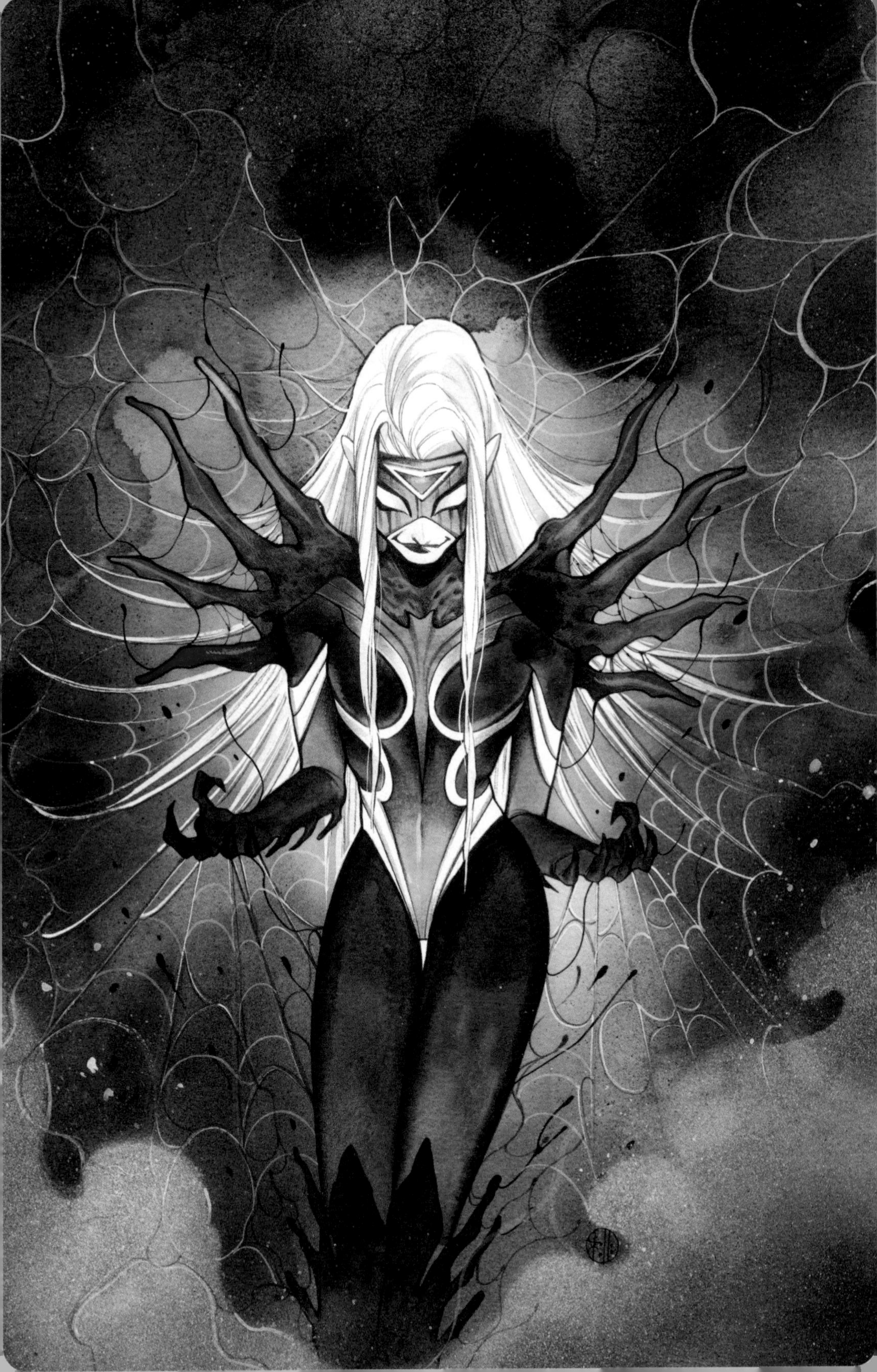

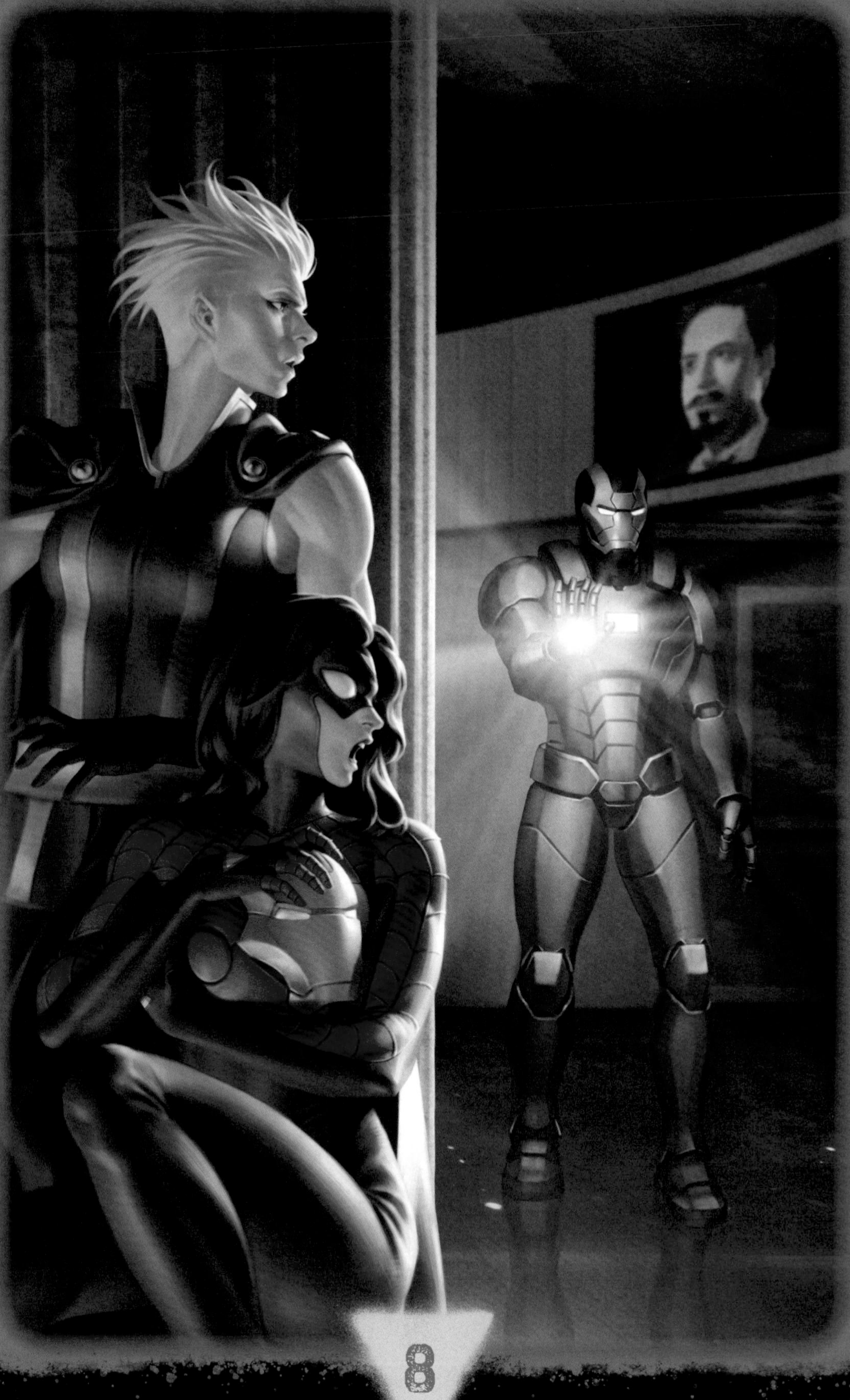

8

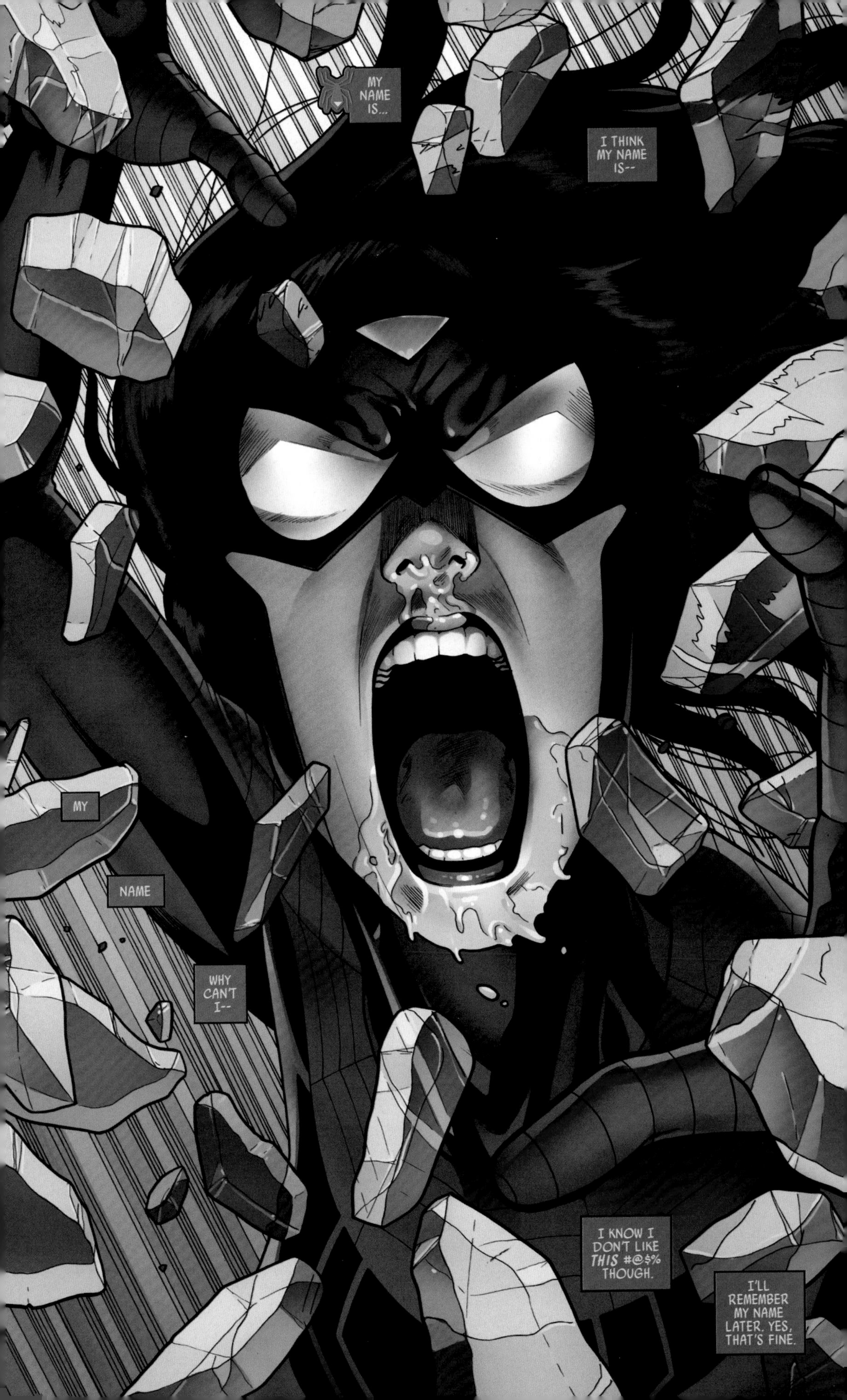

MY NAME IS...
I THINK MY NAME IS--
MY
NAME
WHY CAN'T I--
I KNOW I DON'T LIKE *THIS* #@$% THOUGH.
I'LL REMEMBER MY NAME LATER. YES, THAT'S FINE.

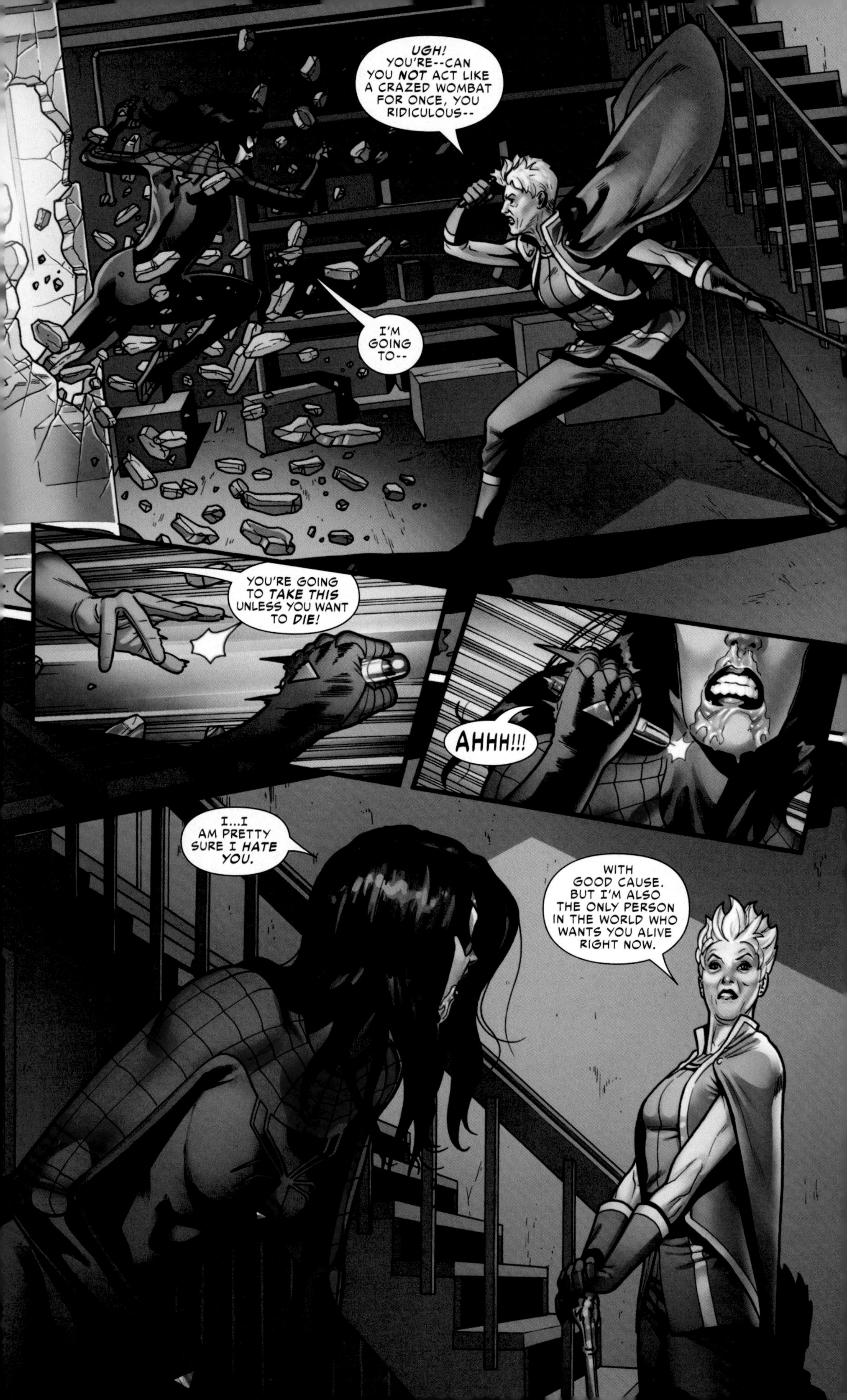
UGH! YOU'RE--CAN YOU NOT ACT LIKE A CRAZED WOMBAT FOR ONCE, YOU RIDICULOUS--
I'M GOING TO--
YOU'RE GOING TO TAKE THIS UNLESS YOU WANT TO DIE!
AHHH!!!
I...I AM PRETTY SURE I HATE YOU.
WITH GOOD CAUSE. BUT I'M ALSO THE ONLY PERSON IN THE WORLD WHO WANTS YOU ALIVE RIGHT NOW.

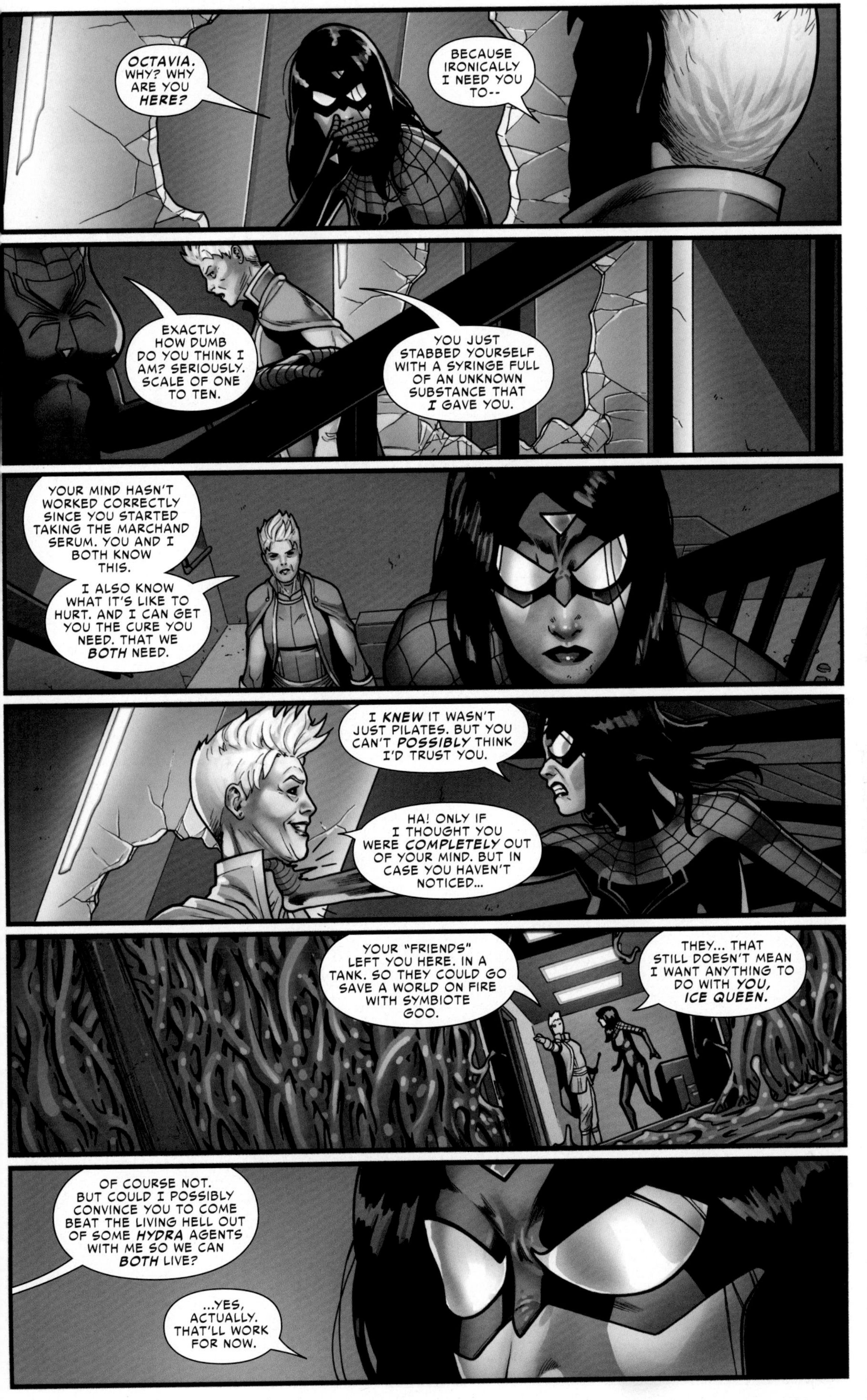
OCTAVIA. WHY? WHY ARE YOU HERE?
BECAUSE IRONICALLY I NEED YOU TO--
EXACTLY HOW DUMB DO YOU THINK I AM? SERIOUSLY. SCALE OF ONE TO TEN.
YOU JUST STABBED YOURSELF WITH A SYRINGE FULL OF AN UNKNOWN SUBSTANCE THAT I GAVE YOU.
YOUR MIND HASN'T WORKED CORRECTLY SINCE YOU STARTED TAKING THE MARCHAND SERUM. YOU AND I BOTH KNOW THIS.
I ALSO KNOW WHAT IT'S LIKE TO HURT. AND I CAN GET YOU THE CURE YOU NEED. THAT WE BOTH NEED.
I KNEW IT WASN'T JUST PILATES. BUT YOU CAN'T POSSIBLY THINK I'D TRUST YOU.
HA! ONLY IF I THOUGHT YOU WERE COMPLETELY OUT OF YOUR MIND. BUT IN CASE YOU HAVEN'T NOTICED...
YOUR "FRIENDS" LEFT YOU HERE. IN A TANK. SO THEY COULD GO SAVE A WORLD ON FIRE WITH SYMBIOTE GOO.
THEY... THAT STILL DOESN'T MEAN I WANT ANYTHING TO DO WITH YOU, ICE QUEEN.
OF COURSE NOT. BUT COULD I POSSIBLY CONVINCE YOU TO COME BEAT THE LIVING HELL OUT OF SOME HYDRA AGENTS WITH ME SO WE CAN BOTH LIVE?
...YES, ACTUALLY. THAT'LL WORK FOR NOW.

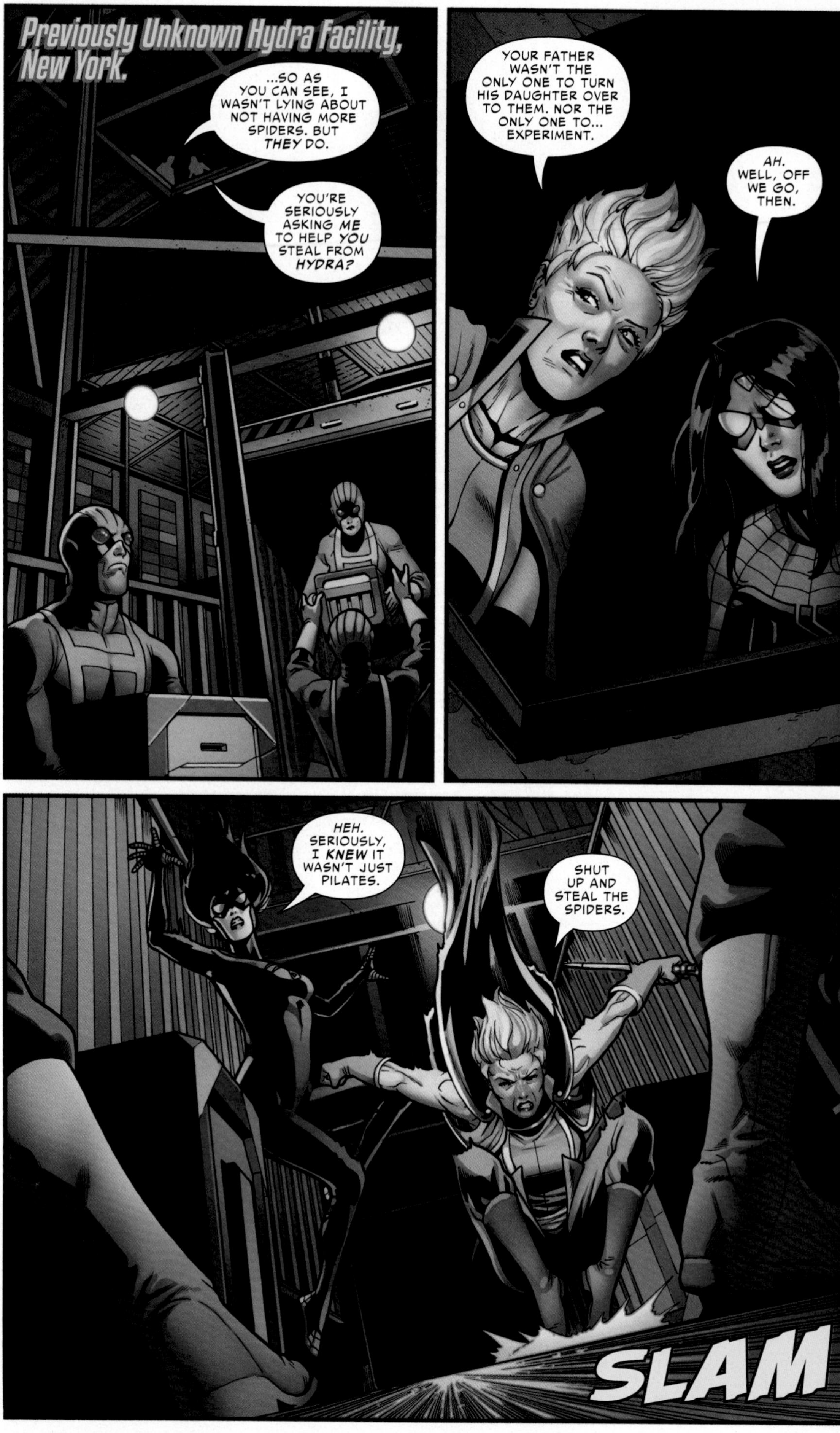
Previously Unknown Hydra Facility, New York.
...SO AS YOU CAN SEE, I WASN'T LYING ABOUT NOT HAVING MORE SPIDERS. BUT *THEY* DO.
YOU'RE SERIOUSLY ASKING *ME* TO HELP *YOU* STEAL FROM *HYDRA?*
YOUR FATHER WASN'T THE ONLY ONE TO TURN HIS DAUGHTER OVER TO THEM. NOR THE ONLY ONE TO... EXPERIMENT.
AH. WELL, OFF WE GO, THEN.
HEH. SERIOUSLY, I *KNEW* IT WASN'T JUST PILATES.
SHUT UP AND STEAL THE SPIDERS.
SLAM

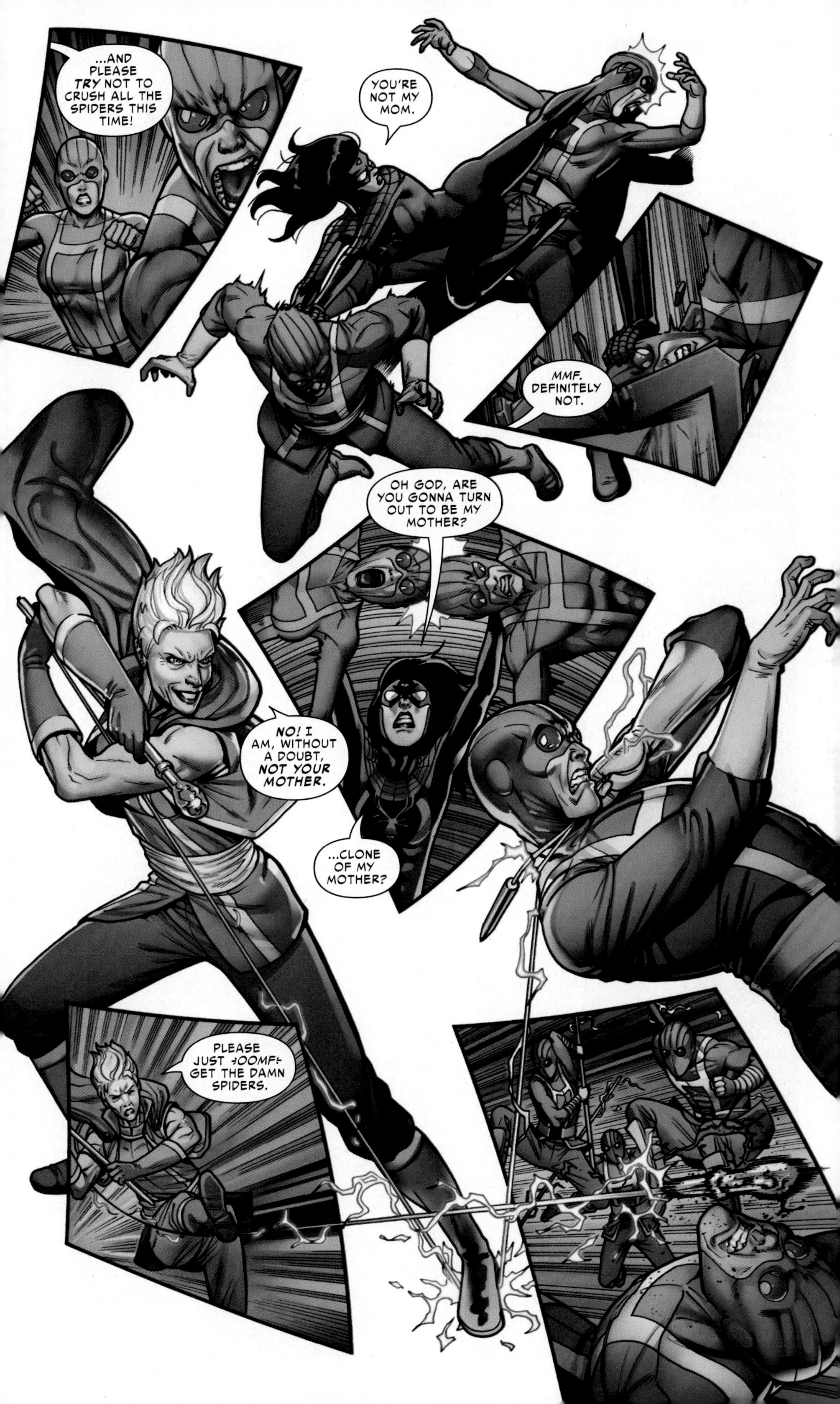
...AND PLEASE TRY NOT TO CRUSH ALL THE SPIDERS THIS TIME!
YOU'RE NOT MY MOM.
MMF. DEFINITELY NOT.
OH GOD, ARE YOU GONNA TURN OUT TO BE MY MOTHER?
NO! I AM, WITHOUT A DOUBT, NOT YOUR MOTHER.
...CLONE OF MY MOTHER?
PLEASE JUST ÷OOMF÷ GET THE DAMN SPIDERS.

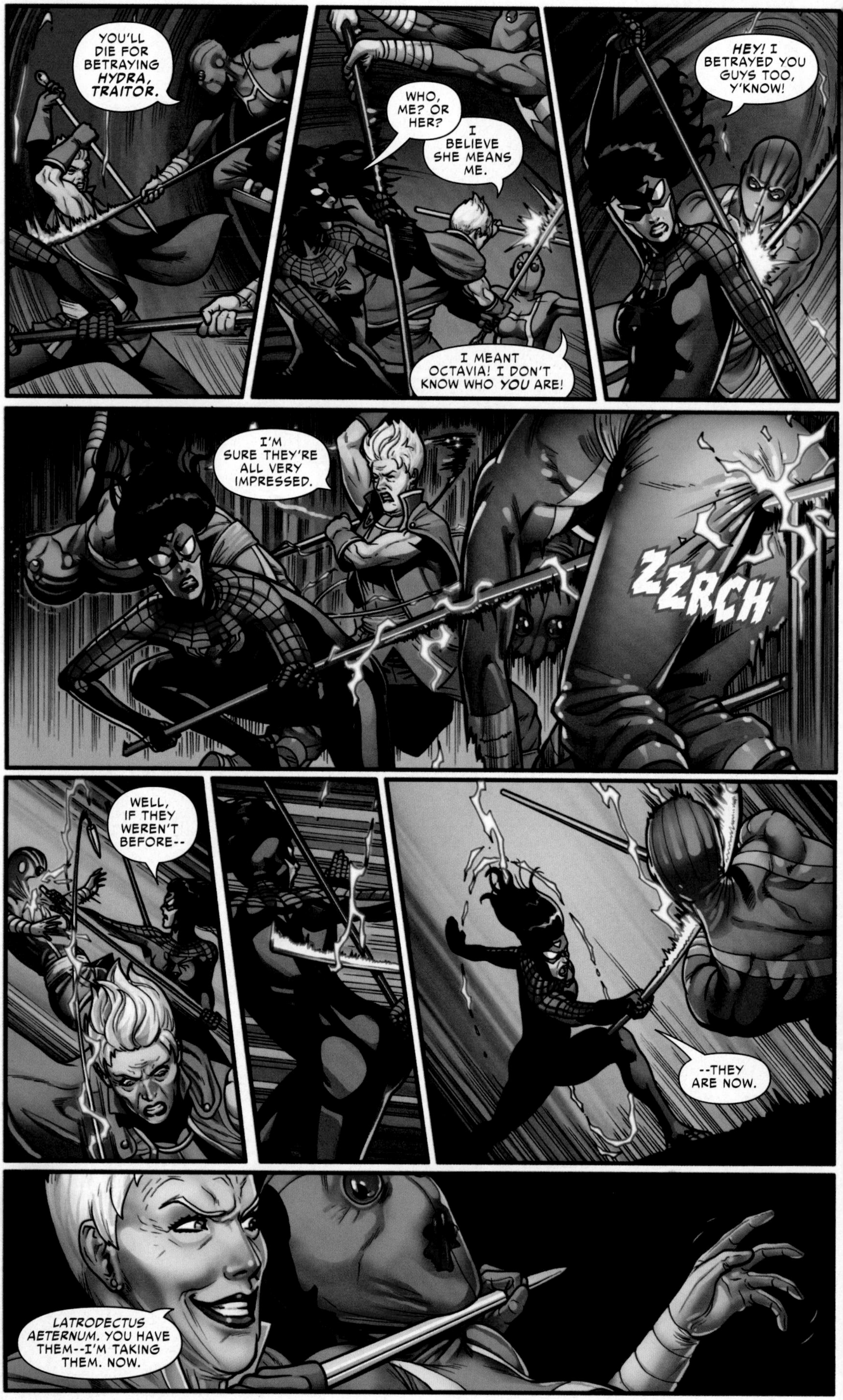
YOU'LL DIE FOR BETRAYING *HYDRA*, *TRAITOR*.
WHO, ME? OR HER?
I BELIEVE SHE MEANS ME.
I MEANT OCTAVIA! I DON'T KNOW WHO *YOU* ARE!
HEY! I BETRAYED YOU GUYS TOO, Y'KNOW!
I'M SURE THEY'RE ALL VERY IMPRESSED.
ZZRCH
WELL, IF THEY WEREN'T BEFORE--
--THEY ARE NOW.
LATRODECTUS AETERNUM. YOU HAVE THEM--I'M TAKING THEM. NOW.

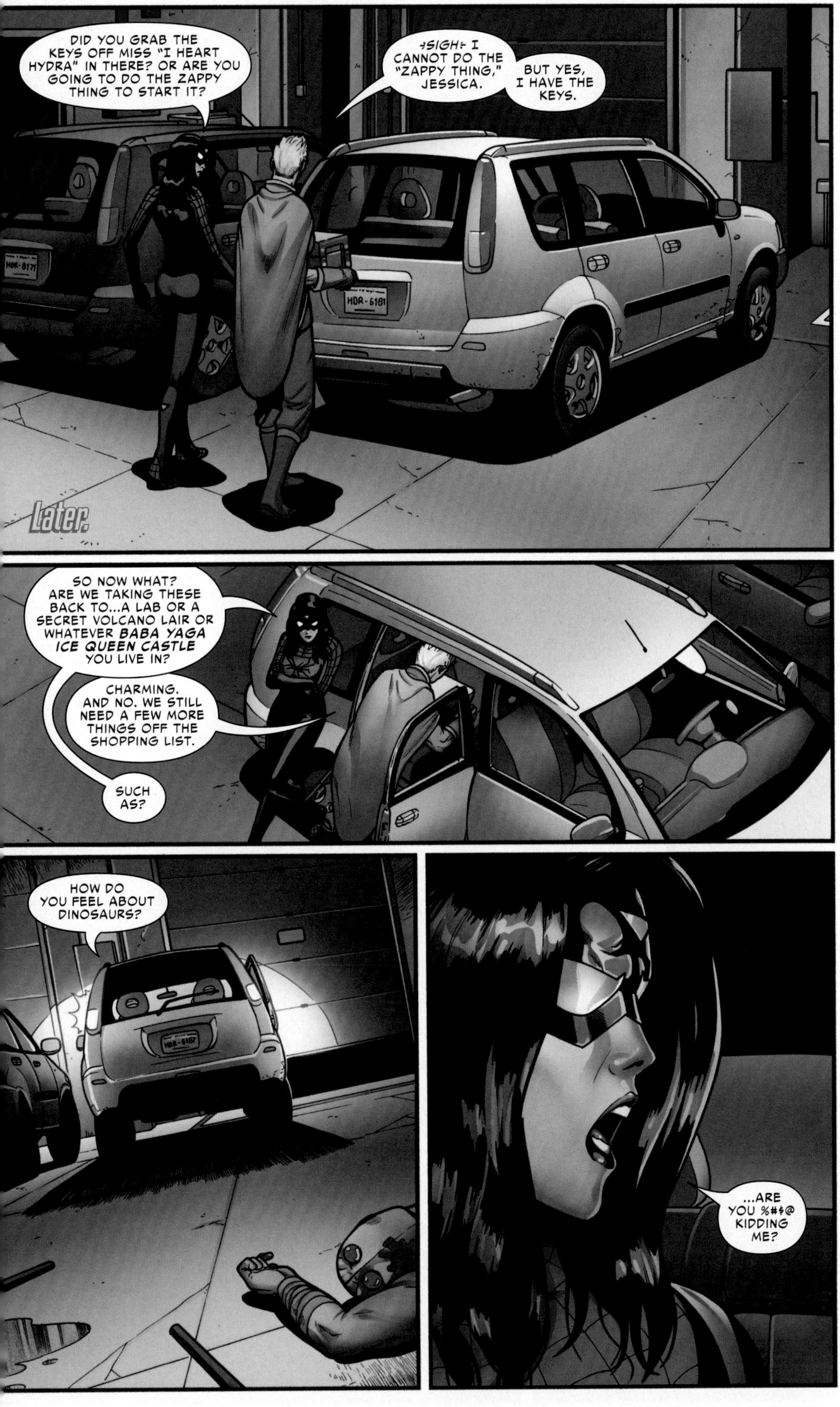
DID YOU GRAB THE KEYS OFF MISS "I HEART HYDRA" IN THERE? OR ARE YOU GOING TO DO THE ZAPPY THING TO START IT?
SIGH I CANNOT DO THE "ZAPPY THING," JESSICA.
BUT YES, I HAVE THE KEYS.
LATER.
SO NOW WHAT? ARE WE TAKING THESE BACK TO...A LAB OR A SECRET VOLCANO LAIR OR WHATEVER BABA YAGA ICE QUEEN CASTLE YOU LIVE IN?
CHARMING. AND NO. WE STILL NEED A FEW MORE THINGS OFF THE SHOPPING LIST.
SUCH AS?
HOW DO YOU FEEL ABOUT DINOSAURS?
...ARE YOU %#$@ KIDDING ME?

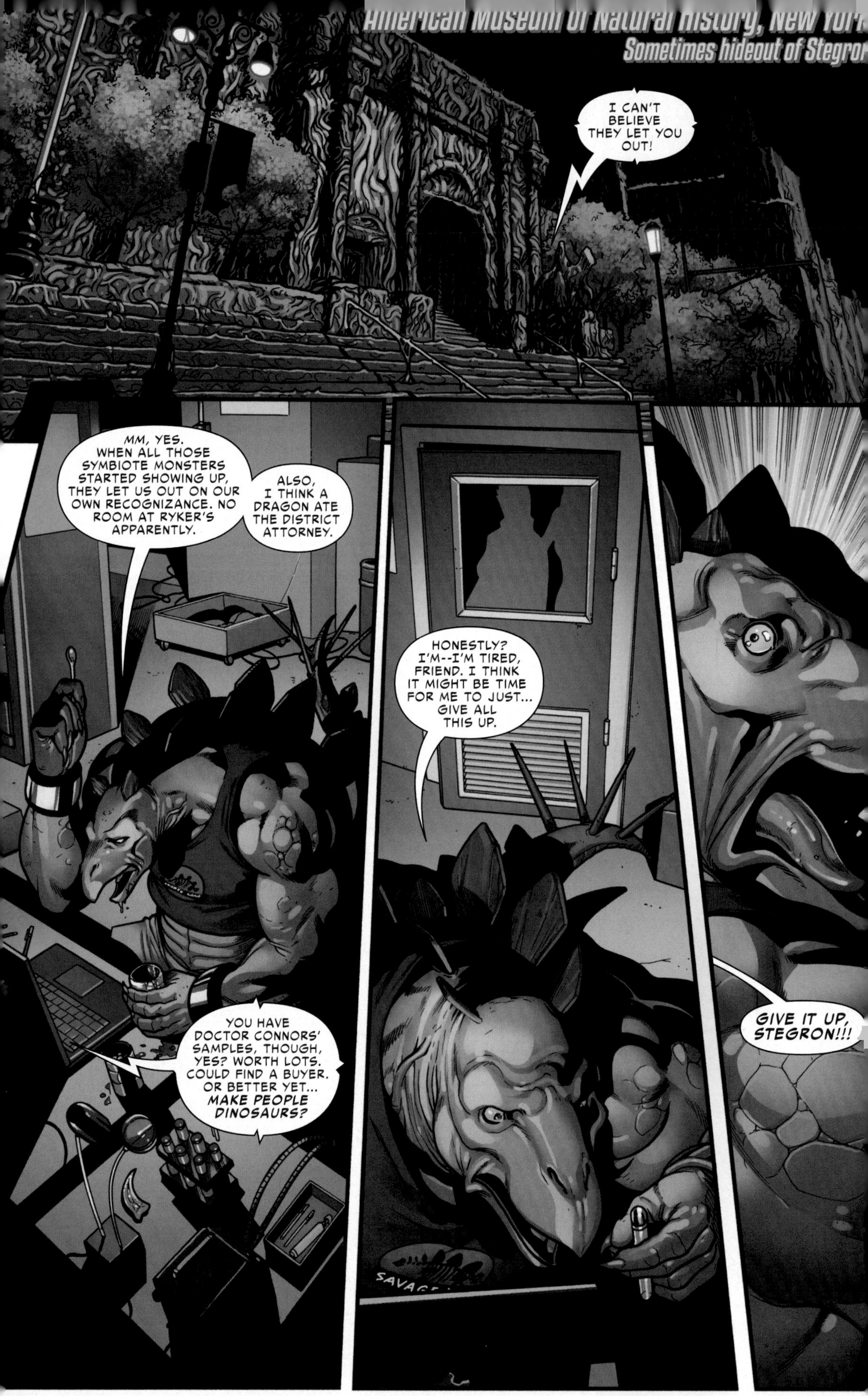

American Museum of Natural History, New York
Sometimes hideout of Stegron
I CAN'T BELIEVE THEY LET YOU OUT!
MM, YES. WHEN ALL THOSE SYMBIOTE MONSTERS STARTED SHOWING UP, THEY LET US OUT ON OUR OWN RECOGNIZANCE. NO ROOM AT RYKER'S APPARENTLY.
ALSO, I THINK A DRAGON ATE THE DISTRICT ATTORNEY.
YOU HAVE DOCTOR CONNORS' SAMPLES, THOUGH, YES? WORTH LOTS. COULD FIND A BUYER. OR BETTER YET... MAKE PEOPLE DINOSAURS?
HONESTLY? I'M--I'M TIRED, FRIEND. I THINK IT MIGHT BE TIME FOR ME TO JUST... GIVE ALL THIS UP.
GIVE IT UP, STEGRON!!!

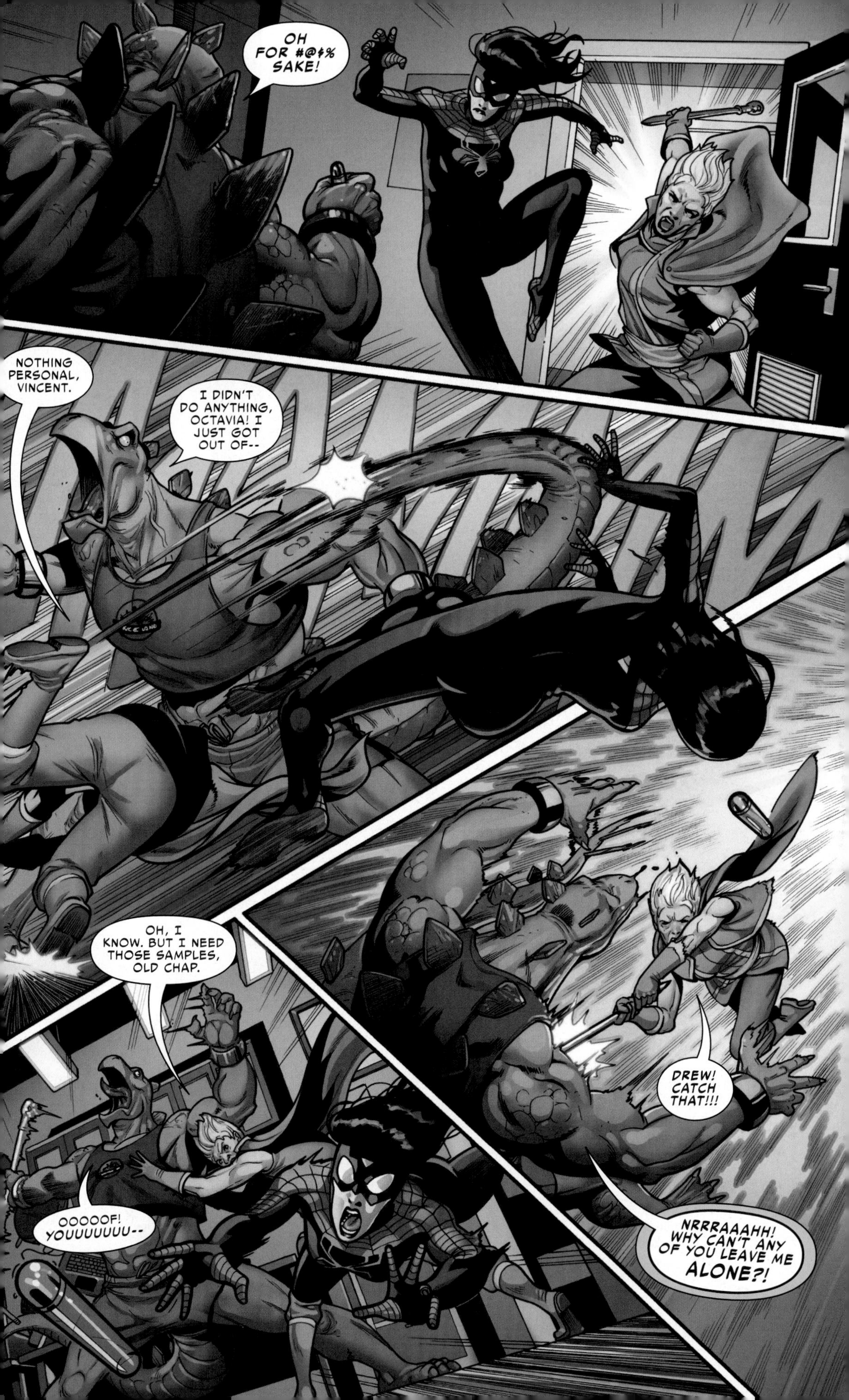
OH FOR #@$% SAKE!
NOTHING PERSONAL, VINCENT.
I DIDN'T DO ANYTHING, OCTAVIA! I JUST GOT OUT OF--
OH, I KNOW. BUT I NEED THOSE SAMPLES, OLD CHAP.
DREW! CATCH THAT!!!
OOOOOF! YOUUUUUUU--
NRRRAAAHH! WHY CAN'T ANY OF YOU LEAVE ME ALONE?!

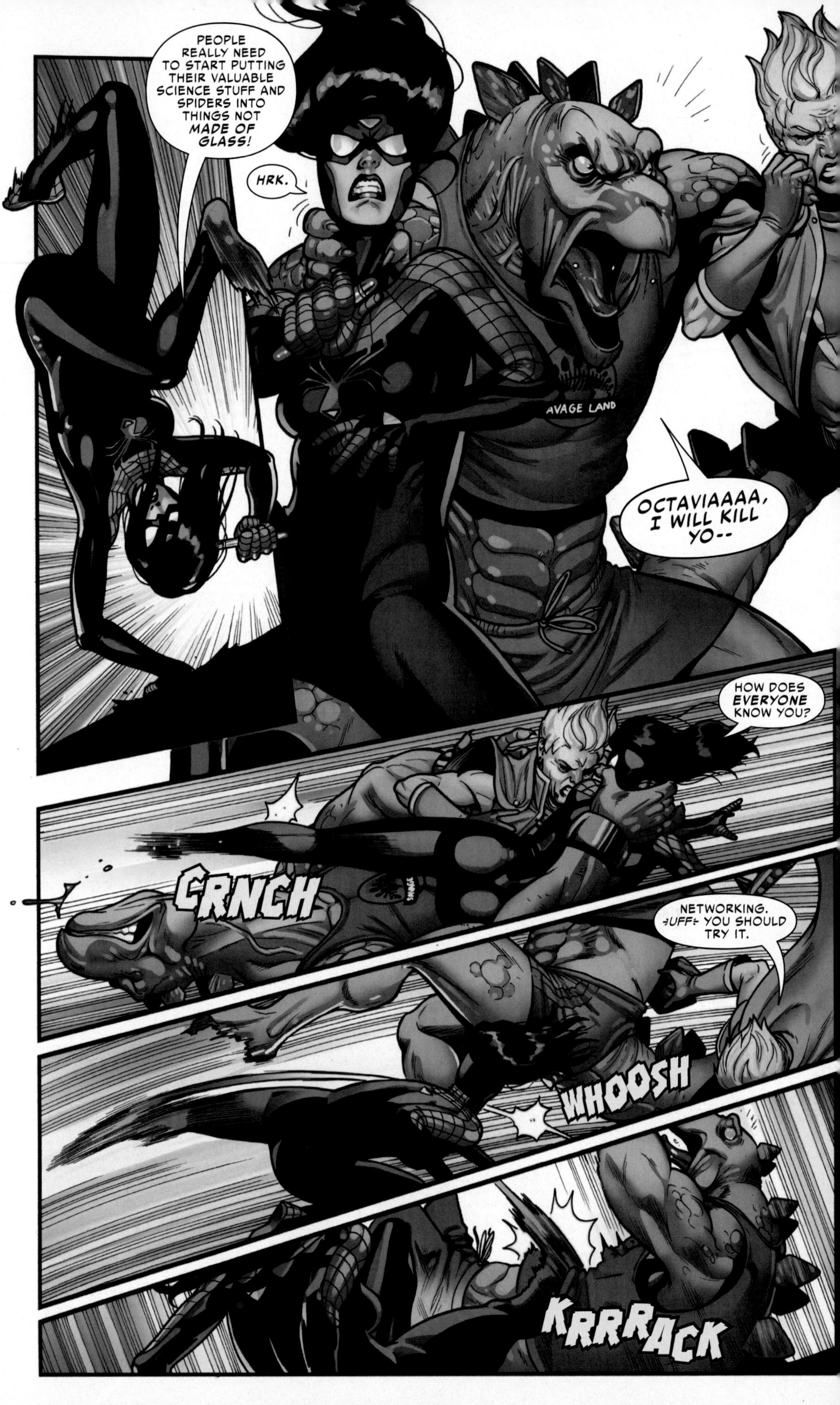
PEOPLE REALLY NEED TO START PUTTING THEIR VALUABLE SCIENCE STUFF AND SPIDERS INTO THINGS NOT MADE OF GLASS!
HRK.
AVAGE LAND
OCTAVIAAAA, I WILL KILL YO--
HOW DOES EVERYONE KNOW YOU?
CRNCH
NETWORKING. *UFF* YOU SHOULD TRY IT.
WHOOSH
KRRRACK

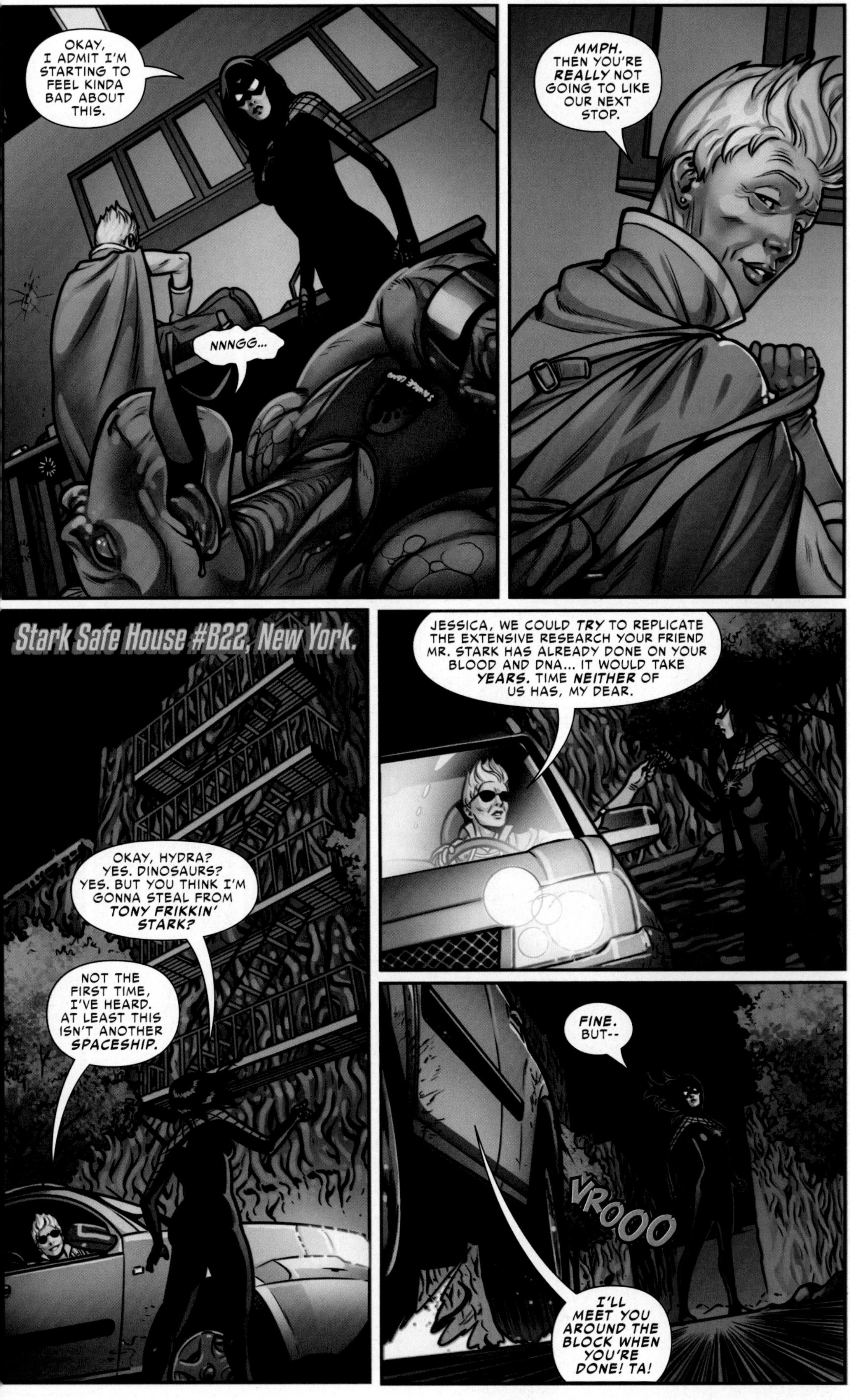
OKAY, I ADMIT I'M STARTING TO FEEL KINDA BAD ABOUT THIS.
NNNGG...
MMPH. THEN YOU'RE REALLY NOT GOING TO LIKE OUR NEXT STOP.
Stark Safe House #B22, New York.
OKAY, HYDRA? YES. DINOSAURS? YES. BUT YOU THINK I'M GONNA STEAL FROM TONY FRIKKIN' STARK?
NOT THE FIRST TIME, I'VE HEARD. AT LEAST THIS ISN'T ANOTHER SPACESHIP.
JESSICA, WE COULD TRY TO REPLICATE THE EXTENSIVE RESEARCH YOUR FRIEND MR. STARK HAS ALREADY DONE ON YOUR BLOOD AND DNA... IT WOULD TAKE YEARS. TIME NEITHER OF US HAS, MY DEAR.
FINE. BUT--
VROOO
I'LL MEET YOU AROUND THE BLOCK WHEN YOU'RE DONE! TA!

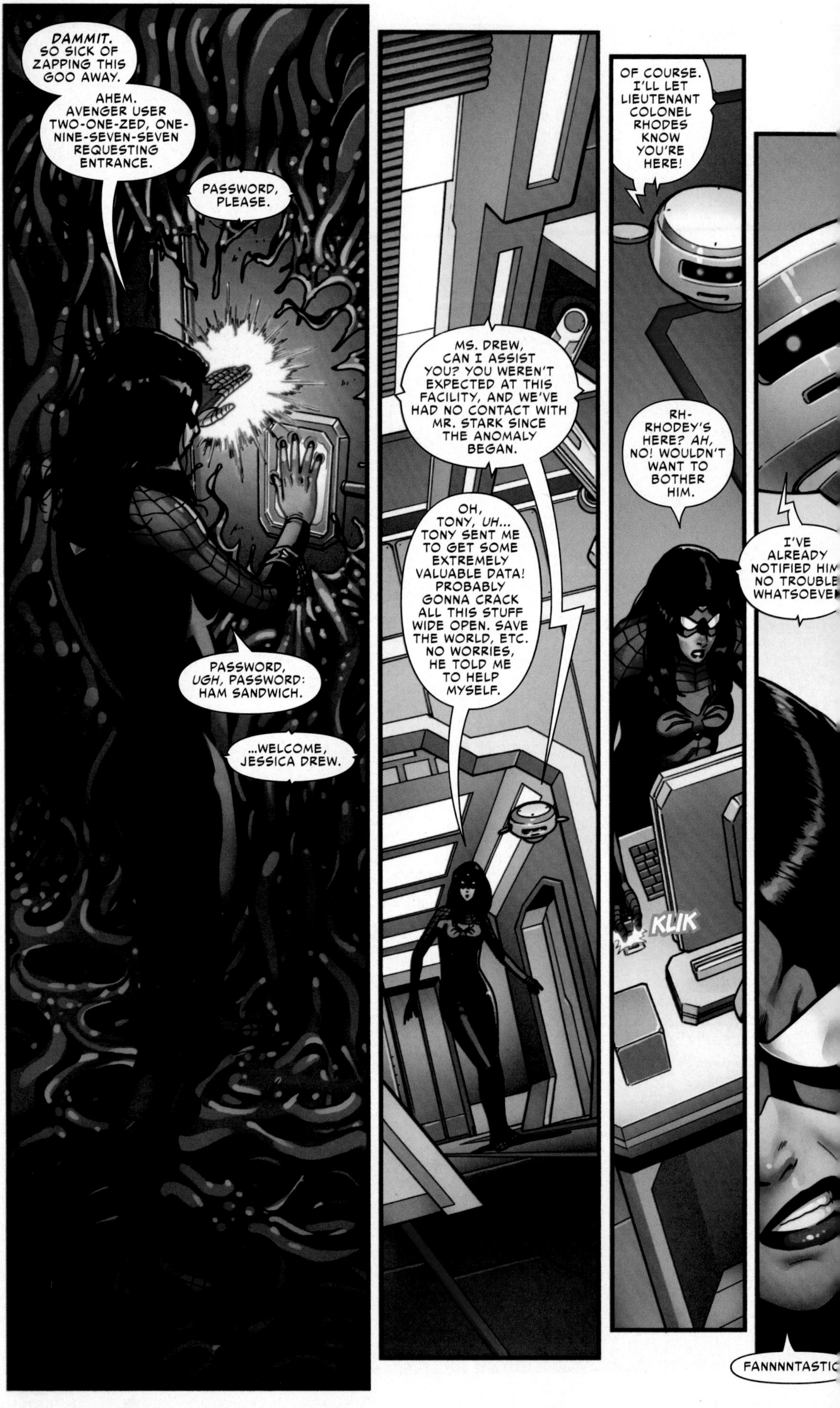
DAMMIT. SO SICK OF ZAPPING THIS GOO AWAY.
AHEM. AVENGER USER TWO-ONE-ZED, ONE-NINE-SEVEN-SEVEN REQUESTING ENTRANCE.
PASSWORD, PLEASE.
PASSWORD, UGH, PASSWORD: HAM SANDWICH.
...WELCOME, JESSICA DREW.
MS. DREW, CAN I ASSIST YOU? YOU WEREN'T EXPECTED AT THIS FACILITY, AND WE'VE HAD NO CONTACT WITH MR. STARK SINCE THE ANOMALY BEGAN.
OH, TONY, UH... TONY SENT ME TO GET SOME EXTREMELY VALUABLE DATA! PROBABLY GONNA CRACK ALL THIS STUFF WIDE OPEN. SAVE THE WORLD, ETC. NO WORRIES, HE TOLD ME TO HELP MYSELF.
OF COURSE. I'LL LET LIEUTENANT COLONEL RHODES KNOW YOU'RE HERE!
RH-RHODEY'S HERE? AH, NO! WOULDN'T WANT TO BOTHER HIM.
KLIK
I'VE ALREADY NOTIFIED HIM NO TROUBLE WHATSOEVE
FANNNNTASTIC

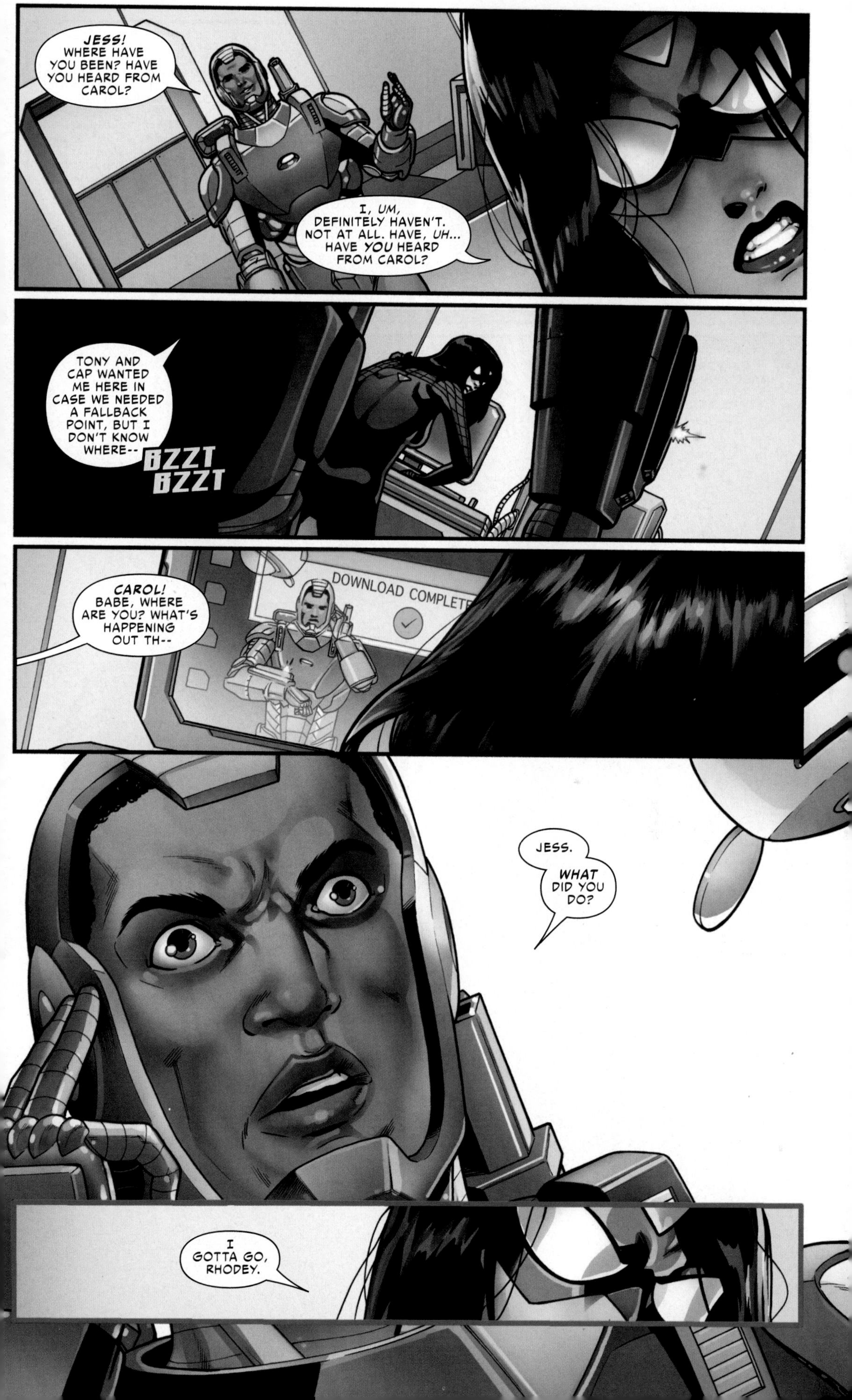
JESS! WHERE HAVE YOU BEEN? HAVE YOU HEARD FROM CAROL?
I, UM, DEFINITELY HAVEN'T. NOT AT ALL. HAVE, UH... HAVE YOU HEARD FROM CAROL?
TONY AND CAP WANTED ME HERE IN CASE WE NEEDED A FALLBACK POINT, BUT I DON'T KNOW WHERE--
BZZT BZZT
DOWNLOAD COMPLETE
CAROL! BABE, WHERE ARE YOU? WHAT'S HAPPENING OUT TH--
JESS.
WHAT DID YOU DO?
I GOTTA GO, RHODEY.

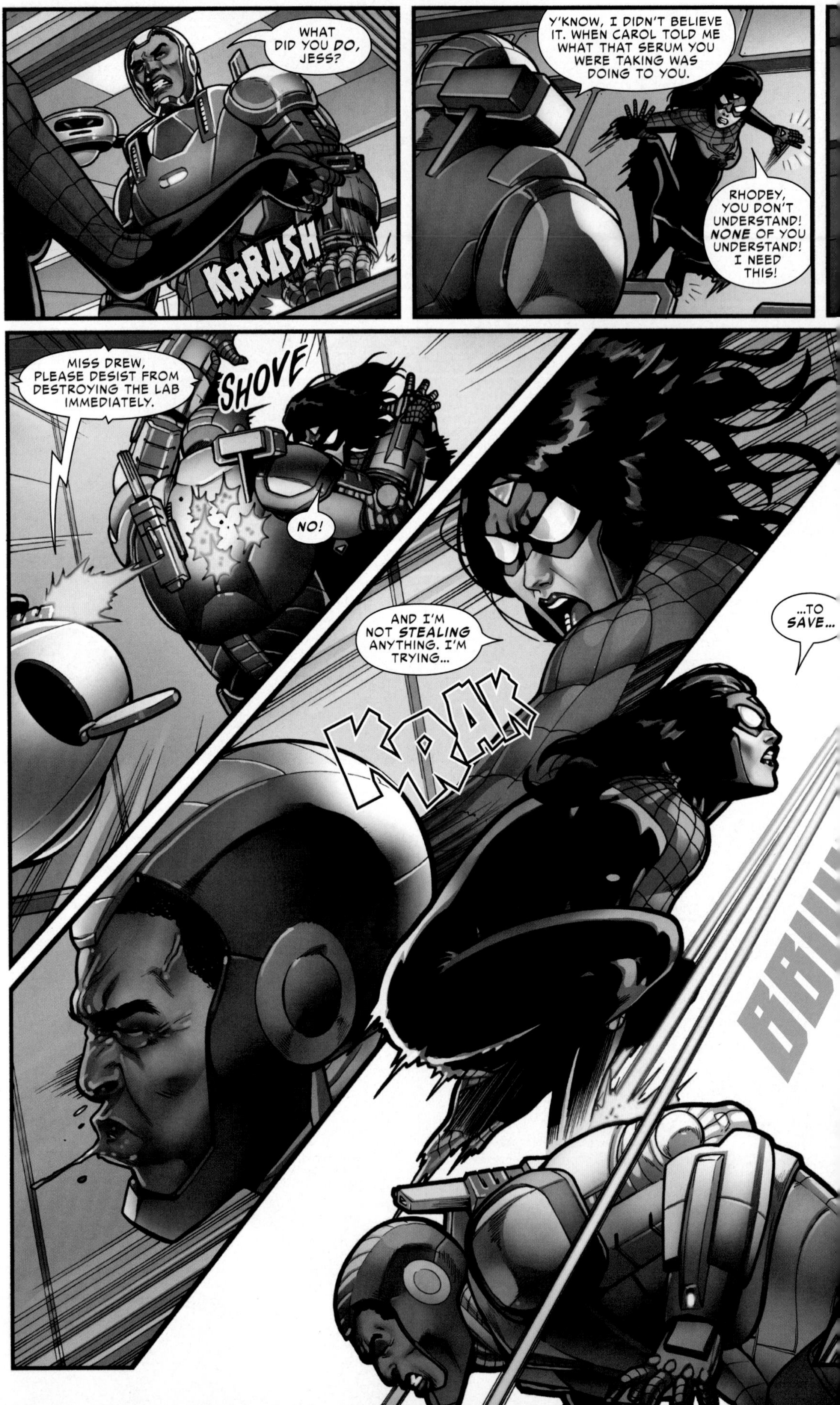

WHAT DID YOU DO, JESS?
KRRASH
Y'KNOW, I DIDN'T BELIEVE IT. WHEN CAROL TOLD ME WHAT THAT SERUM YOU WERE TAKING WAS DOING TO YOU.
RHODEY, YOU DON'T UNDERSTAND! NONE OF YOU UNDERSTAND! I NEED THIS!
MISS DREW, PLEASE DESIST FROM DESTROYING THE LAB IMMEDIATELY.
SHOVE
NO!
AND I'M NOT STEALING ANYTHING. I'M TRYING...
KRAK
...TO SAVE...

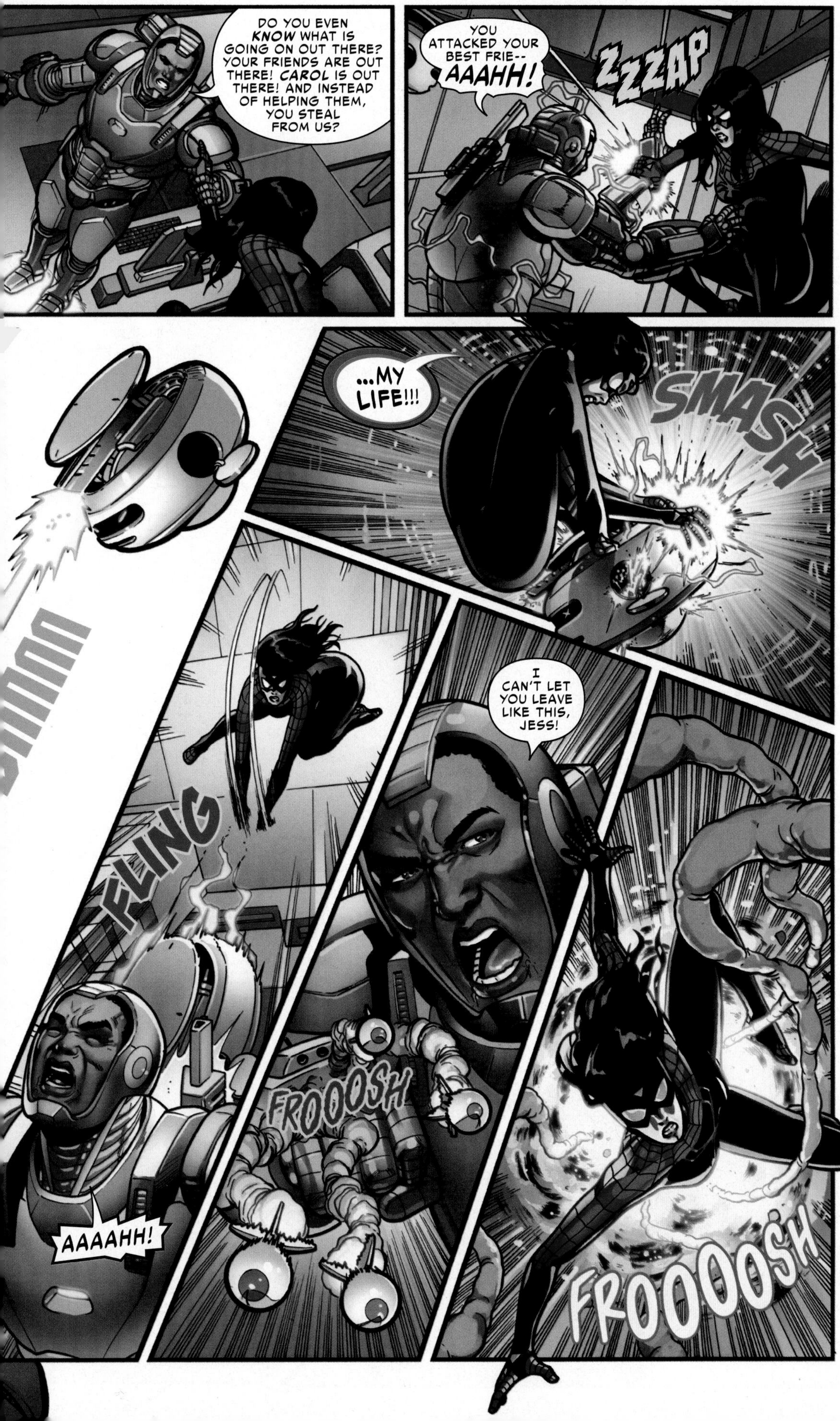
DO YOU EVEN KNOW WHAT IS GOING ON OUT THERE? YOUR FRIENDS ARE OUT THERE! CAROL IS OUT THERE! AND INSTEAD OF HELPING THEM, YOU STEAL FROM US?
YOU ATTACKED YOUR BEST FRIE-- AAAHH!
ZZZAP
...MY LIFE!!!
SMASH
FLING
AAAAHH!
I CAN'T LET YOU LEAVE LIKE THIS, JESS!
FROOOSH
FROOOOSH

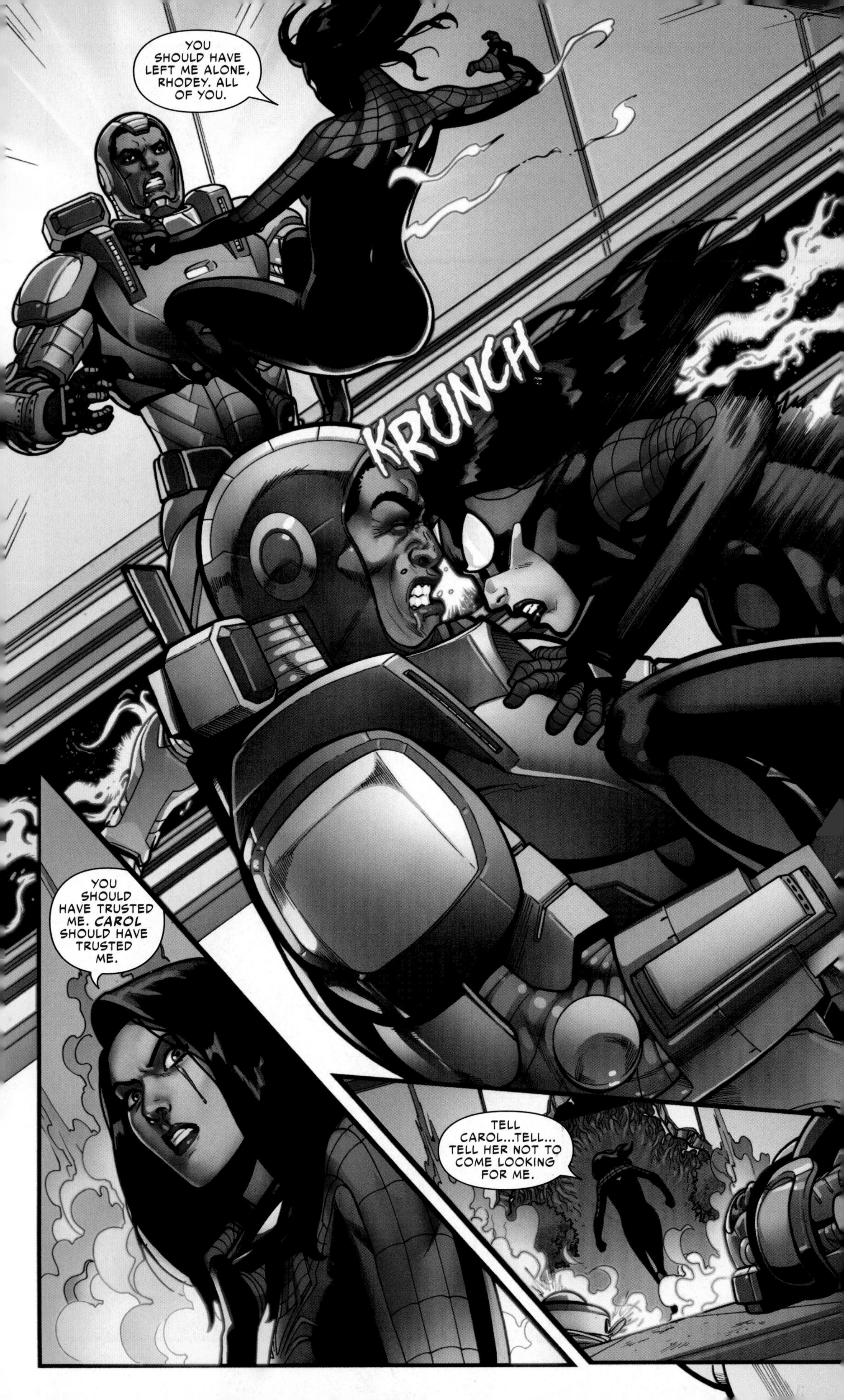
YOU SHOULD HAVE LEFT ME ALONE, RHODEY. ALL OF YOU.
KRUNCH
YOU SHOULD HAVE TRUSTED ME. CAROL SHOULD HAVE TRUSTED ME.
TELL CAROL...TELL... TELL HER NOT TO COME LOOKING FOR ME.

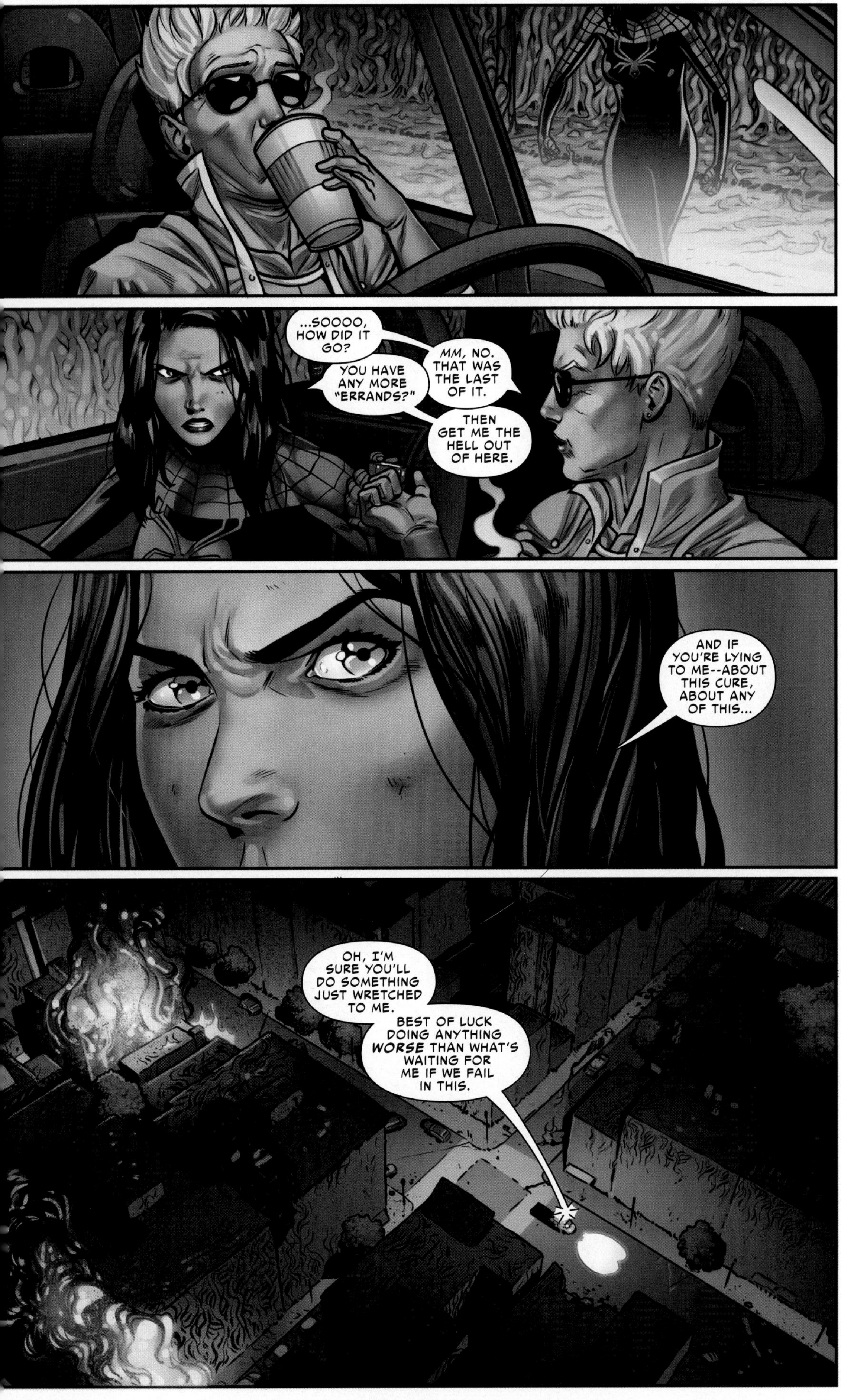
...SOOOO, HOW DID IT GO?
MM, NO. THAT WAS THE LAST OF IT.
YOU HAVE ANY MORE "ERRANDS?"
THEN GET ME THE HELL OUT OF HERE.
AND IF YOU'RE LYING TO ME--ABOUT THIS CURE, ABOUT ANY OF THIS...
OH, I'M SURE YOU'LL DO SOMETHING JUST WRETCHED TO ME.
BEST OF LUCK DOING ANYTHING WORSE THAN WHAT'S WAITING FOR ME IF WE FAIL IN THIS.

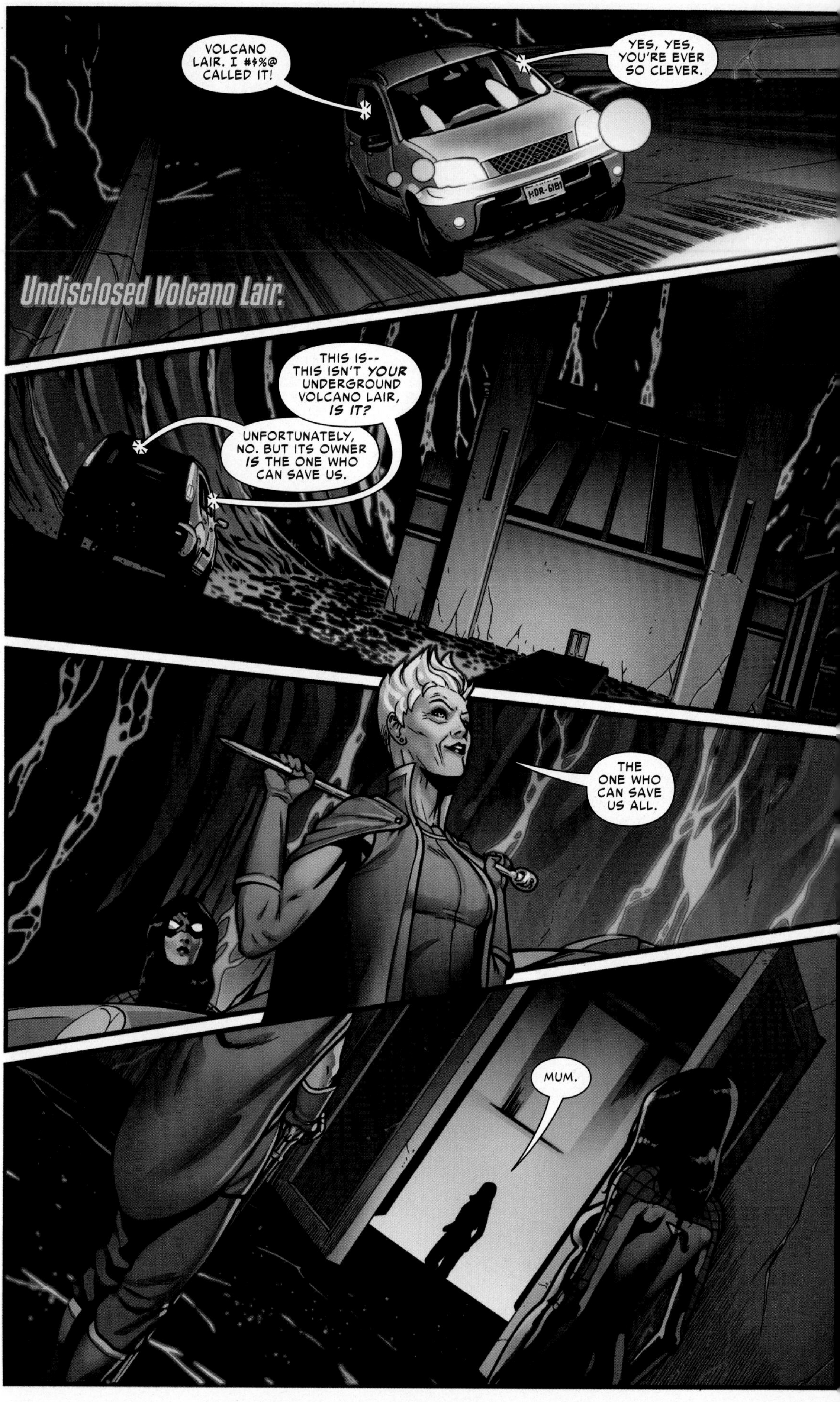
VOLCANO LAIR. I #$%@ CALLED IT!
YES, YES, YOU'RE EVER SO CLEVER.
Undisclosed Volcano Lair.
THIS IS-- THIS ISN'T YOUR UNDERGROUND VOLCANO LAIR, IS IT?
UNFORTUNATELY, NO. BUT ITS OWNER IS THE ONE WHO CAN SAVE US.
THE ONE WHO CAN SAVE US ALL.
MUM.

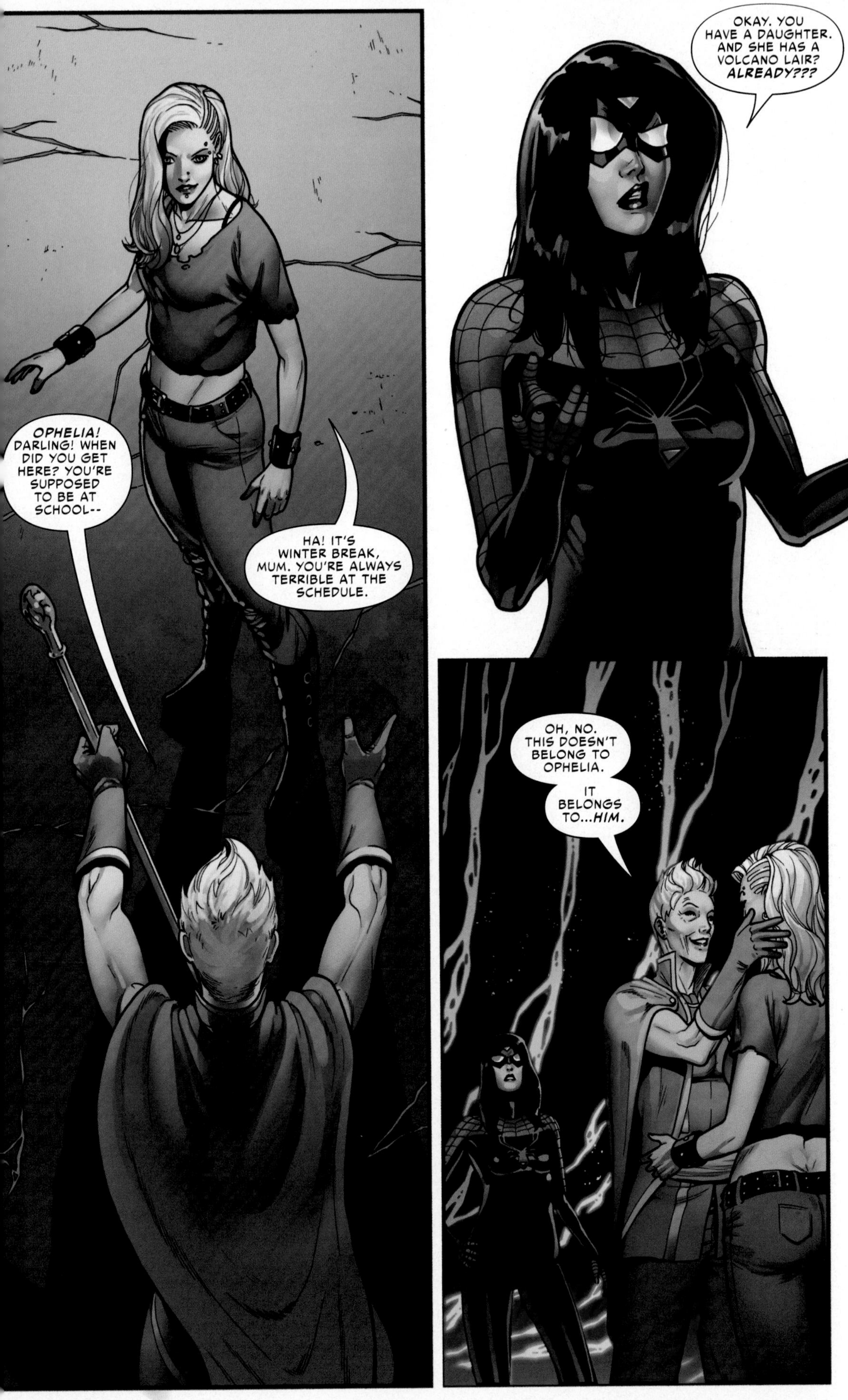

OPHELIA! DARLING! WHEN DID YOU GET HERE? YOU'RE SUPPOSED TO BE AT SCHOOL--
HA! IT'S WINTER BREAK, MUM. YOU'RE ALWAYS TERRIBLE AT THE SCHEDULE.
OKAY. YOU HAVE A DAUGHTER. AND SHE HAS A VOLCANO LAIR? ALREADY???
OH, NO. THIS DOESN'T BELONG TO OPHELIA.
IT BELONGS TO...HIM.

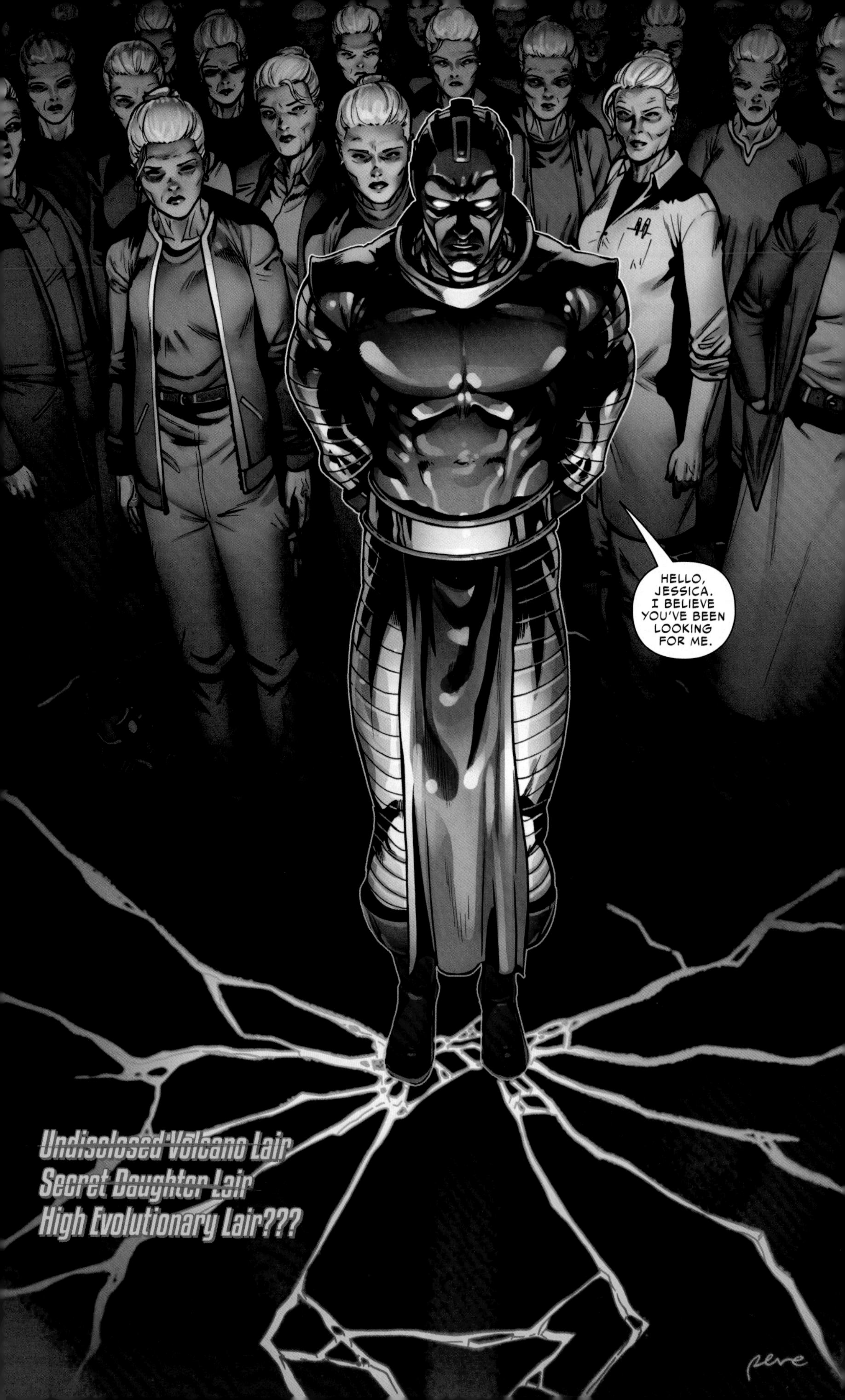
HELLO, JESSICA. I BELIEVE YOU'VE BEEN LOOKING FOR ME.
Undisclosed Volcano Lair
Secret Daughter Lair
High Evolutionary Lair???

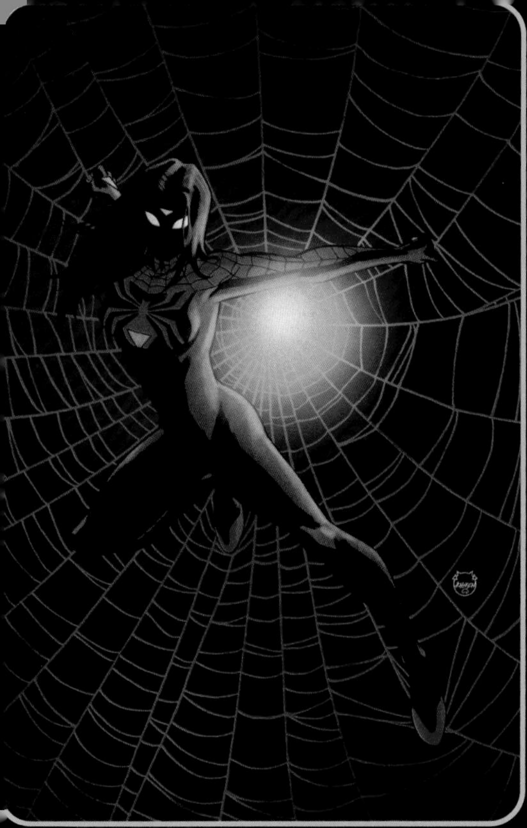

#8 VARIANT BY
DAVE JOHNSON

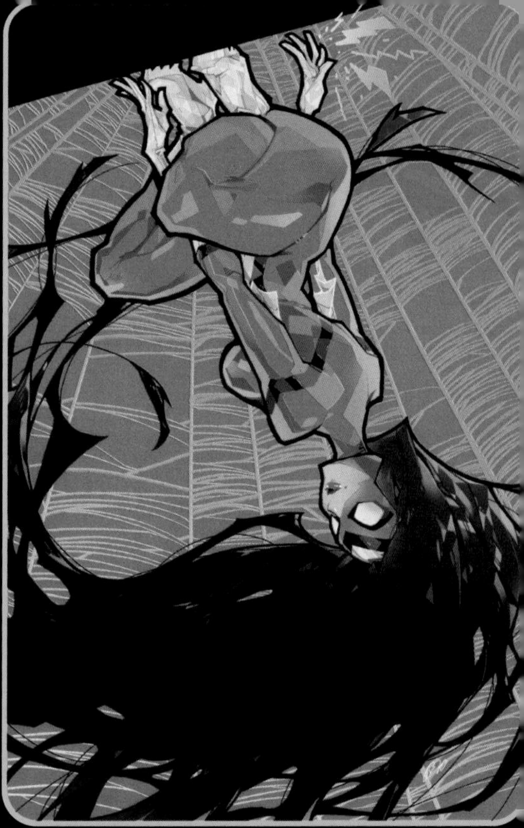

#9 VARIANT BY
ROSE BESCH

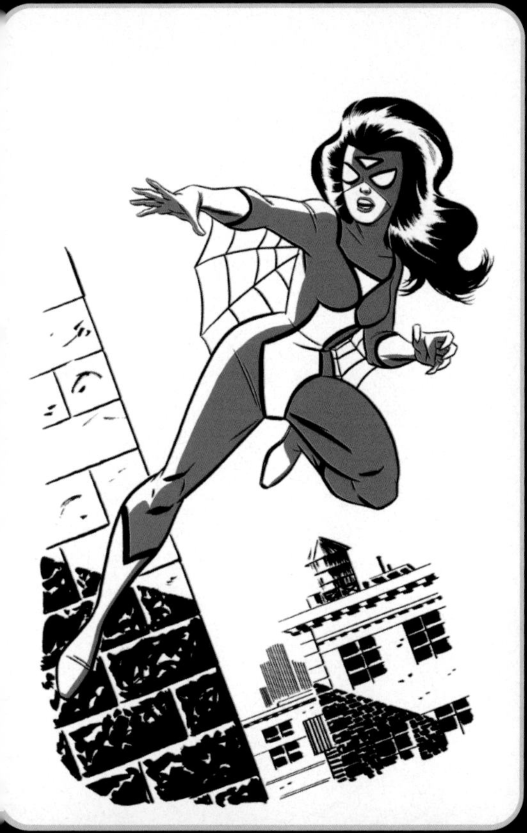

#10 VARIANT BY

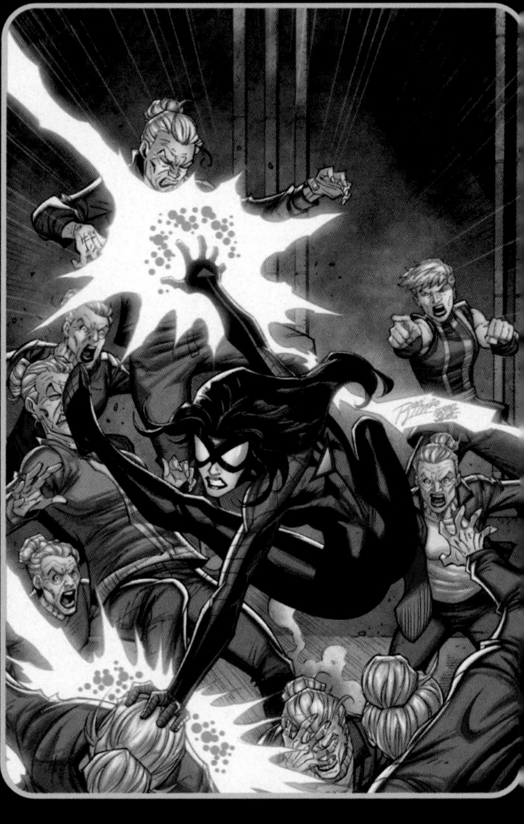

#10 VARIANT BY

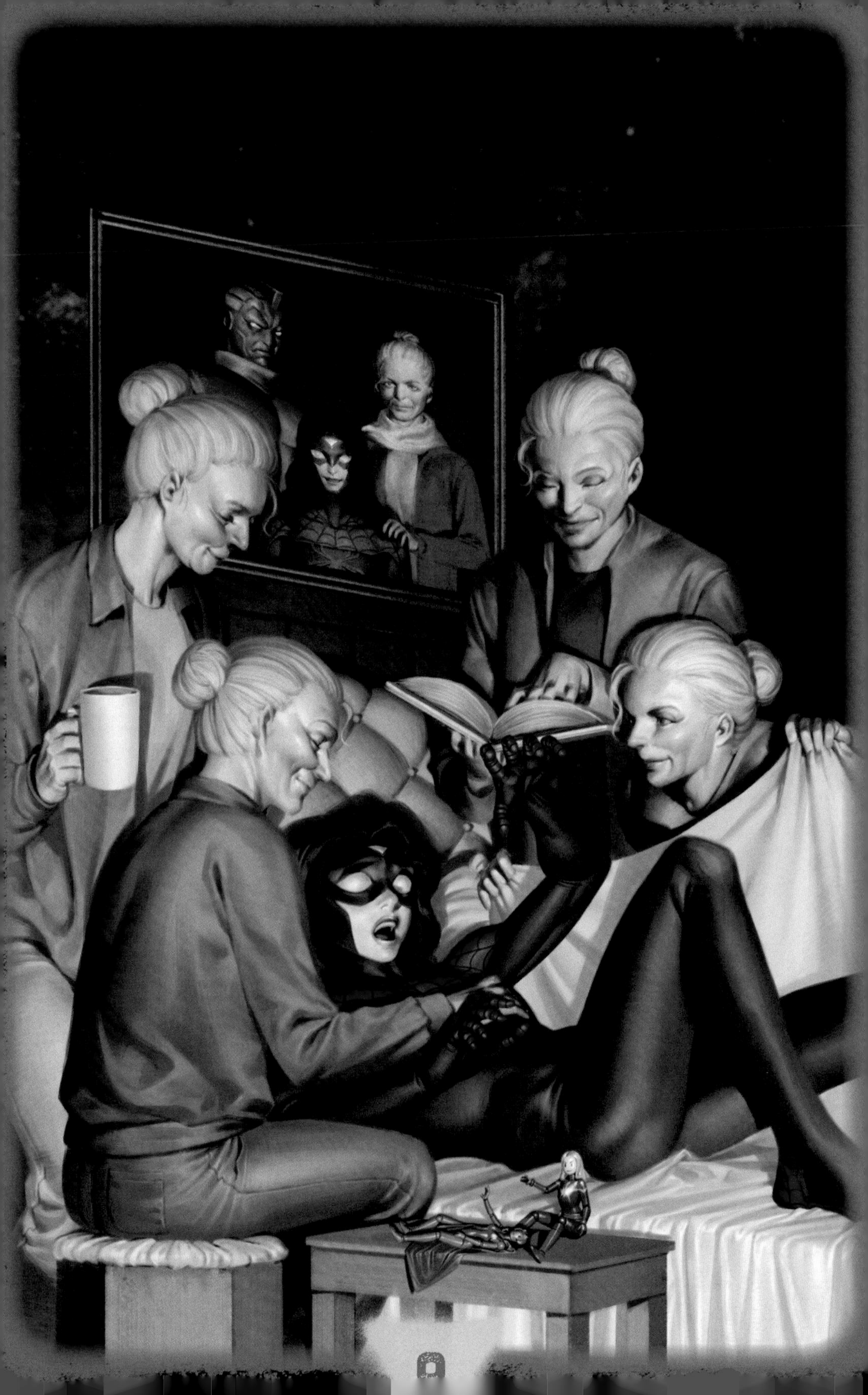

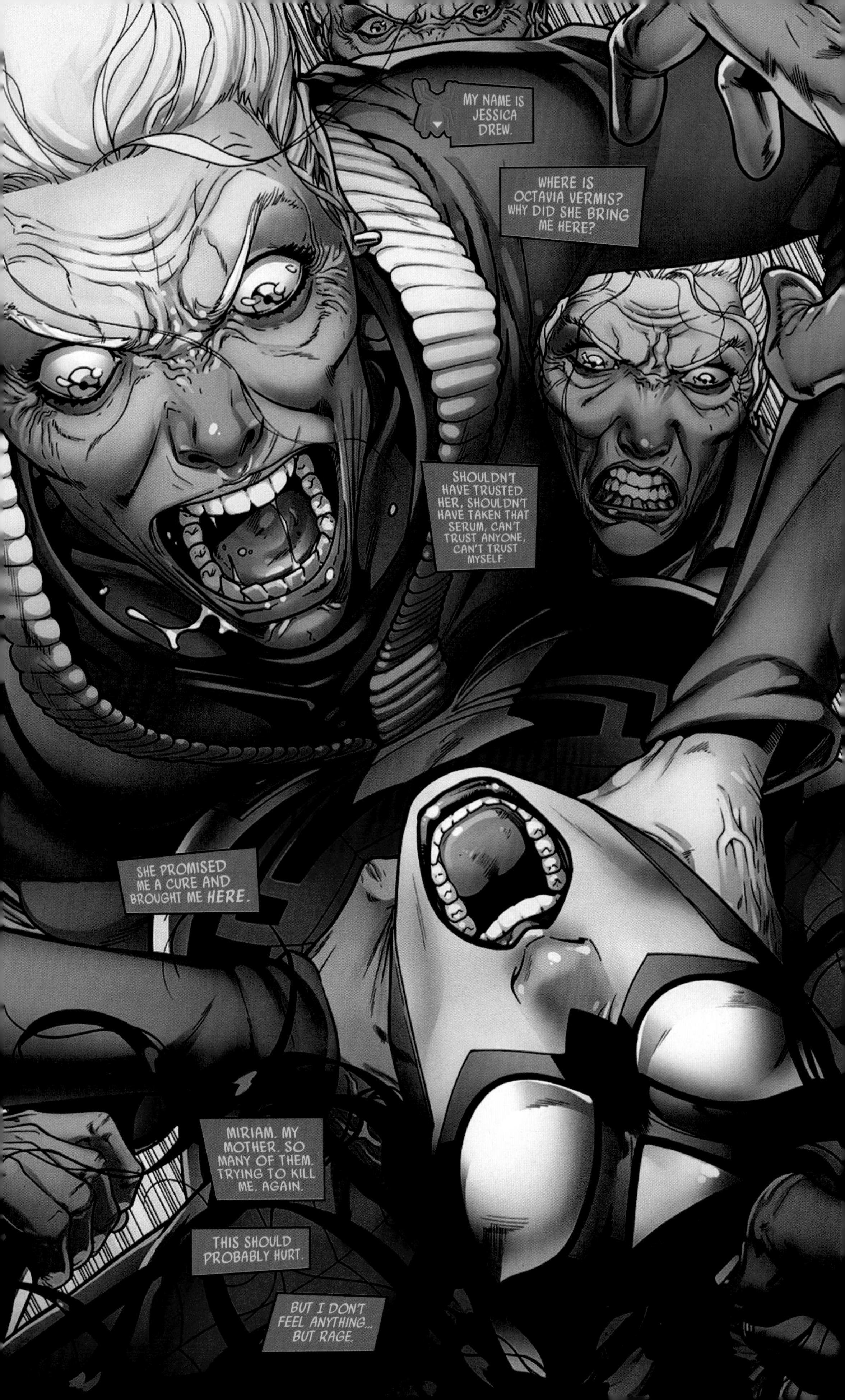

MY NAME IS JESSICA DREW.
WHERE IS OCTAVIA VERMIS? WHY DID SHE BRING ME HERE?
SHOULDN'T HAVE TRUSTED HER, SHOULDN'T HAVE TAKEN THAT SERUM. CAN'T TRUST ANYONE, CAN'T TRUST MYSELF.
SHE PROMISED ME A CURE AND BROUGHT ME *HERE.*
MIRIAM. MY MOTHER. SO MANY OF THEM. TRYING TO KILL ME. AGAIN.
THIS SHOULD PROBABLY HURT.
BUT I DON'T FEEL ANYTHING... BUT RAGE.

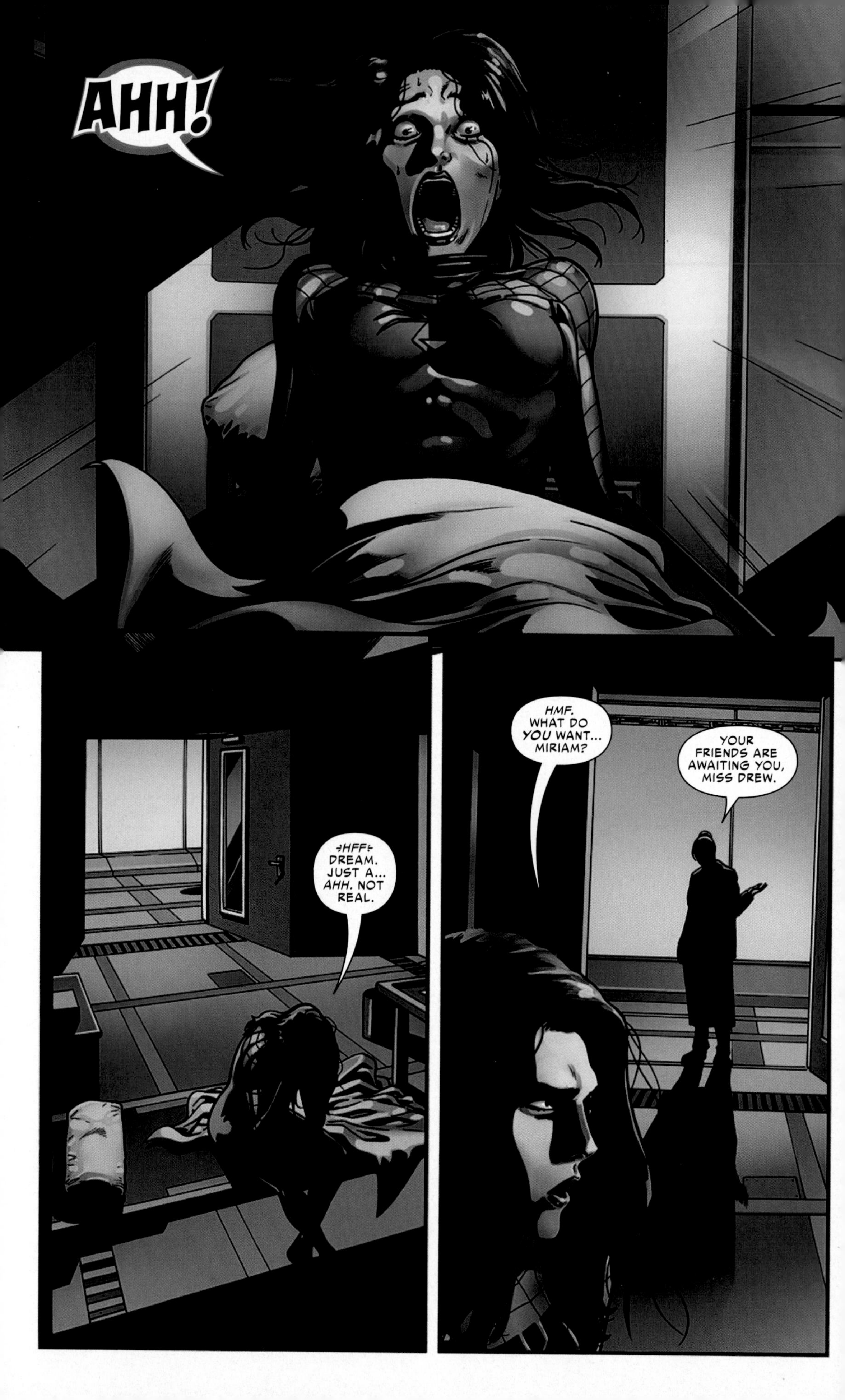
AHH!
=HFF= DREAM. JUST A... AHH. NOT REAL.
HMF. WHAT DO YOU WANT... MIRIAM?
YOUR FRIENDS ARE AWAITING YOU, MISS DREW.

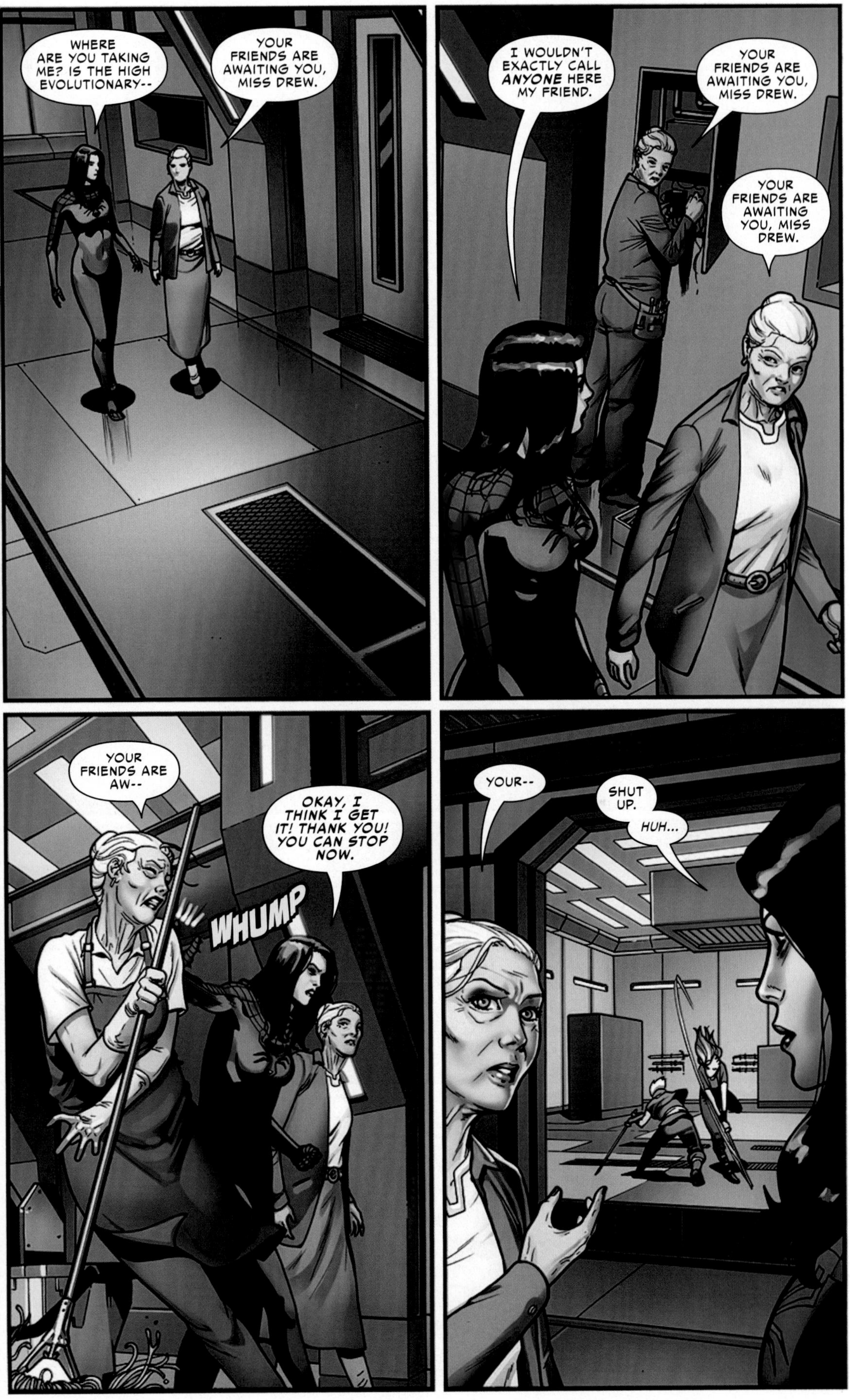

WHERE ARE YOU TAKING ME? IS THE HIGH EVOLUTIONARY--
YOUR FRIENDS ARE AWAITING YOU, MISS DREW.
I WOULDN'T EXACTLY CALL ANYONE HERE MY FRIEND.
YOUR FRIENDS ARE AWAITING YOU, MISS DREW.
YOUR FRIENDS ARE AWAITING YOU, MISS DREW.
YOUR FRIENDS ARE AW--
WHUMP
OKAY, I THINK I GET IT! THANK YOU! YOU CAN STOP NOW.
YOUR--
SHUT UP.
HUH...

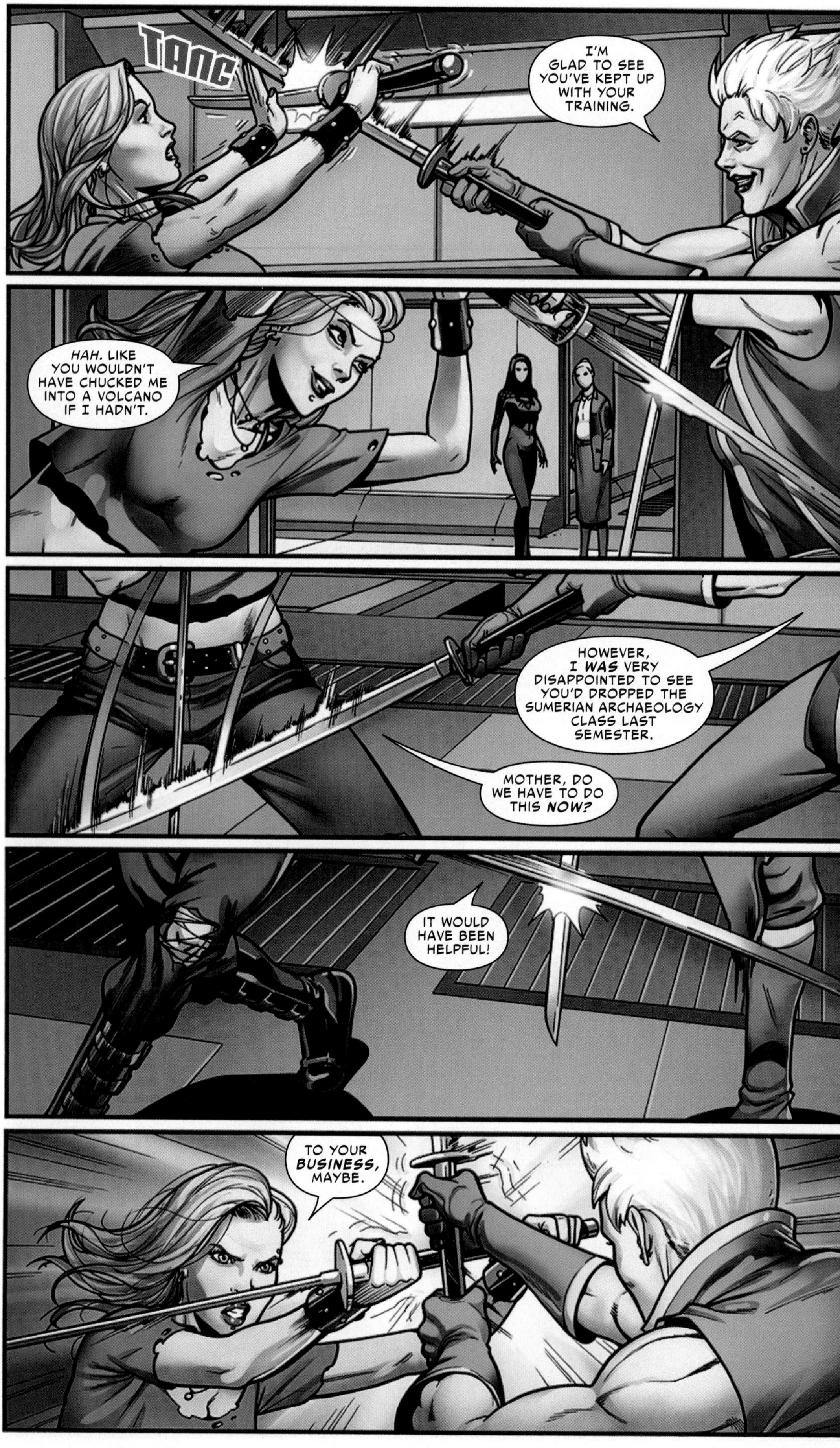
TANC
I'M GLAD TO SEE YOU'VE KEPT UP WITH YOUR TRAINING.
HAH. LIKE YOU WOULDN'T HAVE CHUCKED ME INTO A VOLCANO IF I HADN'T.
HOWEVER, I WAS VERY DISAPPOINTED TO SEE YOU'D DROPPED THE SUMERIAN ARCHAEOLOGY CLASS LAST SEMESTER.
MOTHER, DO WE HAVE TO DO THIS NOW?
IT WOULD HAVE BEEN HELPFUL!
TO YOUR BUSINESS, MAYBE.

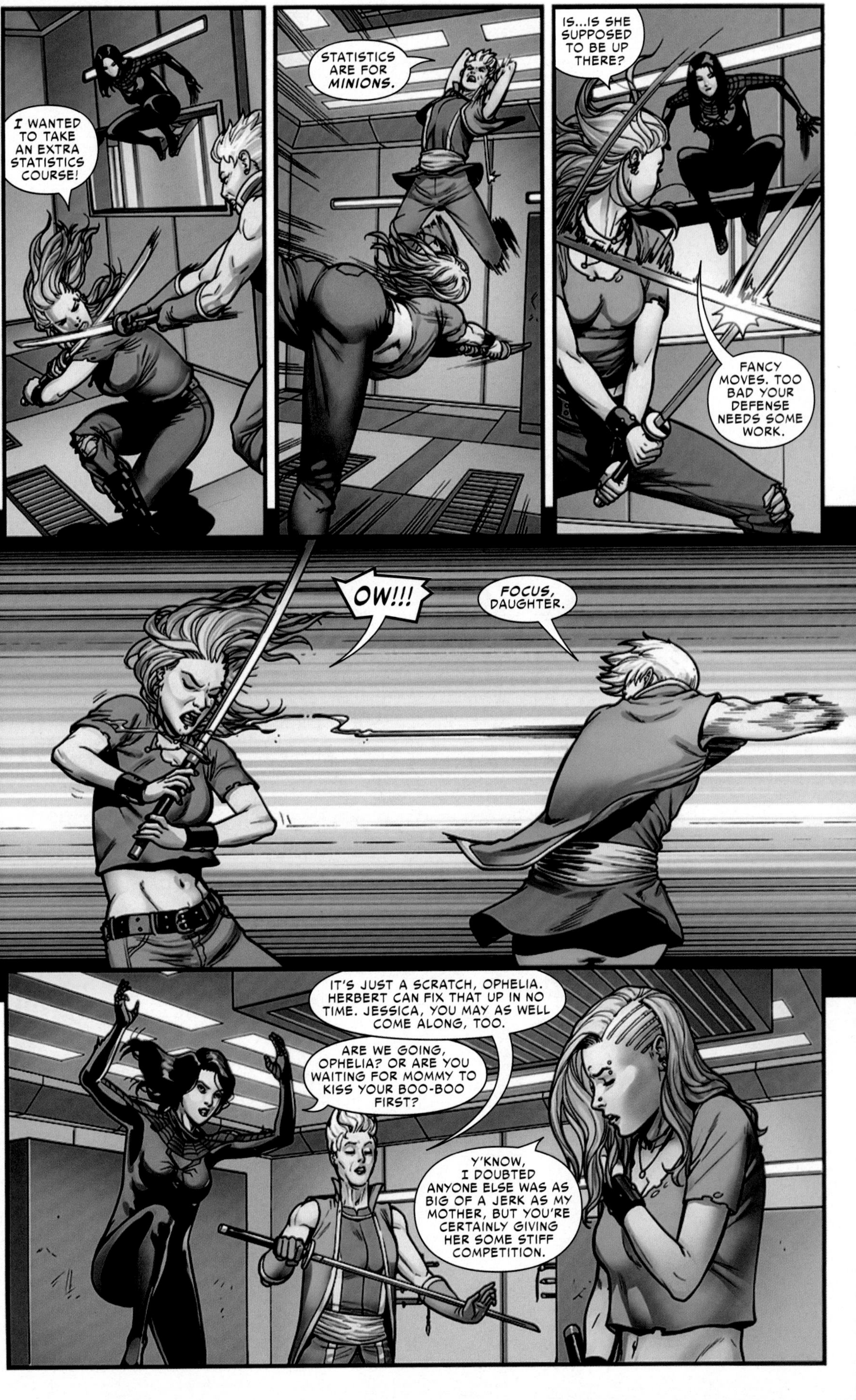
I WANTED TO TAKE AN EXTRA STATISTICS COURSE!
STATISTICS ARE FOR MINIONS.
IS...IS SHE SUPPOSED TO BE UP THERE?
FANCY MOVES. TOO BAD YOUR DEFENSE NEEDS SOME WORK.
OW!!!
FOCUS, DAUGHTER.
IT'S JUST A SCRATCH, OPHELIA. HERBERT CAN FIX THAT UP IN NO TIME. JESSICA, YOU MAY AS WELL COME ALONG, TOO.
ARE WE GOING, OPHELIA? OR ARE YOU WAITING FOR MOMMY TO KISS YOUR BOO-BOO FIRST?
Y'KNOW, I DOUBTED ANYONE ELSE WAS AS BIG OF A JERK AS MY MOTHER, BUT YOU'RE CERTAINLY GIVING HER SOME STIFF COMPETITION.

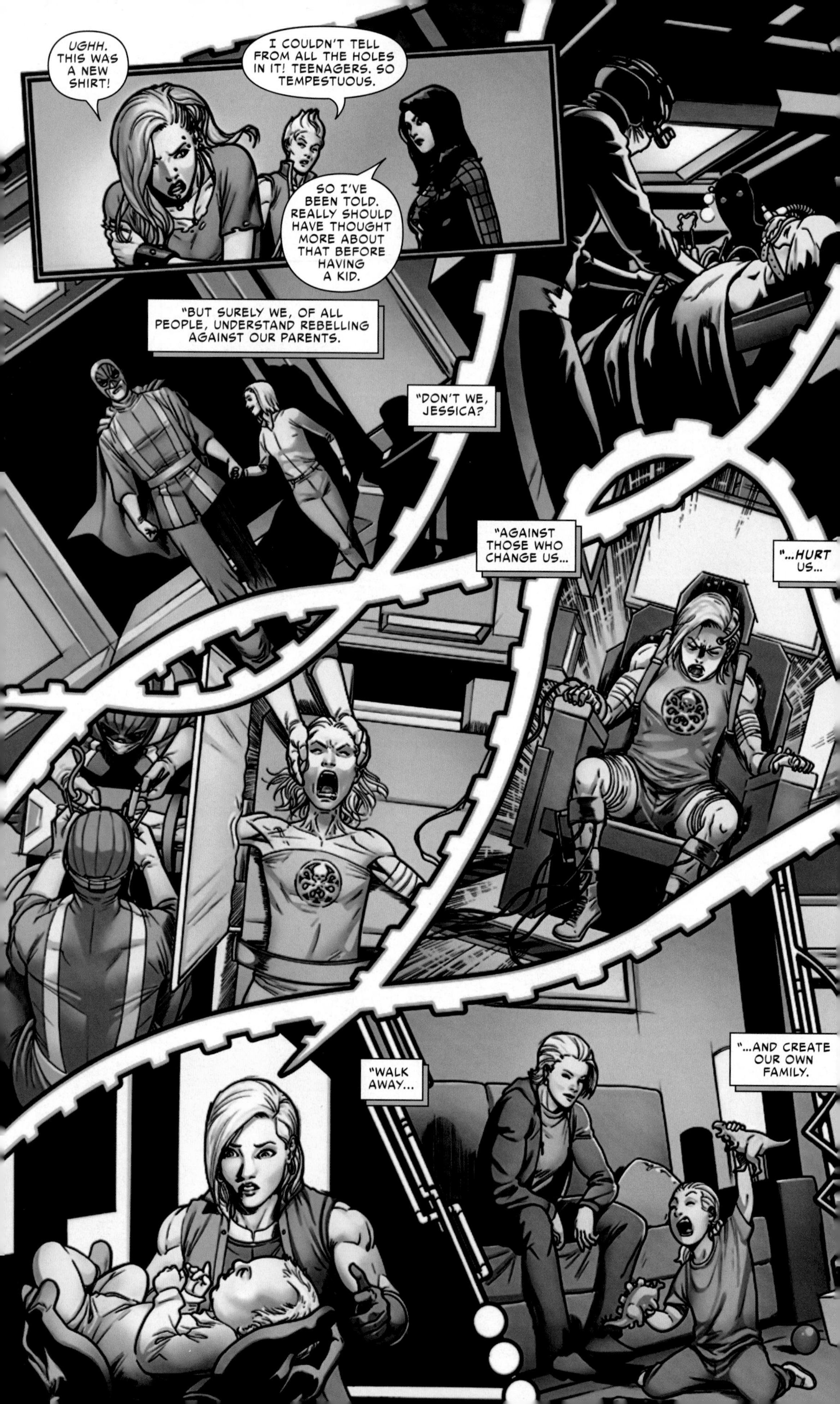
UGHH. THIS WAS A NEW SHIRT!
I COULDN'T TELL FROM ALL THE HOLES IN IT! TEENAGERS. SO TEMPESTUOUS.
SO I'VE BEEN TOLD. REALLY SHOULD HAVE THOUGHT MORE ABOUT THAT BEFORE HAVING A KID.
"BUT SURELY WE, OF ALL PEOPLE, UNDERSTAND REBELLING AGAINST OUR PARENTS.
"DON'T WE, JESSICA?
"AGAINST THOSE WHO CHANGE US...
"...HURT US...
"WALK AWAY...
"...AND CREATE OUR OWN FAMILY.

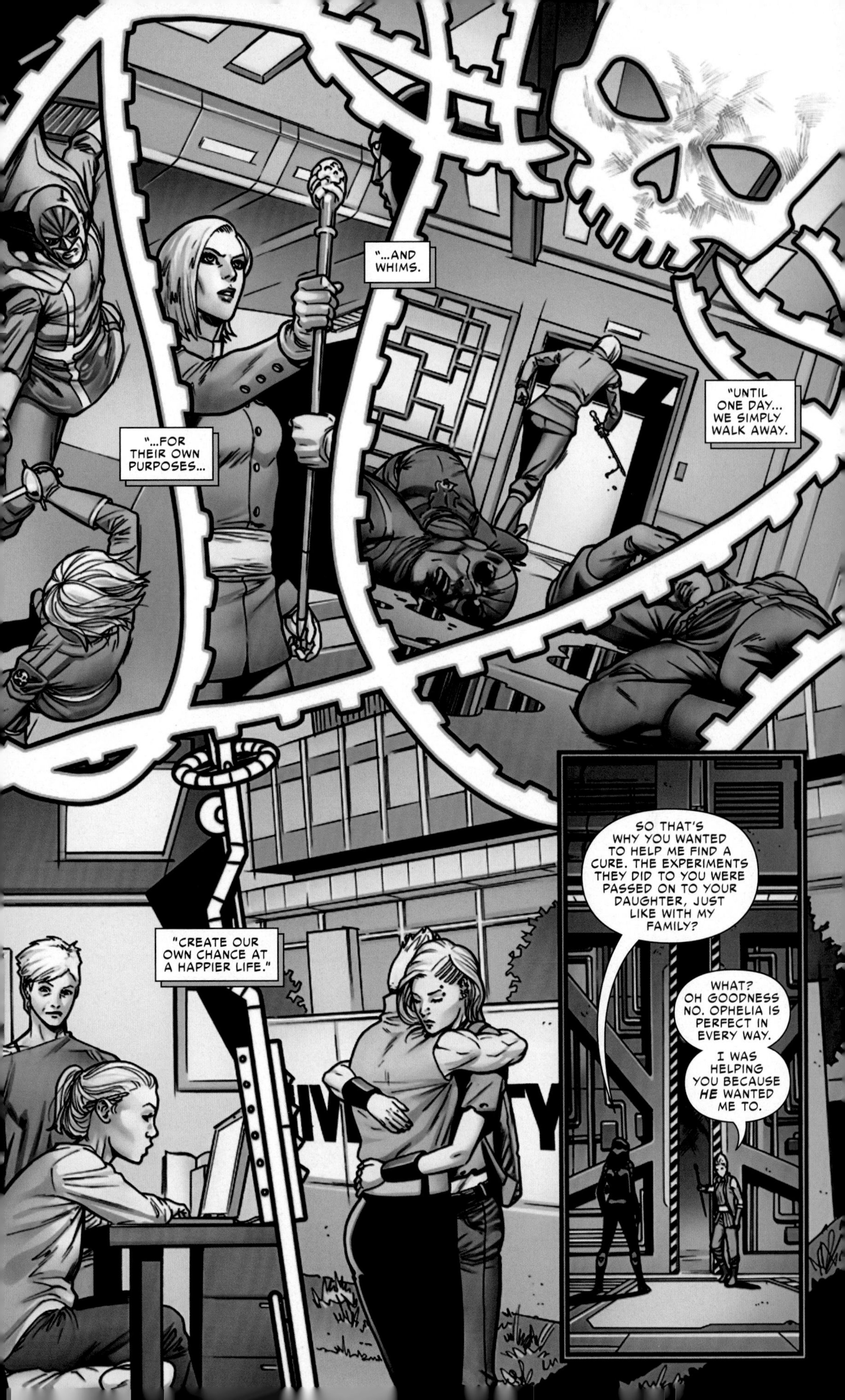
"...FOR THEIR OWN PURPOSES...
"...AND WHIMS.
"UNTIL ONE DAY... WE SIMPLY WALK AWAY.
"CREATE OUR OWN CHANCE AT A HAPPIER LIFE."
SO THAT'S WHY YOU WANTED TO HELP ME FIND A CURE. THE EXPERIMENTS THEY DID TO YOU WERE PASSED ON TO YOUR DAUGHTER, JUST LIKE WITH MY FAMILY?
WHAT? OH GOODNESS NO. OPHELIA IS PERFECT IN EVERY WAY.
I WAS HELPING YOU BECAUSE *HE* WANTED ME TO.

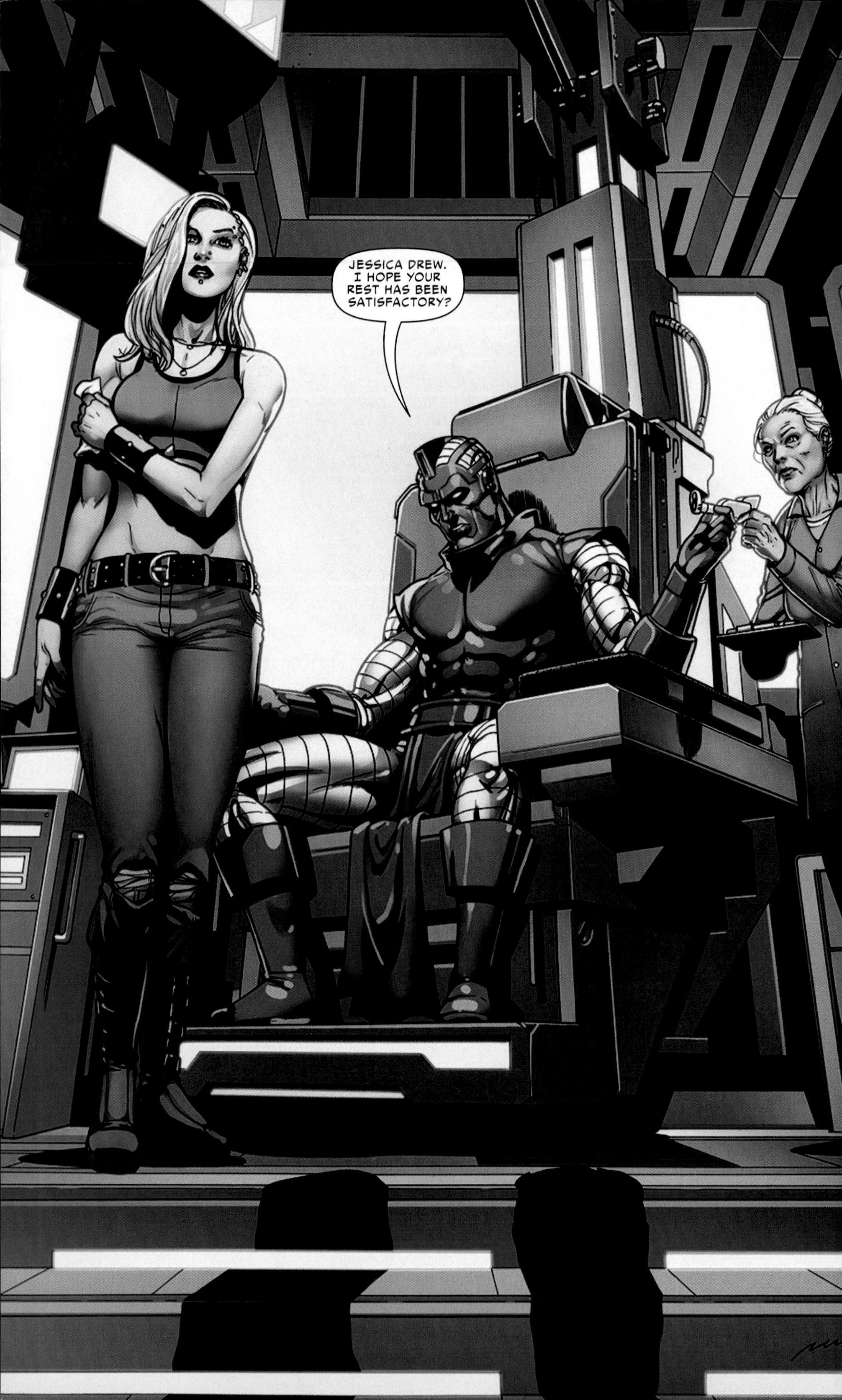
JESSICA DREW. I HOPE YOUR REST HAS BEEN SATISFACTORY?

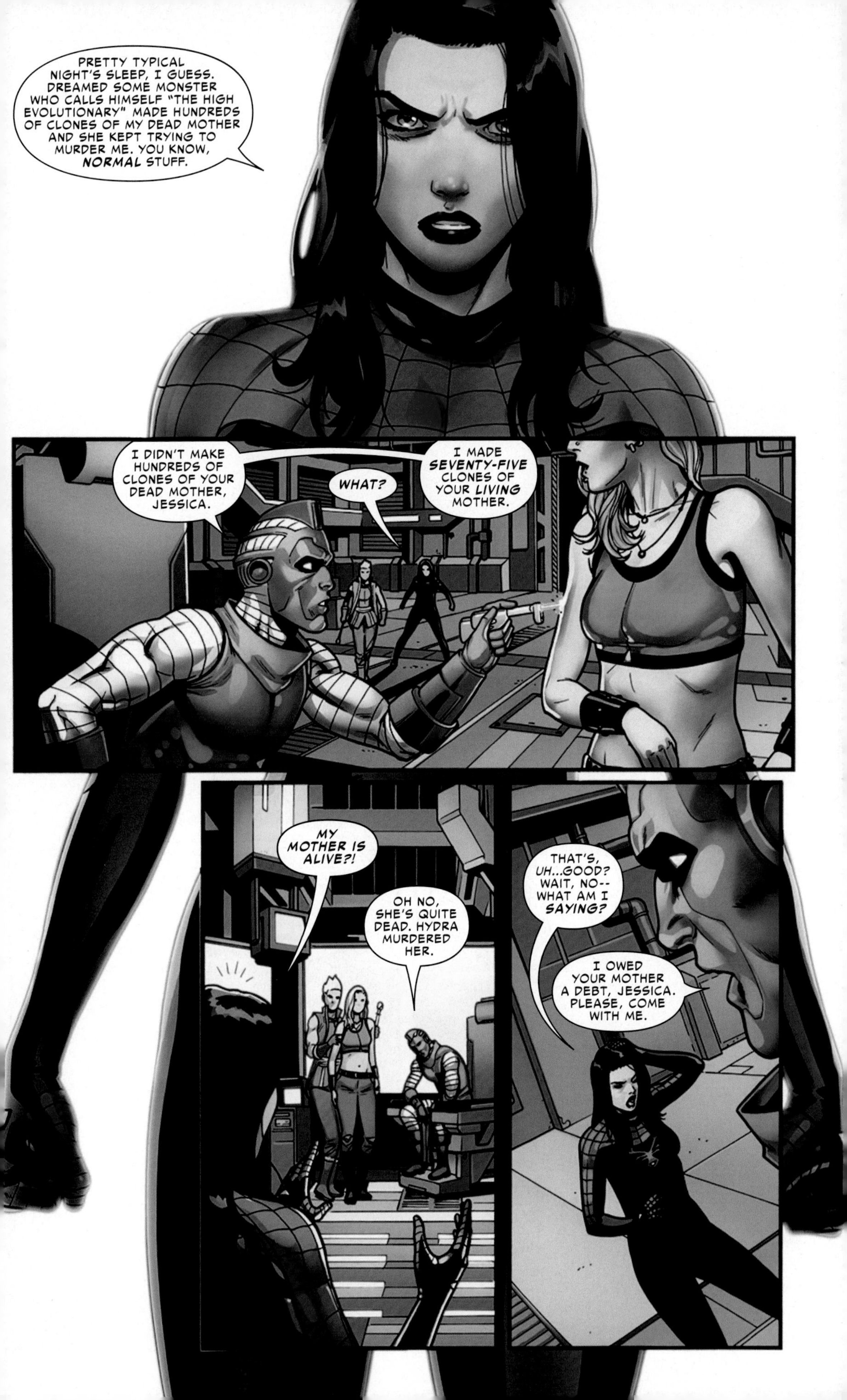
PRETTY TYPICAL NIGHT'S SLEEP, I GUESS. DREAMED SOME MONSTER WHO CALLS HIMSELF "THE HIGH EVOLUTIONARY" MADE HUNDREDS OF CLONES OF MY DEAD MOTHER AND SHE KEPT TRYING TO MURDER ME. YOU KNOW, NORMAL STUFF.
I DIDN'T MAKE HUNDREDS OF CLONES OF YOUR DEAD MOTHER, JESSICA.
WHAT?
I MADE SEVENTY-FIVE CLONES OF YOUR LIVING MOTHER.
MY MOTHER IS ALIVE?!
OH NO, SHE'S QUITE DEAD. HYDRA MURDERED HER.
THAT'S, UH...GOOD? WAIT, NO-- WHAT AM I SAYING?
I OWED YOUR MOTHER A DEBT, JESSICA. PLEASE, COME WITH ME.

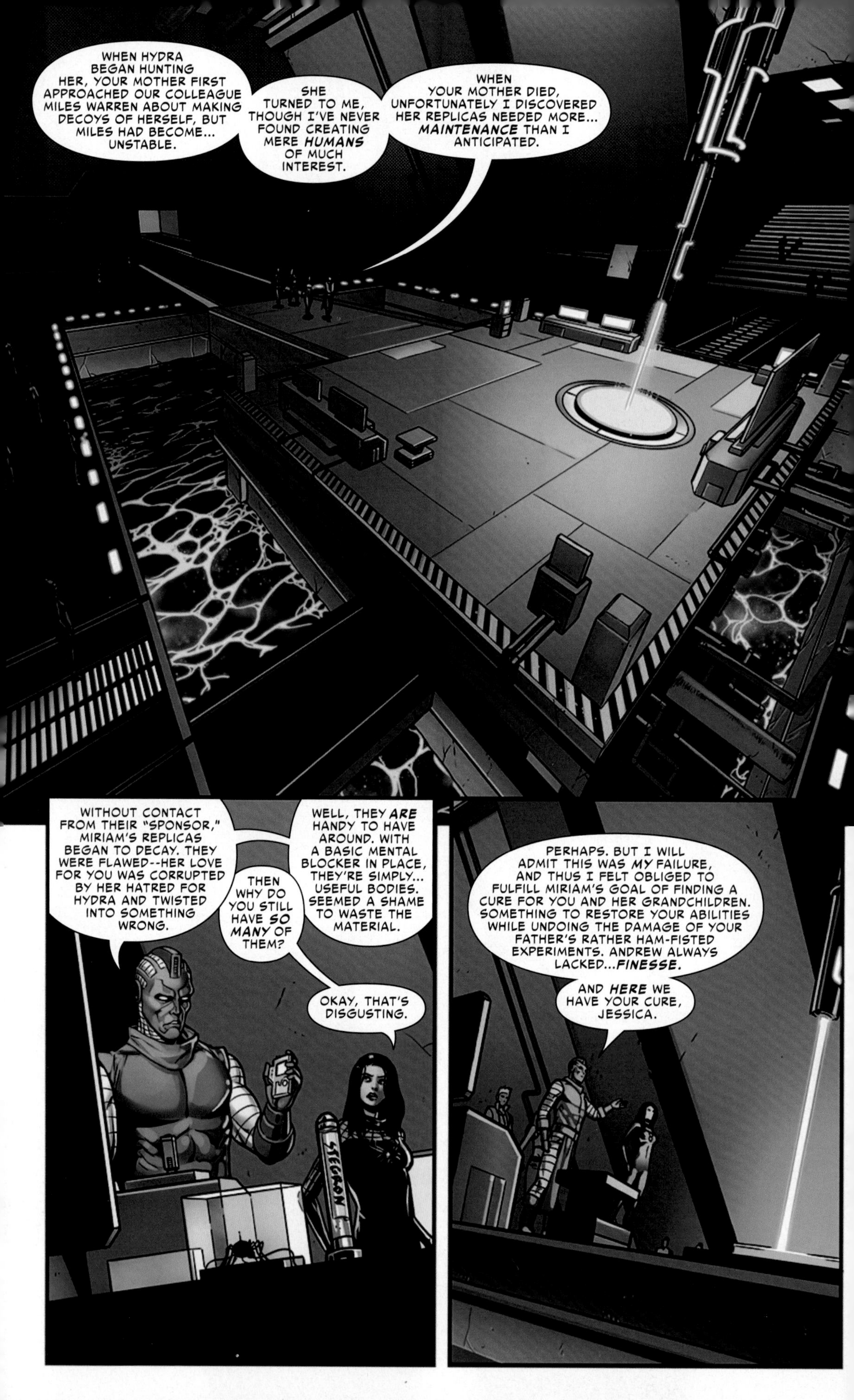
WHEN HYDRA BEGAN HUNTING HER, YOUR MOTHER FIRST APPROACHED OUR COLLEAGUE MILES WARREN ABOUT MAKING DECOYS OF HERSELF, BUT MILES HAD BECOME... UNSTABLE.
SHE TURNED TO ME, THOUGH I'VE NEVER FOUND CREATING MERE *HUMANS* OF MUCH INTEREST.
WHEN YOUR MOTHER DIED, UNFORTUNATELY I DISCOVERED HER REPLICAS NEEDED MORE... *MAINTENANCE* THAN I ANTICIPATED.
WITHOUT CONTACT FROM THEIR "SPONSOR," MIRIAM'S REPLICAS BEGAN TO DECAY. THEY WERE FLAWED--HER LOVE FOR YOU WAS CORRUPTED BY HER HATRED FOR HYDRA AND TWISTED INTO SOMETHING WRONG.
THEN WHY DO YOU STILL HAVE *SO MANY* OF THEM?
WELL, THEY *ARE* HANDY TO HAVE AROUND. WITH A BASIC MENTAL BLOCKER IN PLACE, THEY'RE SIMPLY... USEFUL BODIES. SEEMED A SHAME TO WASTE THE MATERIAL.
OKAY, THAT'S DISGUSTING.
STEGRON
PERHAPS. BUT I WILL ADMIT THIS WAS *MY* FAILURE, AND THUS I FELT OBLIGED TO FULFILL MIRIAM'S GOAL OF FINDING A CURE FOR YOU AND HER GRANDCHILDREN. SOMETHING TO RESTORE YOUR ABILITIES WHILE UNDOING THE DAMAGE OF YOUR FATHER'S RATHER HAM-FISTED EXPERIMENTS. ANDREW ALWAYS LACKED...*FINESSE.*
AND *HERE* WE HAVE YOUR CURE, JESSICA.

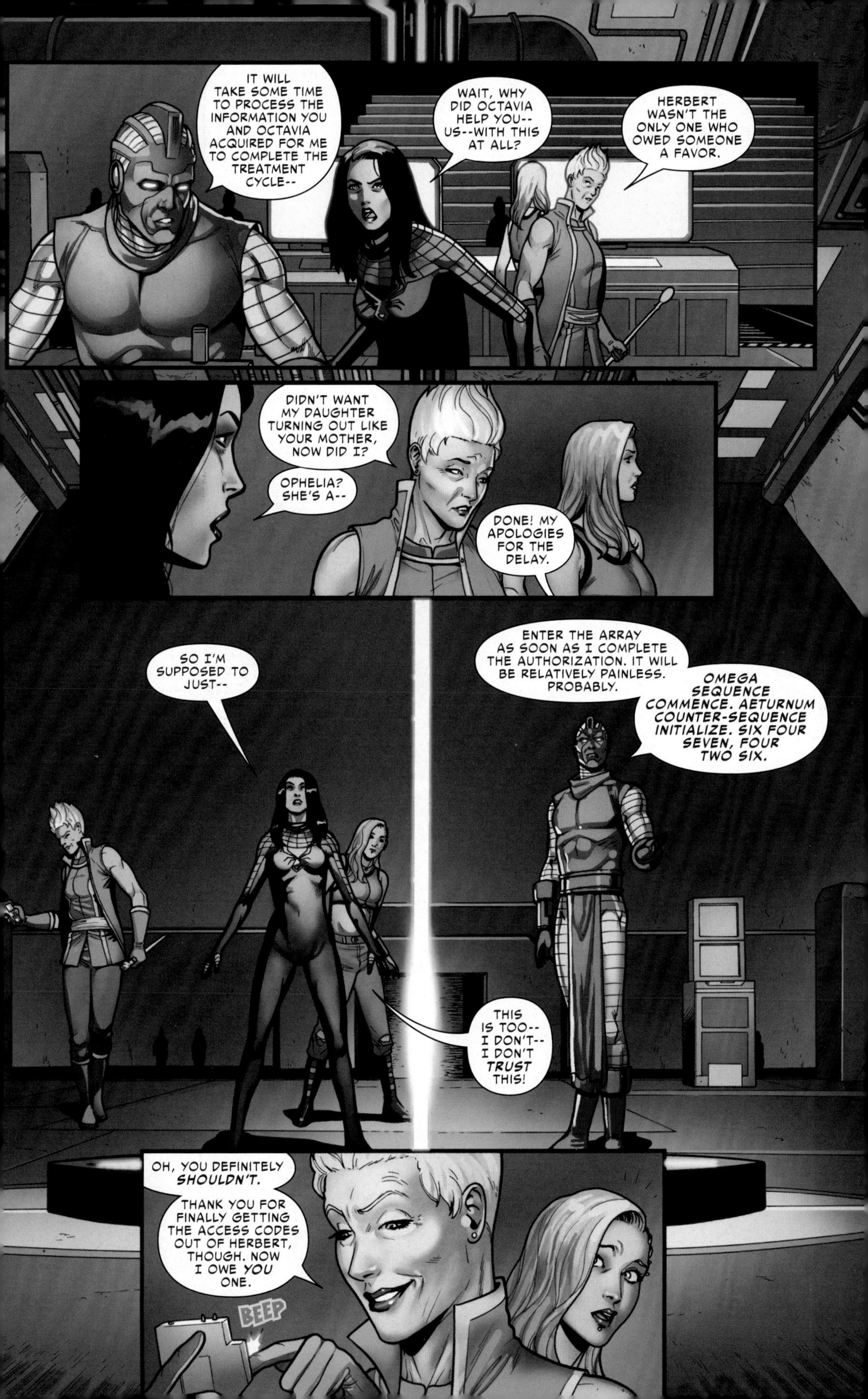
IT WILL TAKE SOME TIME TO PROCESS THE INFORMATION YOU AND OCTAVIA ACQUIRED FOR ME TO COMPLETE THE TREATMENT CYCLE--
WAIT, WHY DID OCTAVIA HELP YOU--US--WITH THIS AT ALL?
HERBERT WASN'T THE ONLY ONE WHO OWED SOMEONE A FAVOR.
DIDN'T WANT MY DAUGHTER TURNING OUT LIKE YOUR MOTHER, NOW DID I?
OPHELIA? SHE'S A--
DONE! MY APOLOGIES FOR THE DELAY.
SO I'M SUPPOSED TO JUST--
ENTER THE ARRAY AS SOON AS I COMPLETE THE AUTHORIZATION. IT WILL BE RELATIVELY PAINLESS. PROBABLY.
OMEGA SEQUENCE COMMENCE. AETURNUM COUNTER-SEQUENCE INITIALIZE. SIX FOUR SEVEN, FOUR TWO SIX.
THIS IS TOO-- I DON'T-- I DON'T TRUST THIS!
OH, YOU DEFINITELY SHOULDN'T.
THANK YOU FOR FINALLY GETTING THE ACCESS CODES OUT OF HERBERT, THOUGH. NOW I OWE YOU ONE.
BEEP

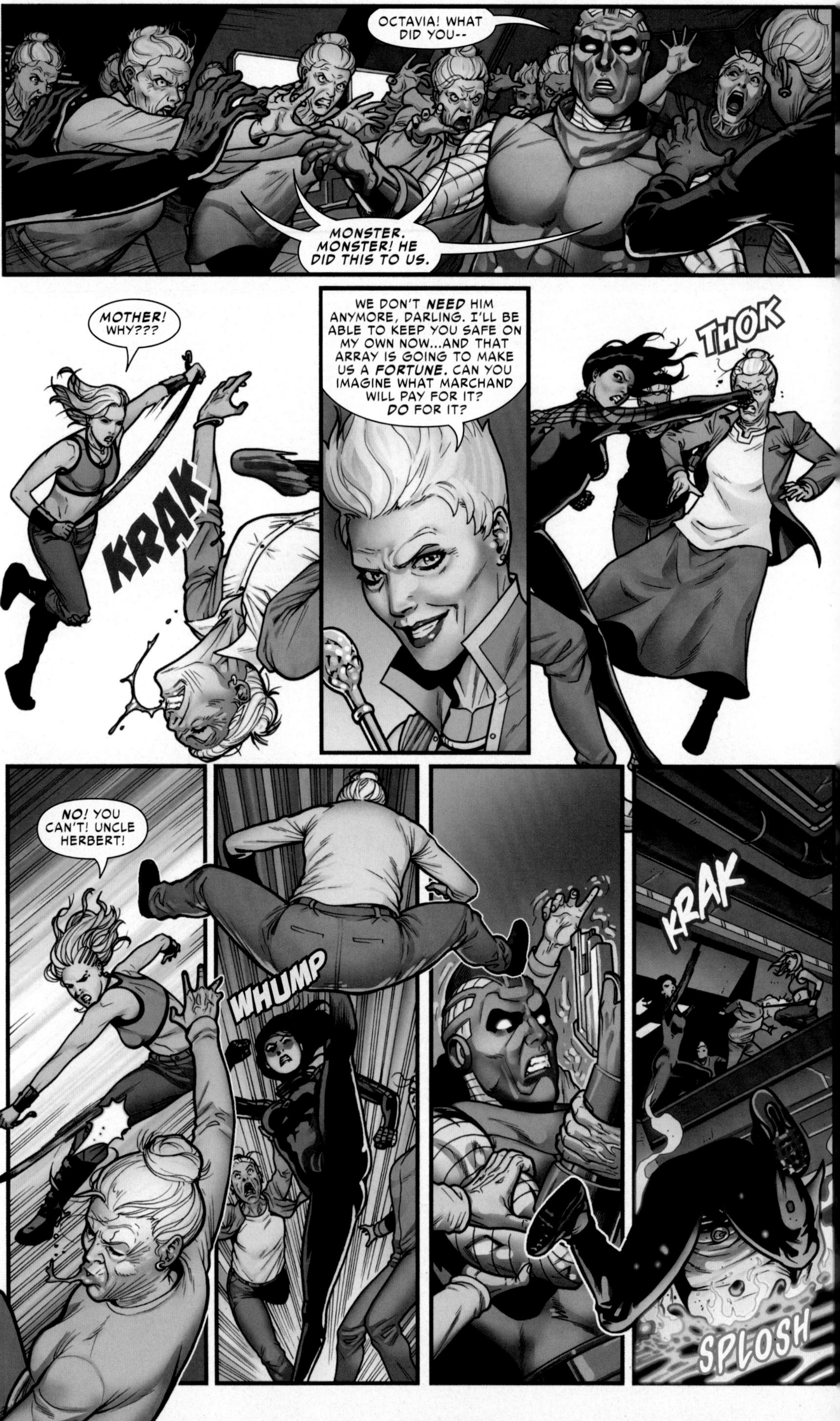

OCTAVIA! WHAT DID YOU--
MONSTER. MONSTER! HE DID THIS TO US.
MOTHER! WHY???
KRAK
WE DON'T NEED HIM ANYMORE, DARLING. I'LL BE ABLE TO KEEP YOU SAFE ON MY OWN NOW...AND THAT ARRAY IS GOING TO MAKE US A FORTUNE. CAN YOU IMAGINE WHAT MARCHAND WILL PAY FOR IT? DO FOR IT?
THOK
NO! YOU CAN'T! UNCLE HERBERT!
WHUMP
KRAK
SPLOSH

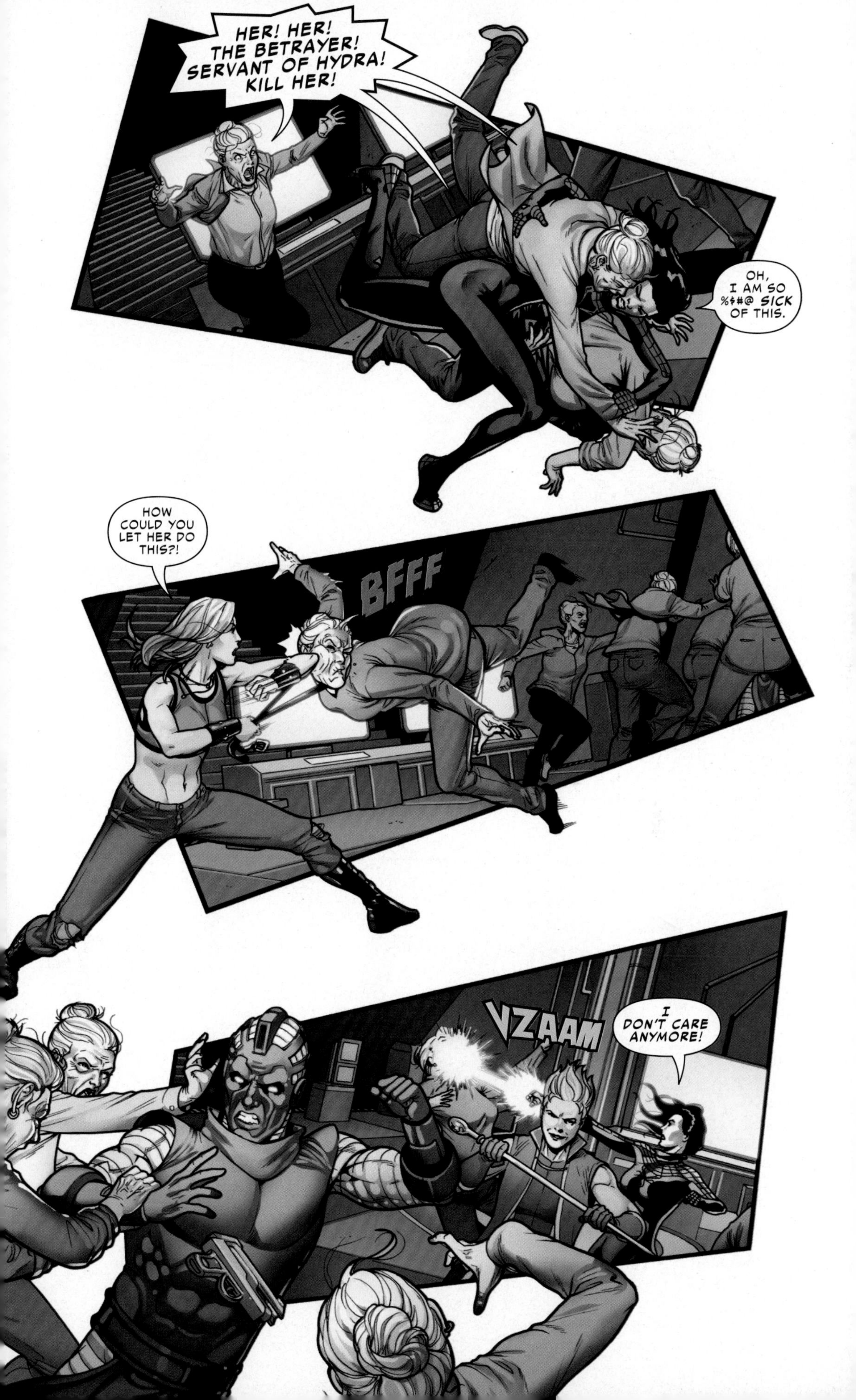
HER! HER! THE BETRAYER! SERVANT OF HYDRA! KILL HER!
OH, I AM SO %$#@ SICK OF THIS.
HOW COULD YOU LET HER DO THIS?!
BFFF
VZAAM
I DON'T CARE ANYMORE!

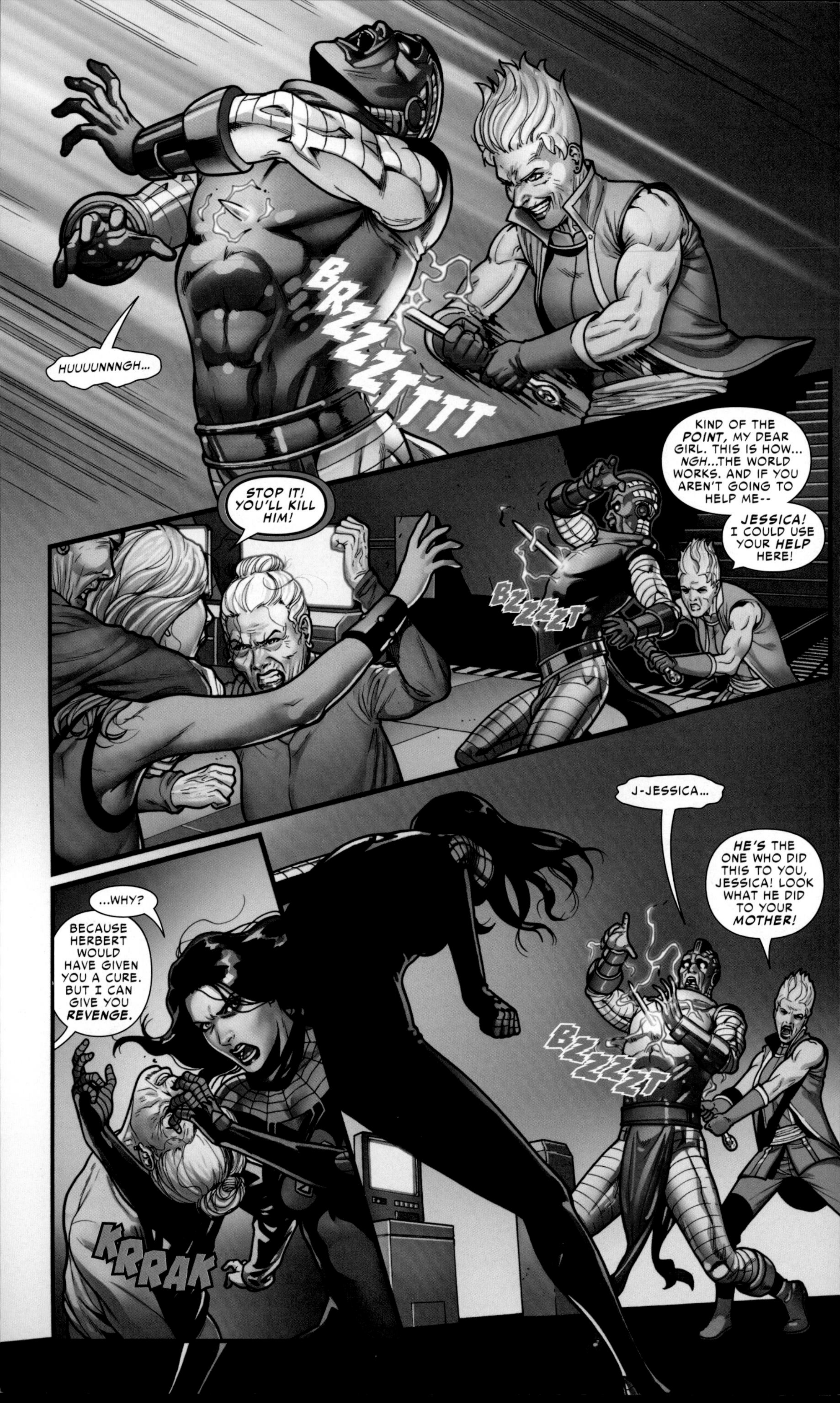

BRZZZZTTTTT
HUUUUNNNGH...
STOP IT! YOU'LL KILL HIM!
KIND OF THE POINT, MY DEAR GIRL. THIS IS HOW... NGH...THE WORLD WORKS. AND IF YOU AREN'T GOING TO HELP ME--
JESSICA! I COULD USE YOUR HELP HERE!
BZZZZZT
J-JESSICA...
HE'S THE ONE WHO DID THIS TO YOU, JESSICA! LOOK WHAT HE DID TO YOUR MOTHER!
...WHY?
BECAUSE HERBERT WOULD HAVE GIVEN YOU A CURE. BUT I CAN GIVE YOU REVENGE.
BZZZZZT
KRRAK

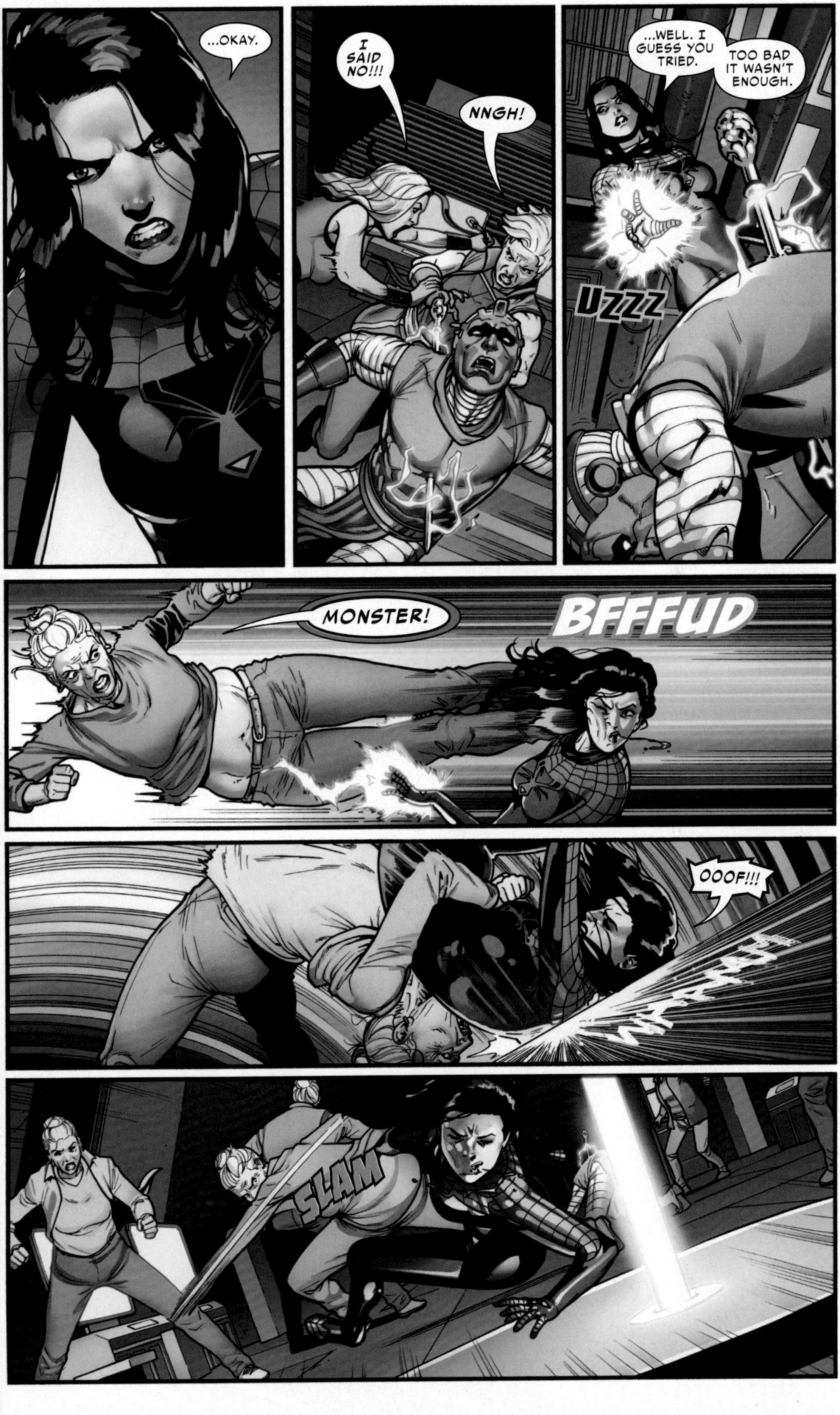
...OKAY.
I SAID NO!!!
NNGH!
...WELL. I GUESS YOU TRIED.
TOO BAD IT WASN'T ENOUGH.
UZZZ
MONSTER!
BFFFUD
OOOF!!!
SLAM

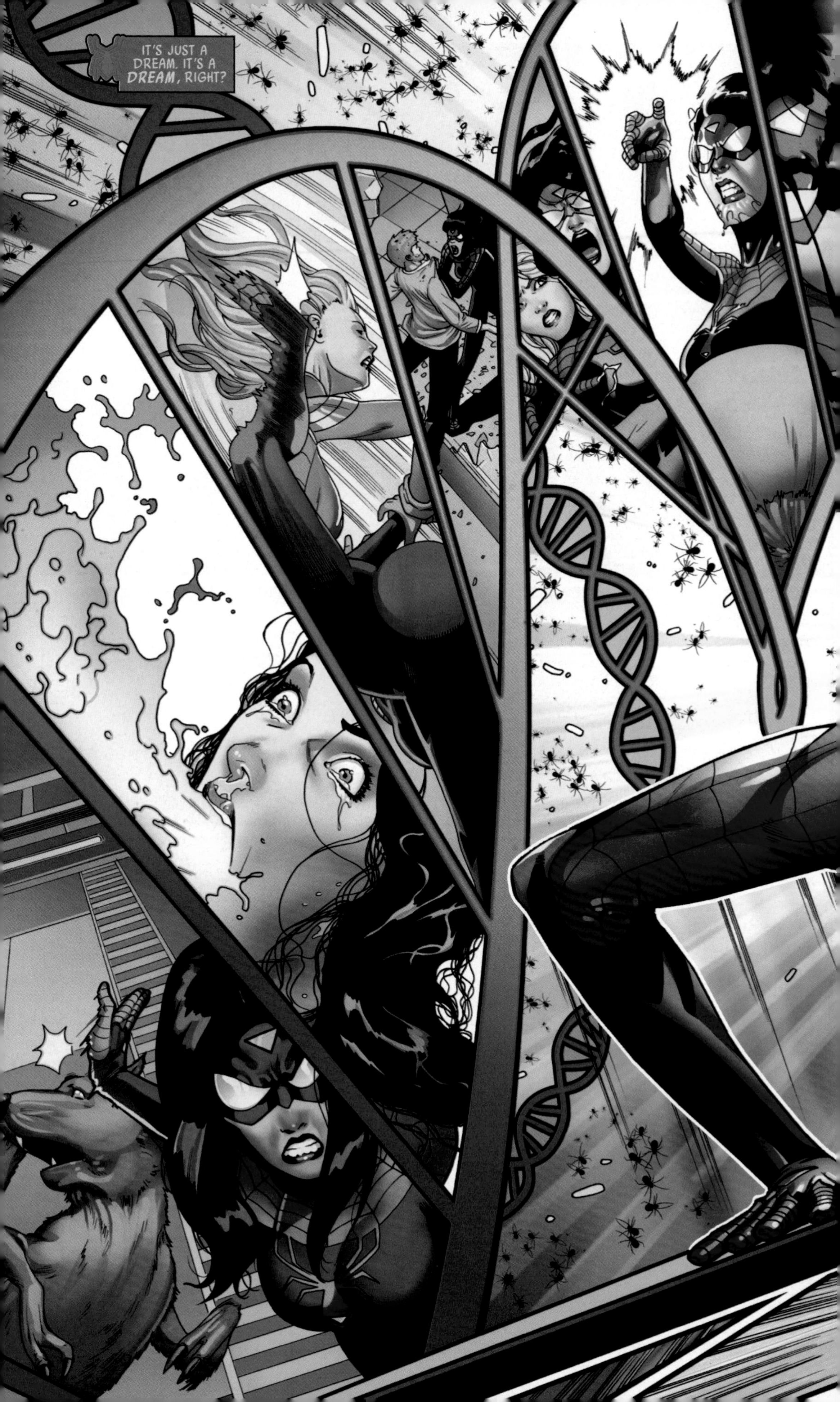
IT'S JUST A DREAM. IT'S A *DREAM*, RIGHT?

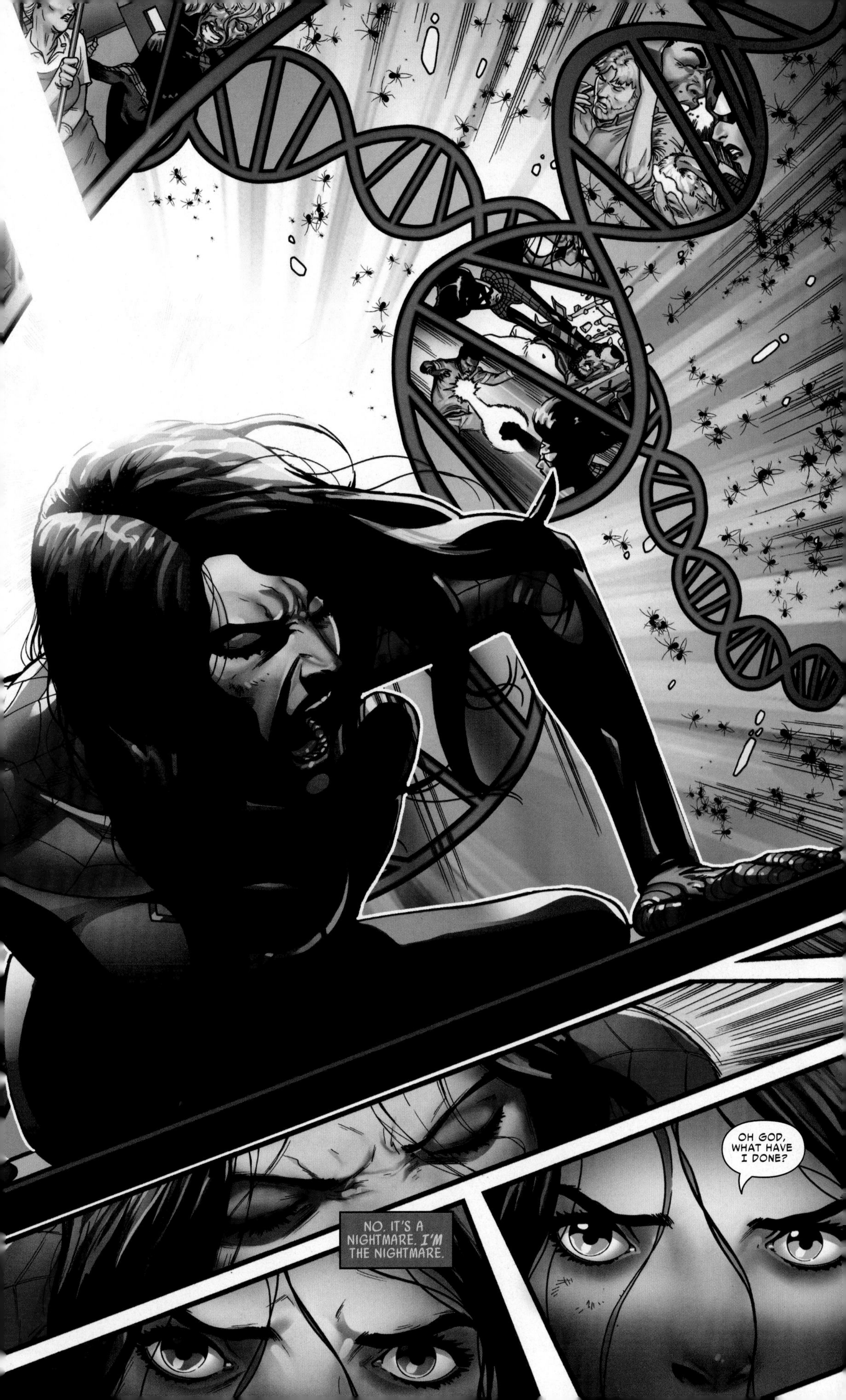
OH GOD, WHAT HAVE I DONE?
NO. IT'S A NIGHTMARE. *I'M* THE NIGHTMARE.

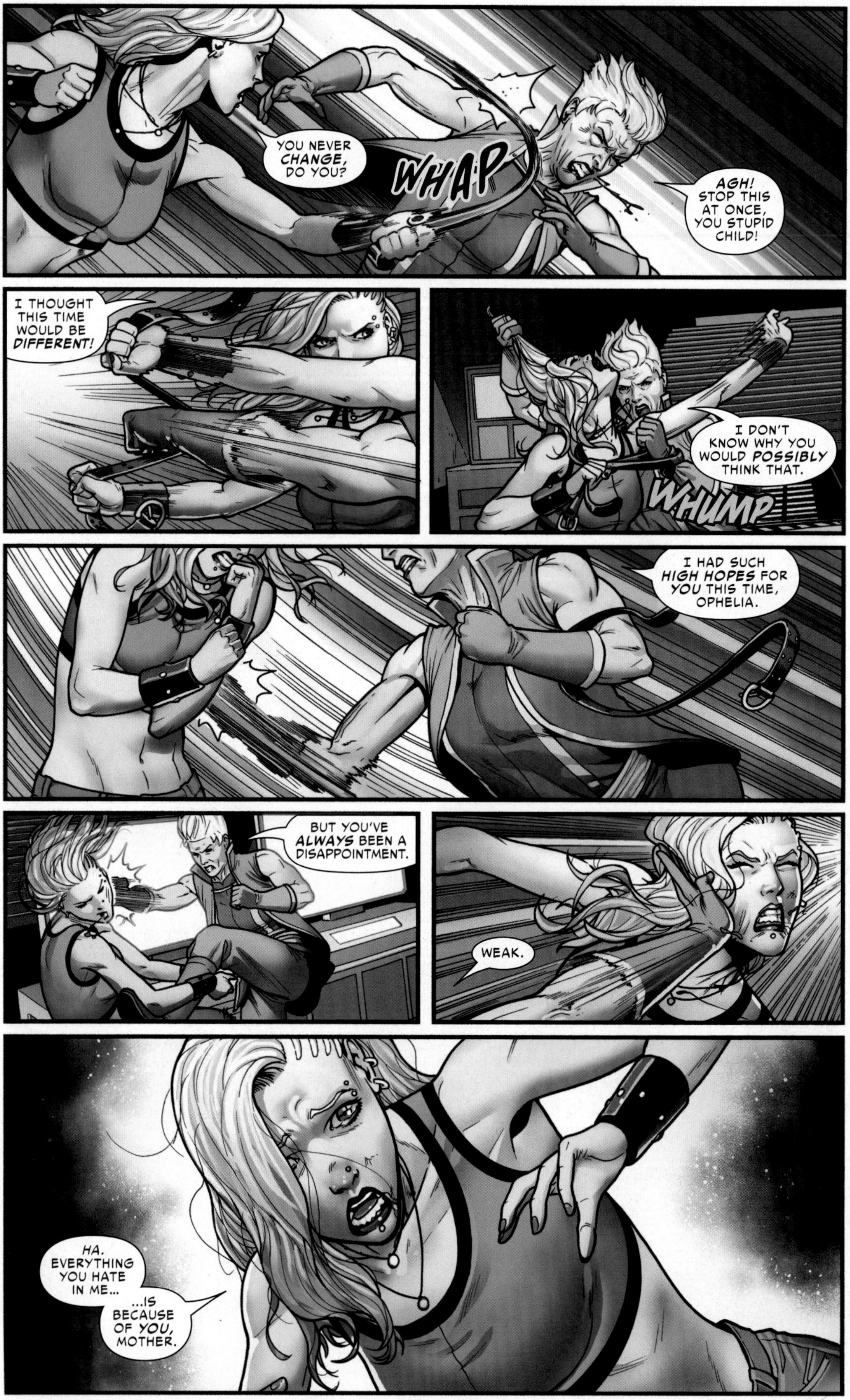

YOU NEVER CHANGE, DO YOU?
WHAP
AGH! STOP THIS AT ONCE, YOU STUPID CHILD!
I THOUGHT THIS TIME WOULD BE DIFFERENT!
I DON'T KNOW WHY YOU WOULD POSSIBLY THINK THAT.
WHUMP
I HAD SUCH HIGH HOPES FOR YOU THIS TIME, OPHELIA.
BUT YOU'VE ALWAYS BEEN A DISAPPOINTMENT.
WEAK.
HA. EVERYTHING YOU HATE IN ME...
...IS BECAUSE OF YOU, MOTHER.

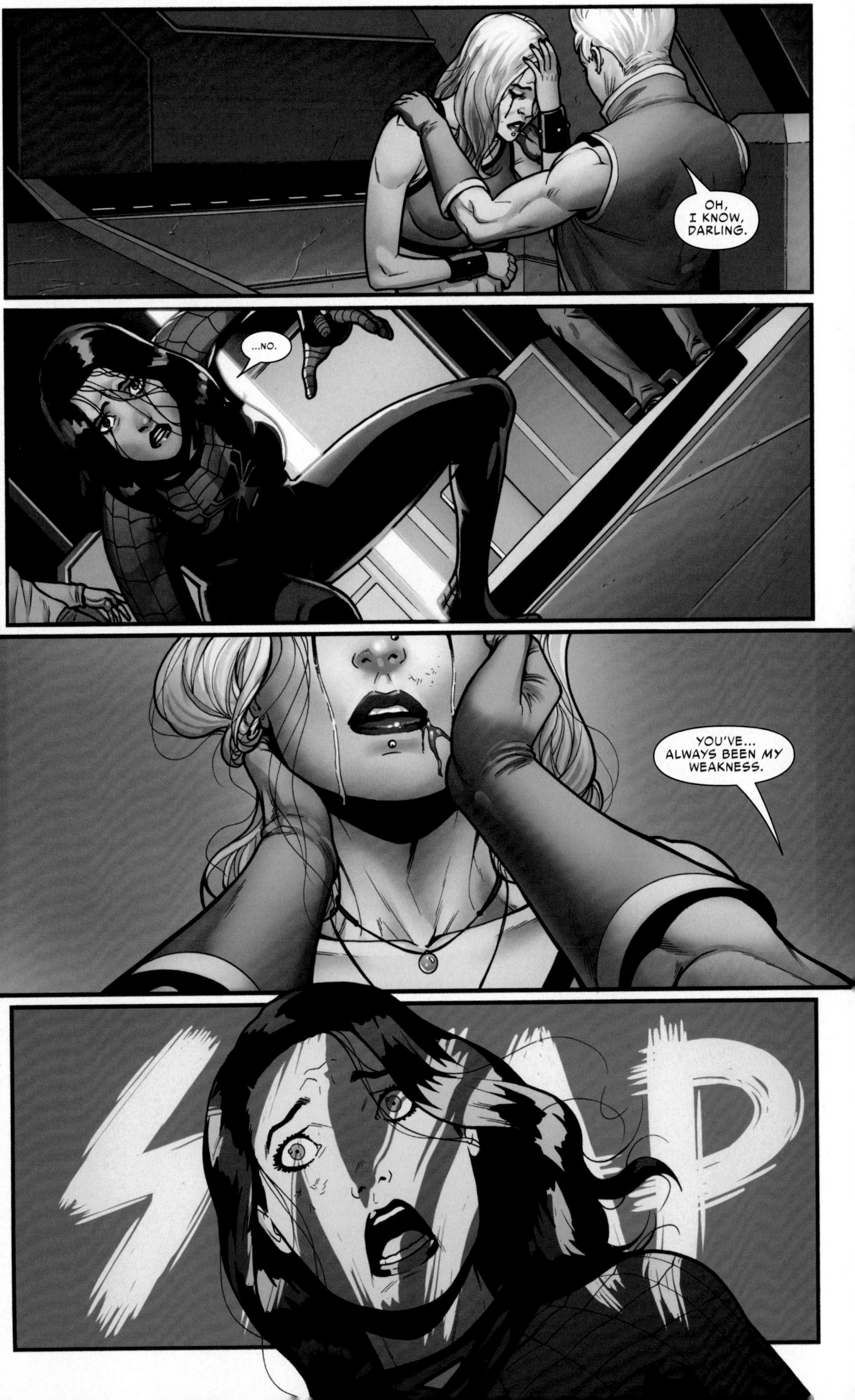
OH, I KNOW, DARLING.
...NO.
YOU'VE... ALWAYS BEEN MY WEAKNESS.
SNAP

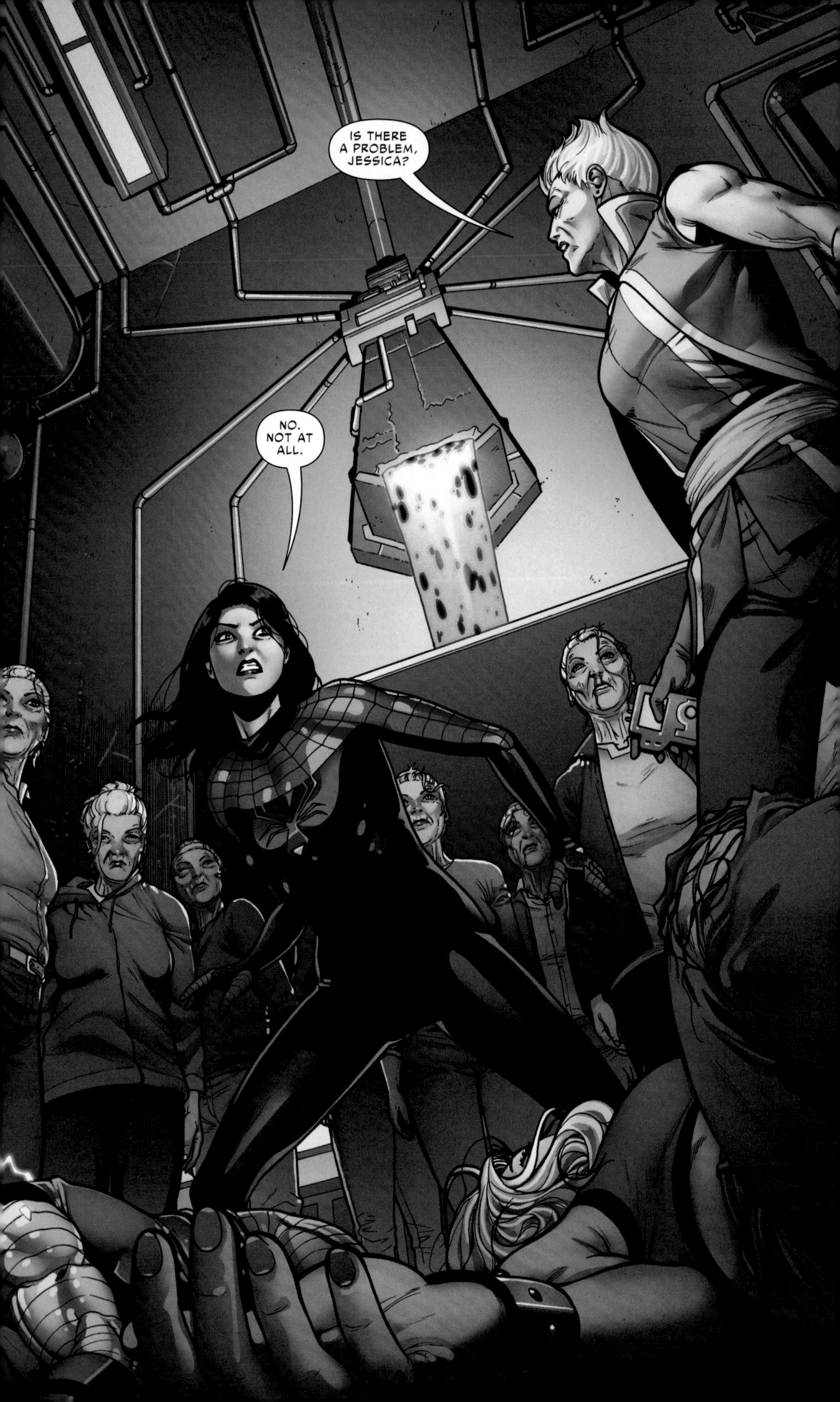
IS THERE A PROBLEM, JESSICA?
NO. NOT AT ALL.

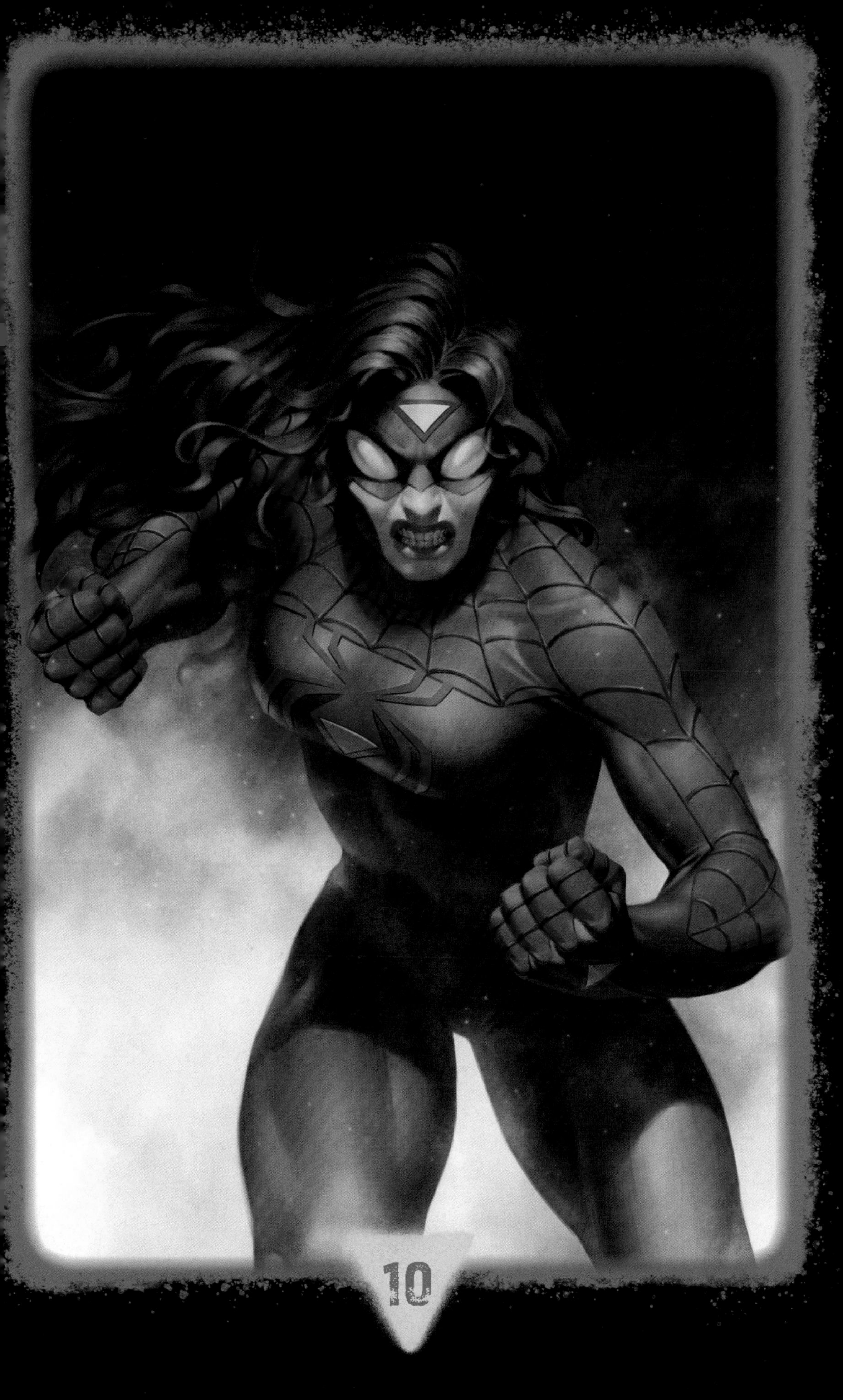
10

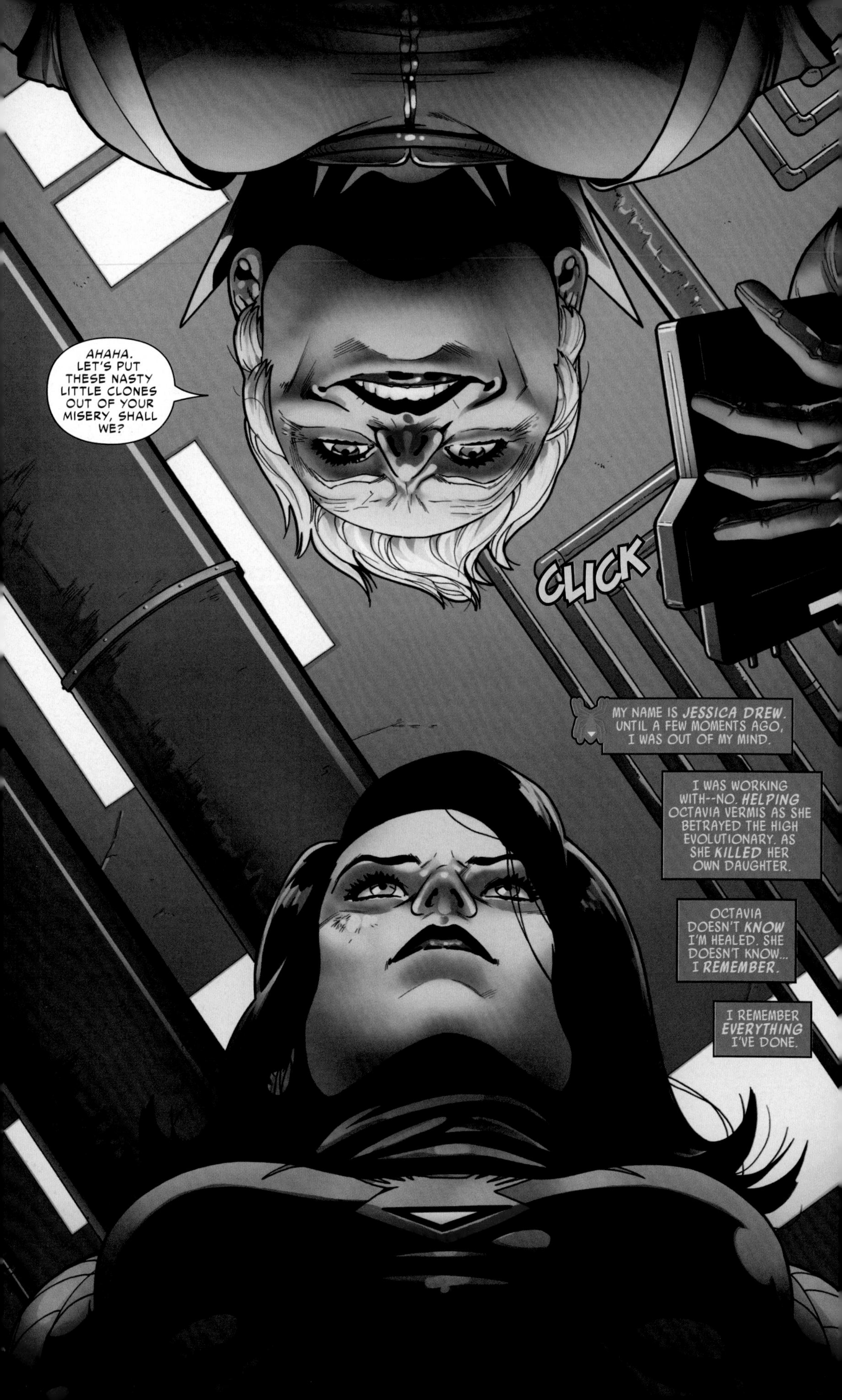
AHAHA. LET'S PUT THESE NASTY LITTLE CLONES OUT OF YOUR MISERY, SHALL WE?
CLICK
MY NAME IS JESSICA DREW. UNTIL A FEW MOMENTS AGO, I WAS OUT OF MY MIND.
I WAS WORKING WITH--NO. HELPING OCTAVIA VERMIS AS SHE BETRAYED THE HIGH EVOLUTIONARY. AS SHE KILLED HER OWN DAUGHTER.
OCTAVIA DOESN'T KNOW I'M HEALED. SHE DOESN'T KNOW... I REMEMBER.
I REMEMBER EVERYTHING I'VE DONE.

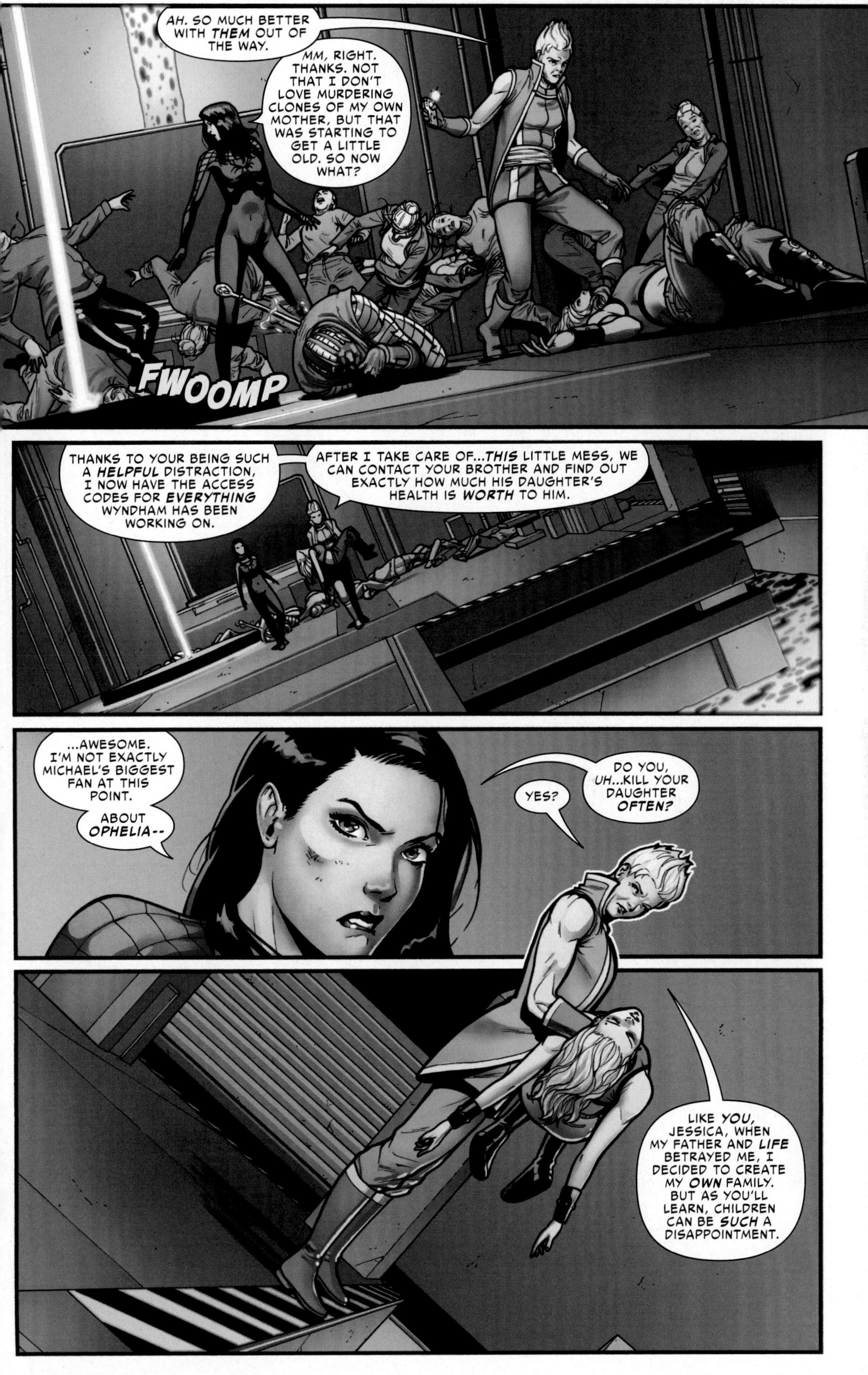
AH. SO MUCH BETTER WITH THEM OUT OF THE WAY.
MM, RIGHT. THANKS. NOT THAT I DON'T LOVE MURDERING CLONES OF MY OWN MOTHER, BUT THAT WAS STARTING TO GET A LITTLE OLD. SO NOW WHAT?
FWOOMP
THANKS TO YOUR BEING SUCH A HELPFUL DISTRACTION, I NOW HAVE THE ACCESS CODES FOR EVERYTHING WYNDHAM HAS BEEN WORKING ON.
AFTER I TAKE CARE OF...THIS LITTLE MESS, WE CAN CONTACT YOUR BROTHER AND FIND OUT EXACTLY HOW MUCH HIS DAUGHTER'S HEALTH IS WORTH TO HIM.
...AWESOME. I'M NOT EXACTLY MICHAEL'S BIGGEST FAN AT THIS POINT.
ABOUT OPHELIA--
YES?
DO YOU, UH...KILL YOUR DAUGHTER OFTEN?
LIKE YOU, JESSICA, WHEN MY FATHER AND LIFE BETRAYED ME, I DECIDED TO CREATE MY OWN FAMILY. BUT AS YOU'LL LEARN, CHILDREN CAN BE SUCH A DISAPPOINTMENT.

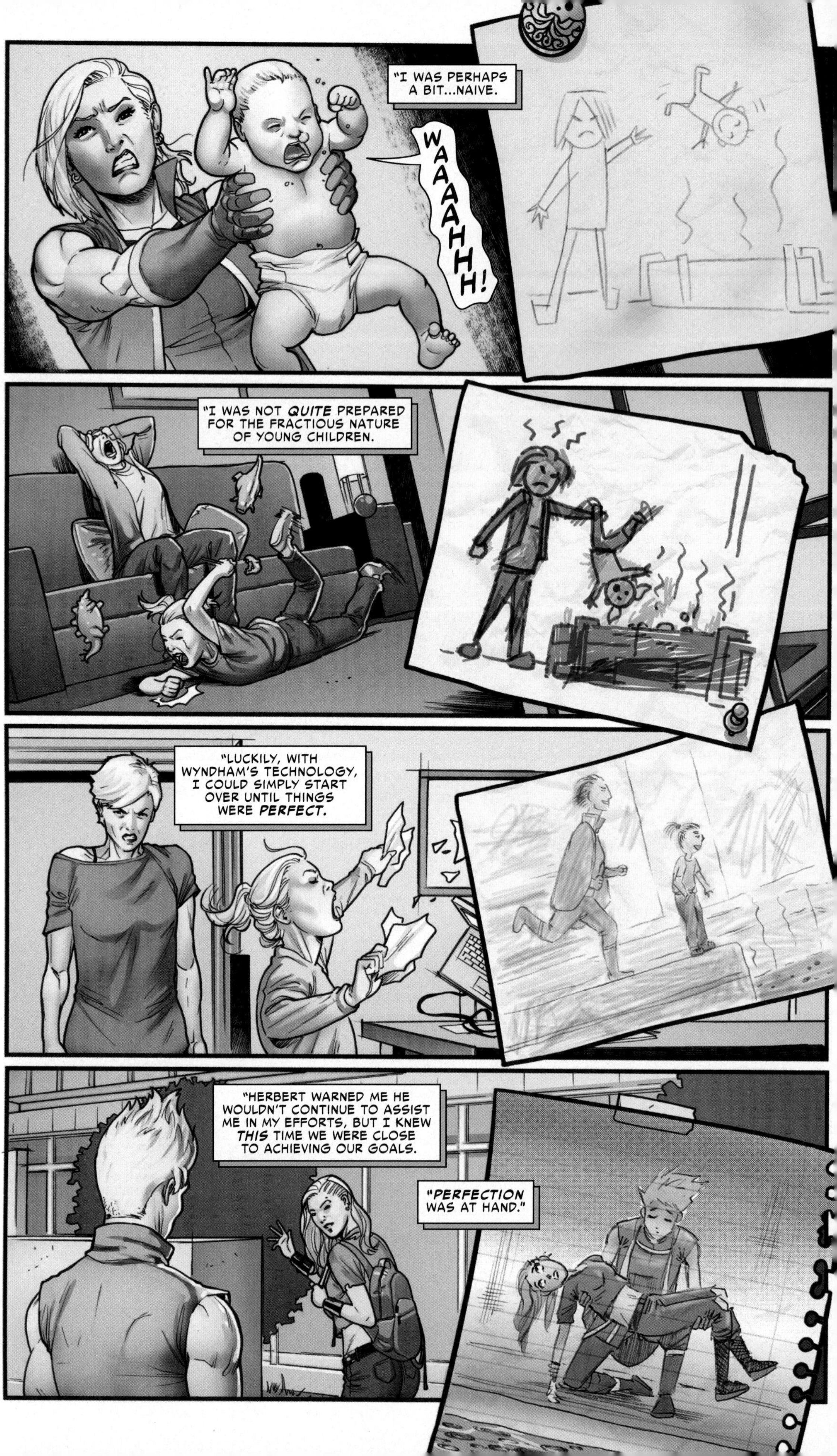
"I WAS PERHAPS A BIT...NAIVE.
WAAAAHHH!
"I WAS NOT QUITE PREPARED FOR THE FRACTIOUS NATURE OF YOUNG CHILDREN.
"LUCKILY, WITH WYNDHAM'S TECHNOLOGY, I COULD SIMPLY START OVER UNTIL THINGS WERE PERFECT.
"HERBERT WARNED ME HE WOULDN'T CONTINUE TO ASSIST ME IN MY EFFORTS, BUT I KNEW THIS TIME WE WERE CLOSE TO ACHIEVING OUR GOALS.
"PERFECTION WAS AT HAND."

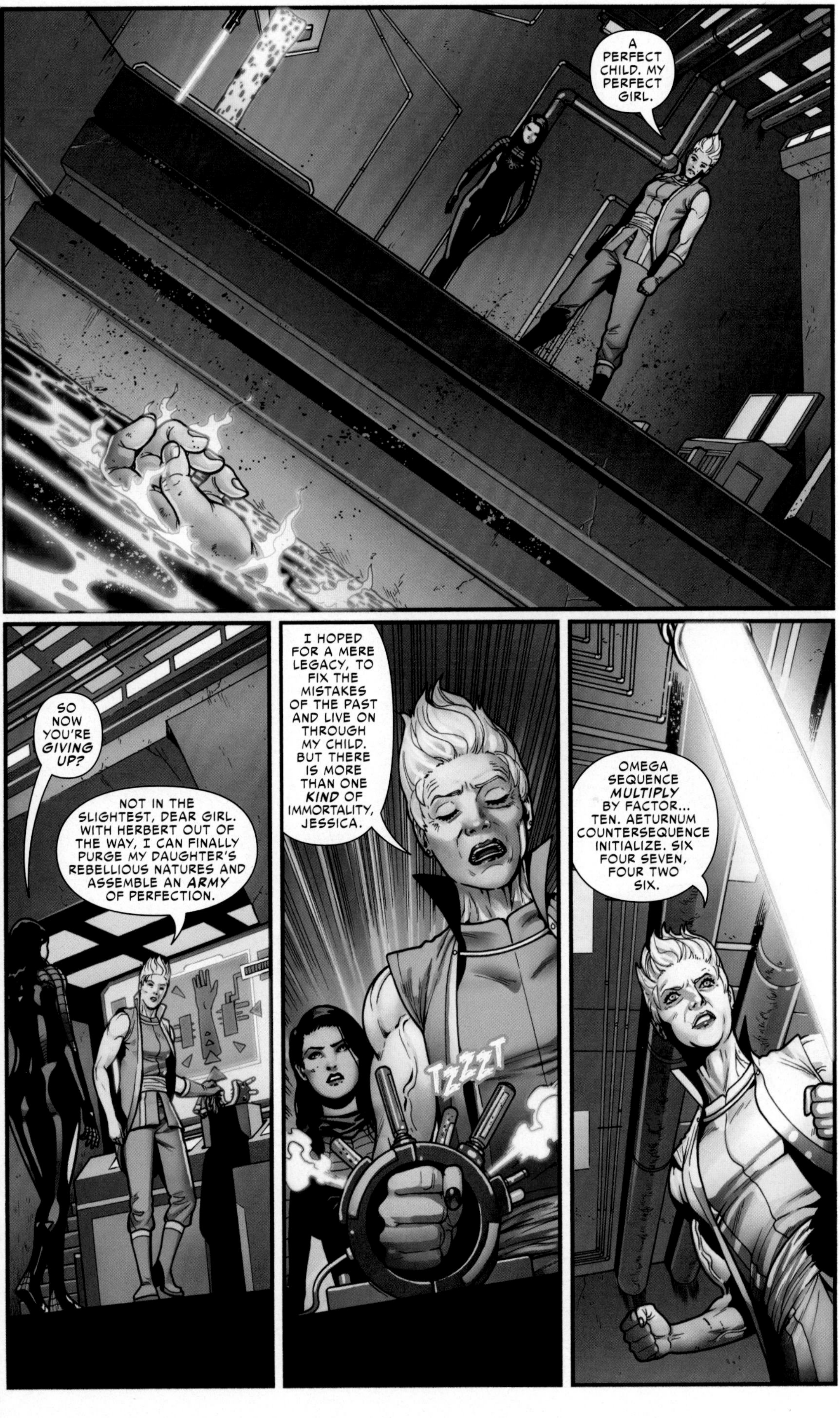

A PERFECT CHILD. MY PERFECT GIRL.
SO NOW YOU'RE GIVING UP?
NOT IN THE SLIGHTEST, DEAR GIRL. WITH HERBERT OUT OF THE WAY, I CAN FINALLY PURGE MY DAUGHTER'S REBELLIOUS NATURES AND ASSEMBLE AN ARMY OF PERFECTION.
I HOPED FOR A MERE LEGACY, TO FIX THE MISTAKES OF THE PAST AND LIVE ON THROUGH MY CHILD. BUT THERE IS MORE THAN ONE KIND OF IMMORTALITY, JESSICA.
TZZZT
OMEGA SEQUENCE MULTIPLY BY FACTOR... TEN. AETURNUM COUNTERSEQUENCE INITIALIZE. SIX FOUR SEVEN, FOUR TWO SIX.

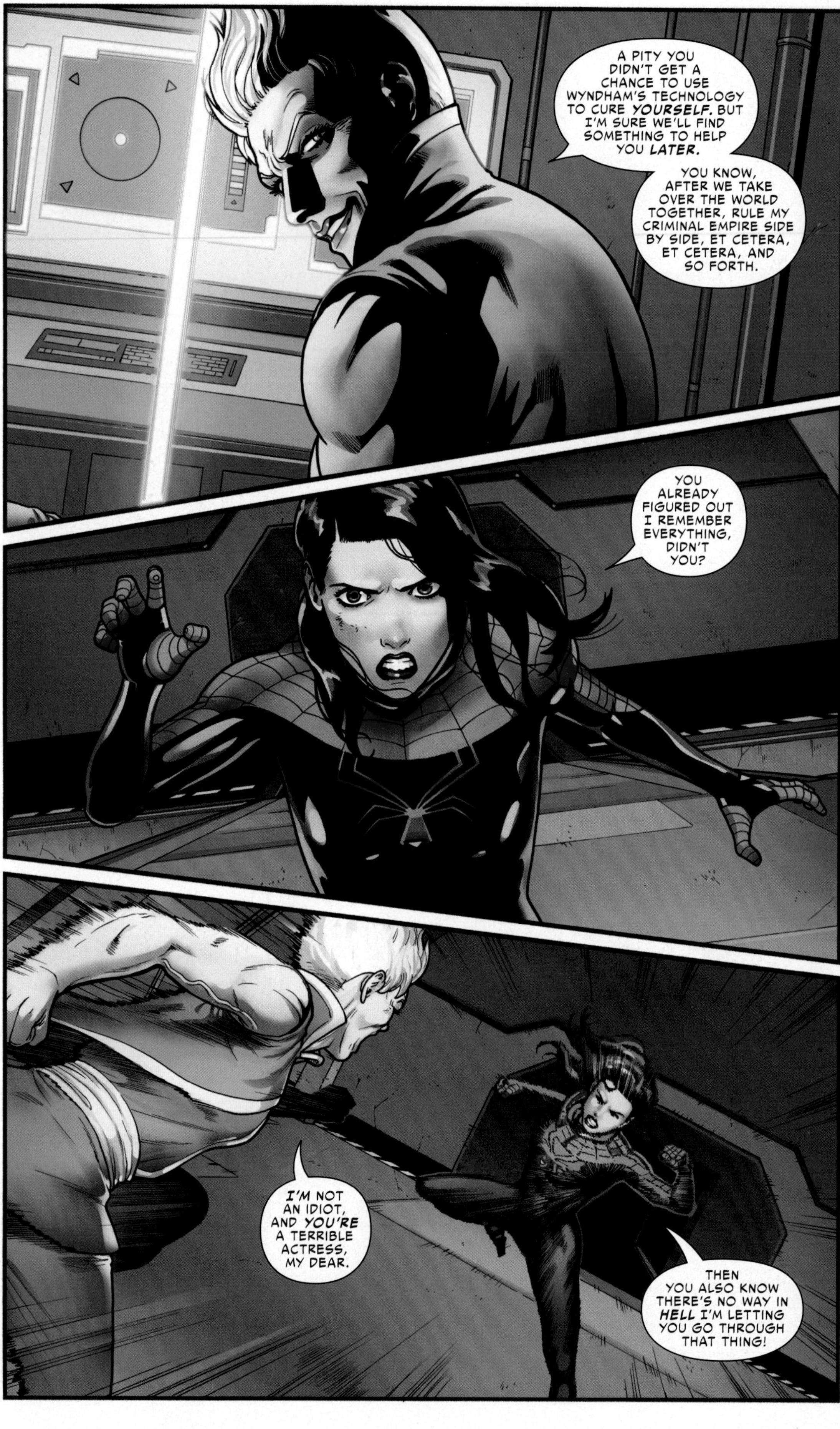

A PITY YOU DIDN'T GET A CHANCE TO USE WYNDHAM'S TECHNOLOGY TO CURE *YOURSELF.* BUT I'M SURE WE'LL FIND SOMETHING TO HELP YOU *LATER.*
YOU KNOW, AFTER WE TAKE OVER THE WORLD TOGETHER, RULE MY CRIMINAL EMPIRE SIDE BY SIDE, ET CETERA, ET CETERA, AND SO FORTH.
YOU ALREADY FIGURED OUT I REMEMBER EVERYTHING, DIDN'T YOU?
I'M NOT AN IDIOT, AND *YOU'RE* A TERRIBLE ACTRESS, MY DEAR.
THEN YOU ALSO KNOW THERE'S NO WAY IN *HELL* I'M LETTING YOU GO THROUGH THAT THING!

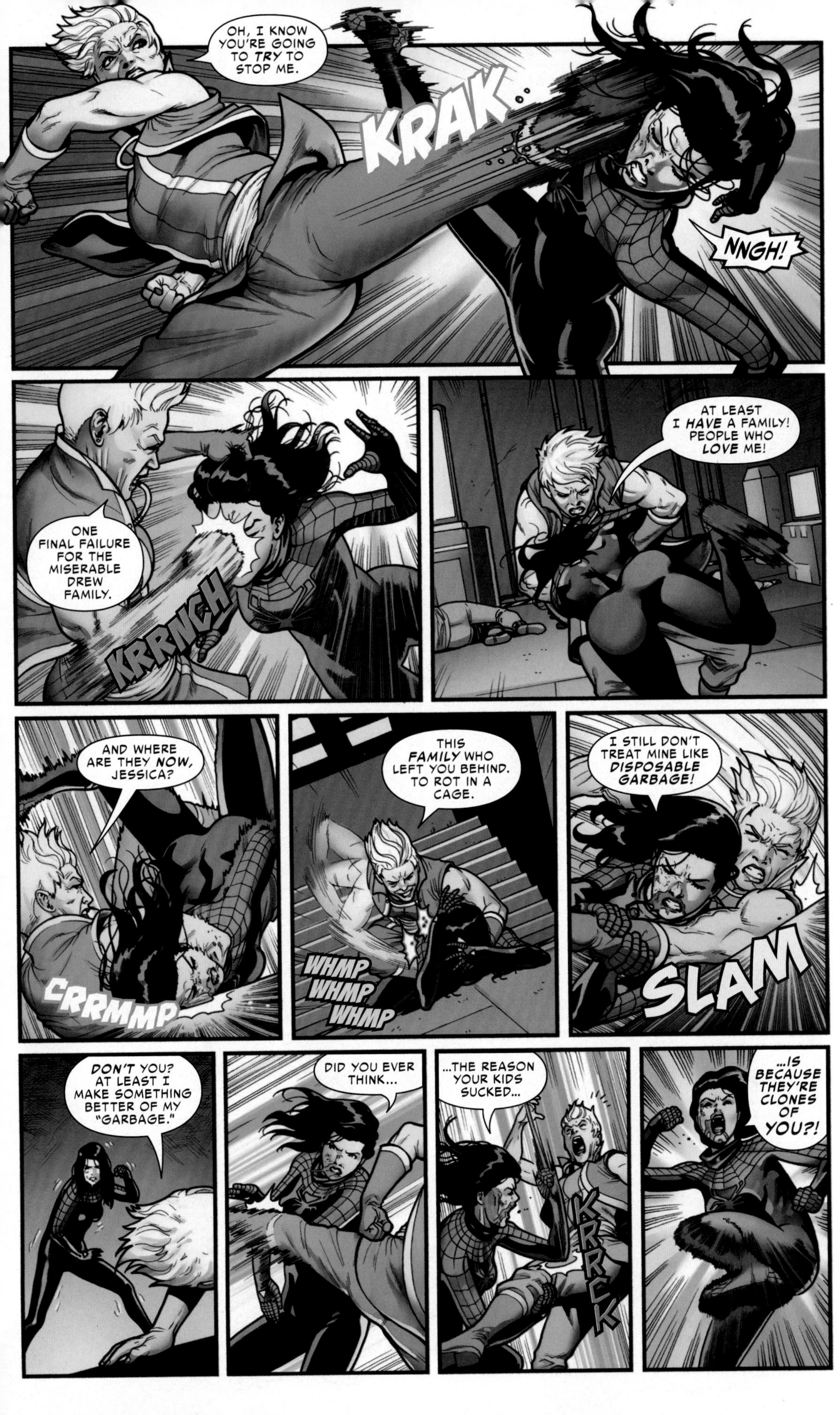
OH, I KNOW YOU'RE GOING TO TRY TO STOP ME.
KRAK
NNGH!
ONE FINAL FAILURE FOR THE MISERABLE DREW FAMILY.
KRRNCH
AT LEAST I HAVE A FAMILY! PEOPLE WHO LOVE ME!
AND WHERE ARE THEY NOW, JESSICA?
CRRMMP
THIS FAMILY WHO LEFT YOU BEHIND. TO ROT IN A CAGE.
WHMP WHMP WHMP
I STILL DON'T TREAT MINE LIKE DISPOSABLE GARBAGE!
SLAM
DON'T YOU? AT LEAST I MAKE SOMETHING BETTER OF MY "GARBAGE."
DID YOU EVER THINK...
...THE REASON YOUR KIDS SUCKED...
KRRCK
...IS BECAUSE THEY'RE CLONES OF YOU?!

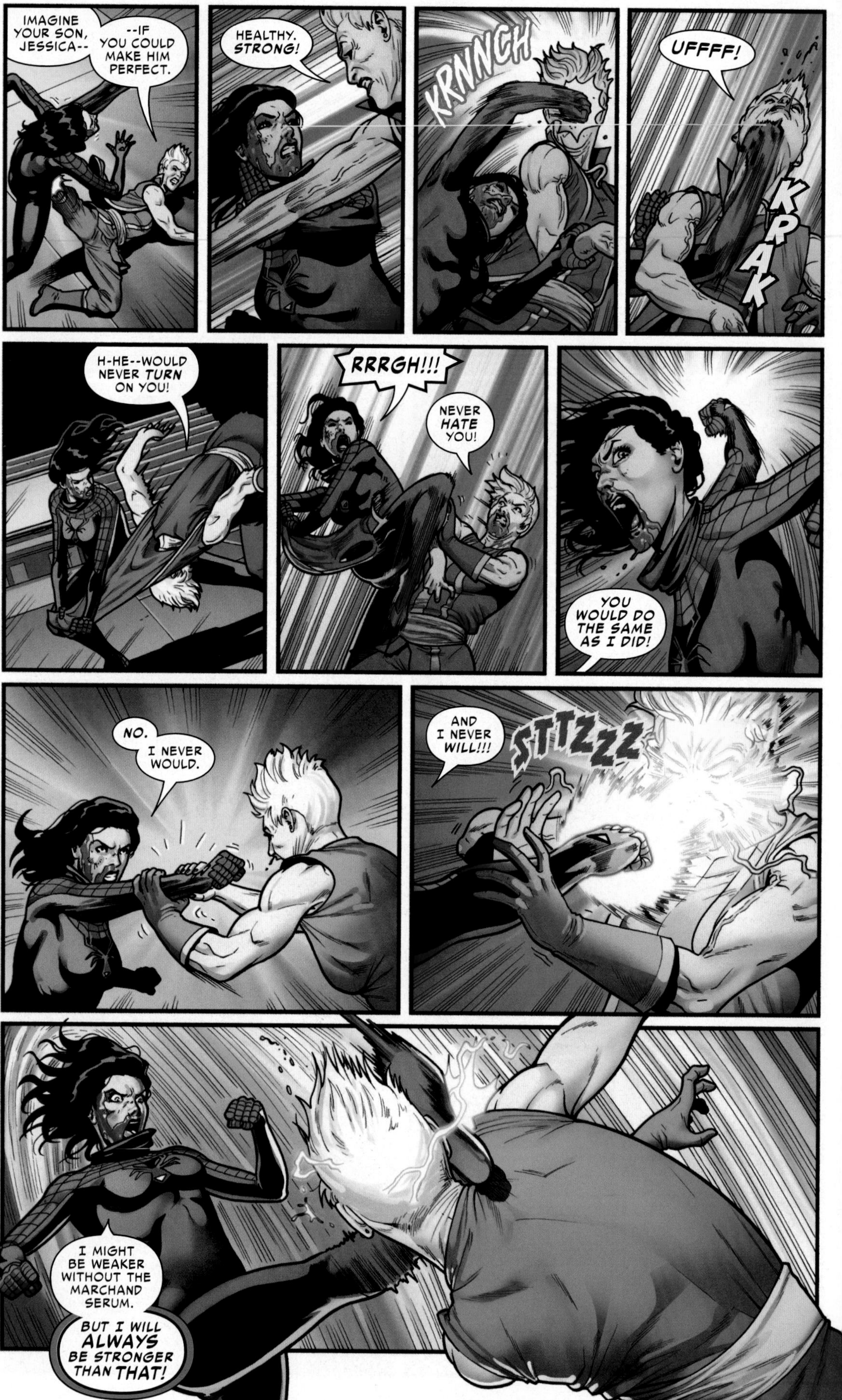
IMAGINE YOUR SON, JESSICA--
--IF YOU COULD MAKE HIM PERFECT.
HEALTHY. STRONG!
KRNNCH
UFFFF!
KRAK
H-HE--WOULD NEVER TURN ON YOU!
RRRGH!!!
NEVER HATE YOU!
YOU WOULD DO THE SAME AS I DID!
NO. I NEVER WOULD.
AND I NEVER WILL!!!
STTZZZ
I MIGHT BE WEAKER WITHOUT THE MARCHAND SERUM.
BUT I WILL ALWAYS BE STRONGER THAN THAT!

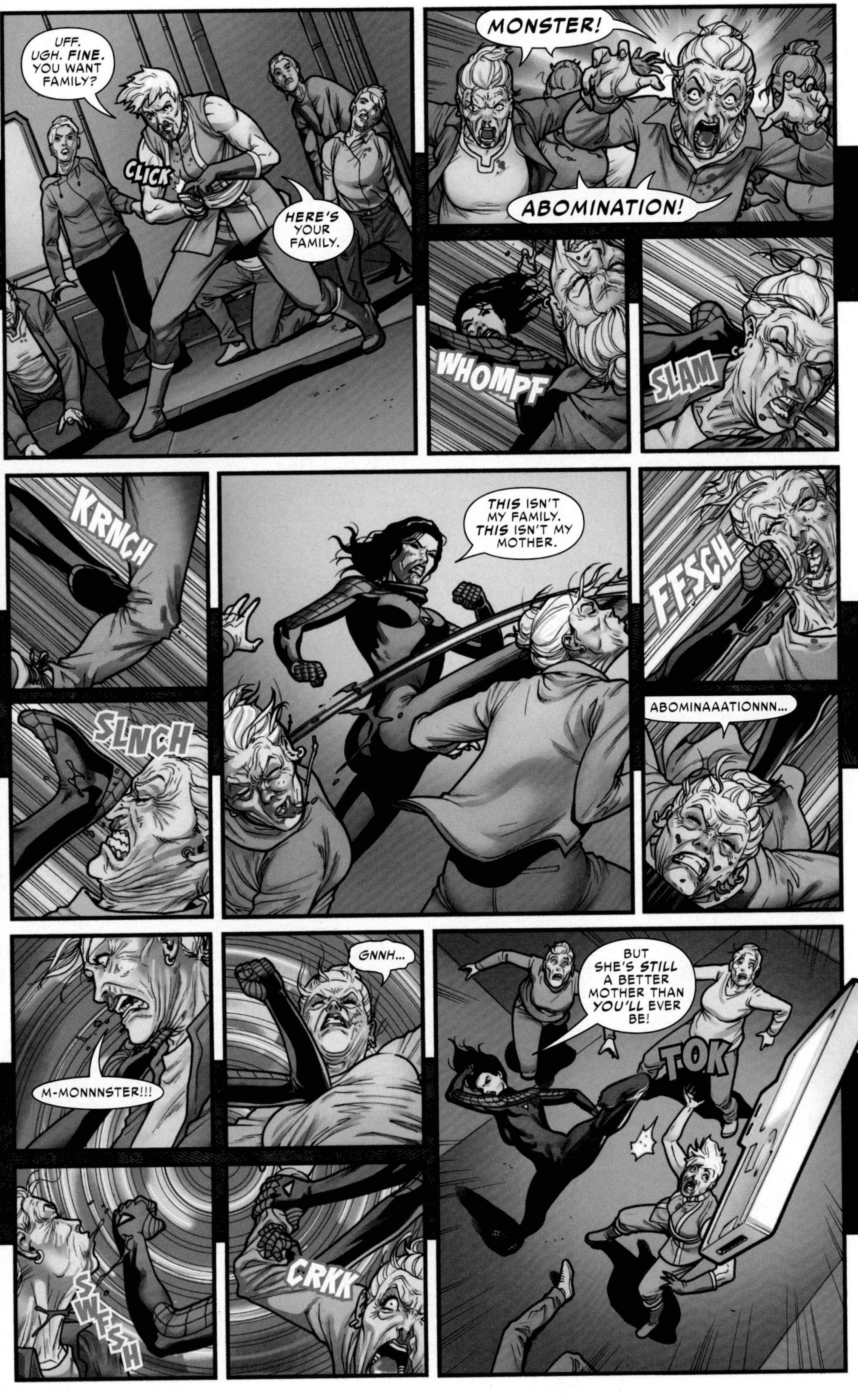
UFF. UGH. FINE. YOU WANT FAMILY?
CLICK
HERE'S YOUR FAMILY.
MONSTER!
ABOMINATION!
WHOMPF
SLAM
KRNCH
THIS ISN'T MY FAMILY. THIS ISN'T MY MOTHER.
FFSCH
SLNCH
ABOMINAAATIONNN...
M-MONNNSTER!!!
GNNH...
BUT SHE'S STILL A BETTER MOTHER THAN YOU'LL EVER BE!
TOK
SWFSH
CRKK

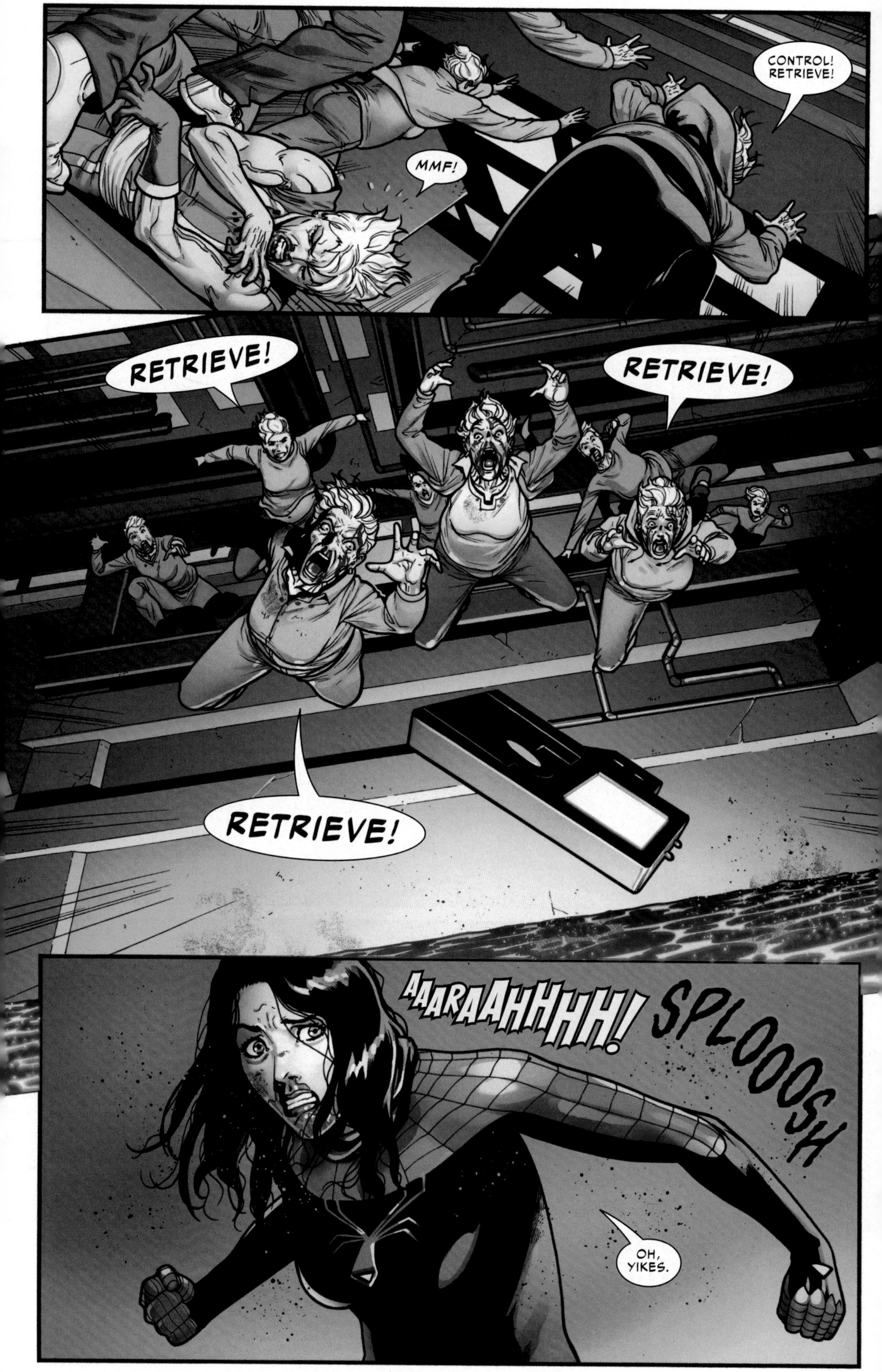
CONTROL! RETRIEVE!
MMF!
RETRIEVE!
RETRIEVE!
RETRIEVE!
AAARAAHHHH!
SPLOOOSH
OH, YIKES.

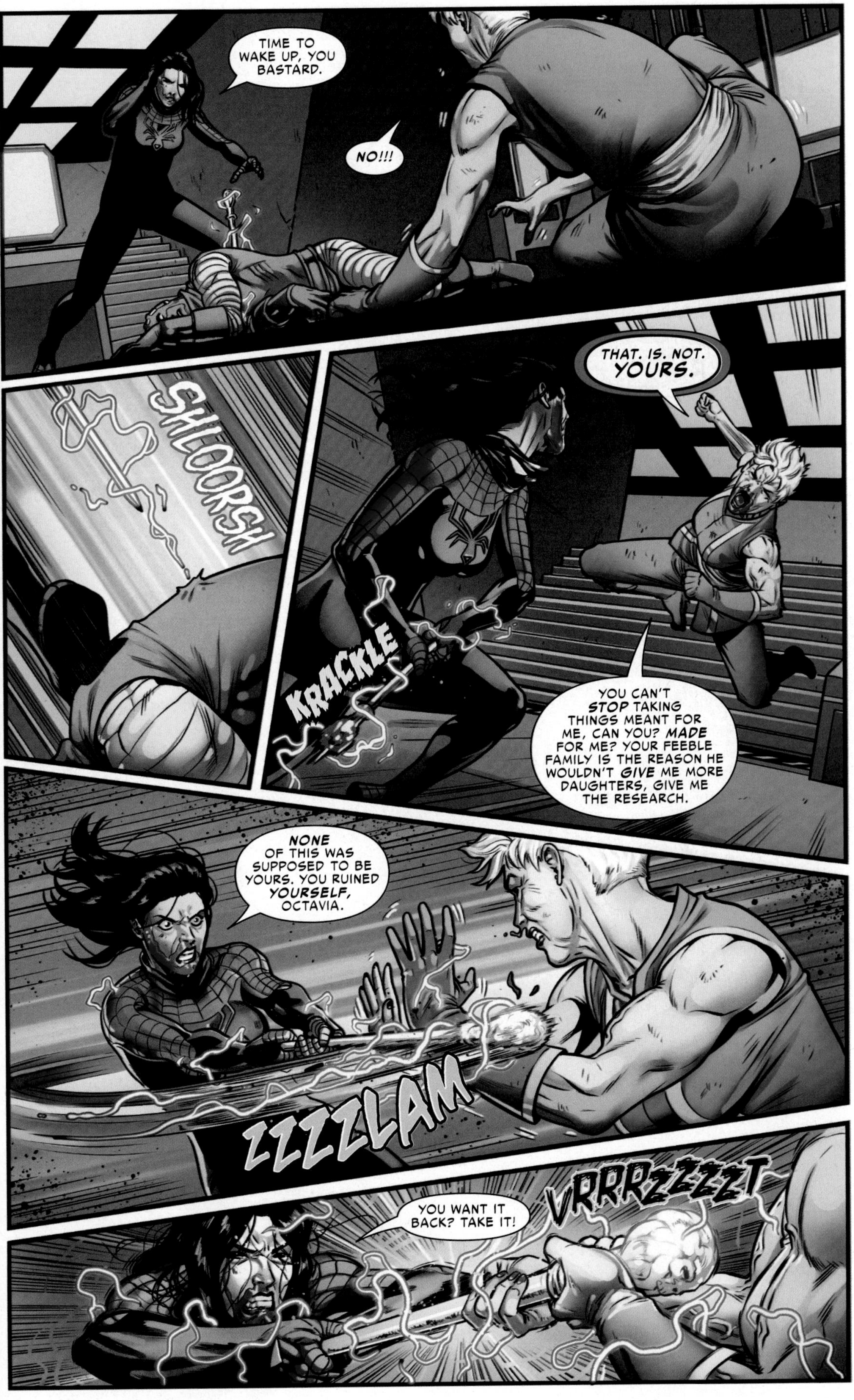
TIME TO WAKE UP, YOU BASTARD.
NO!!!
SHLOORSH
THAT. IS. NOT. YOURS.
KRACKLE
YOU CAN'T STOP TAKING THINGS MEANT FOR ME, CAN YOU? MADE FOR ME? YOUR FEEBLE FAMILY IS THE REASON HE WOULDN'T GIVE ME MORE DAUGHTERS, GIVE ME THE RESEARCH.
NONE OF THIS WAS SUPPOSED TO BE YOURS. YOU RUINED YOURSELF, OCTAVIA.
ZZZZLAM
YOU WANT IT BACK? TAKE IT!
VRRRZZZZT

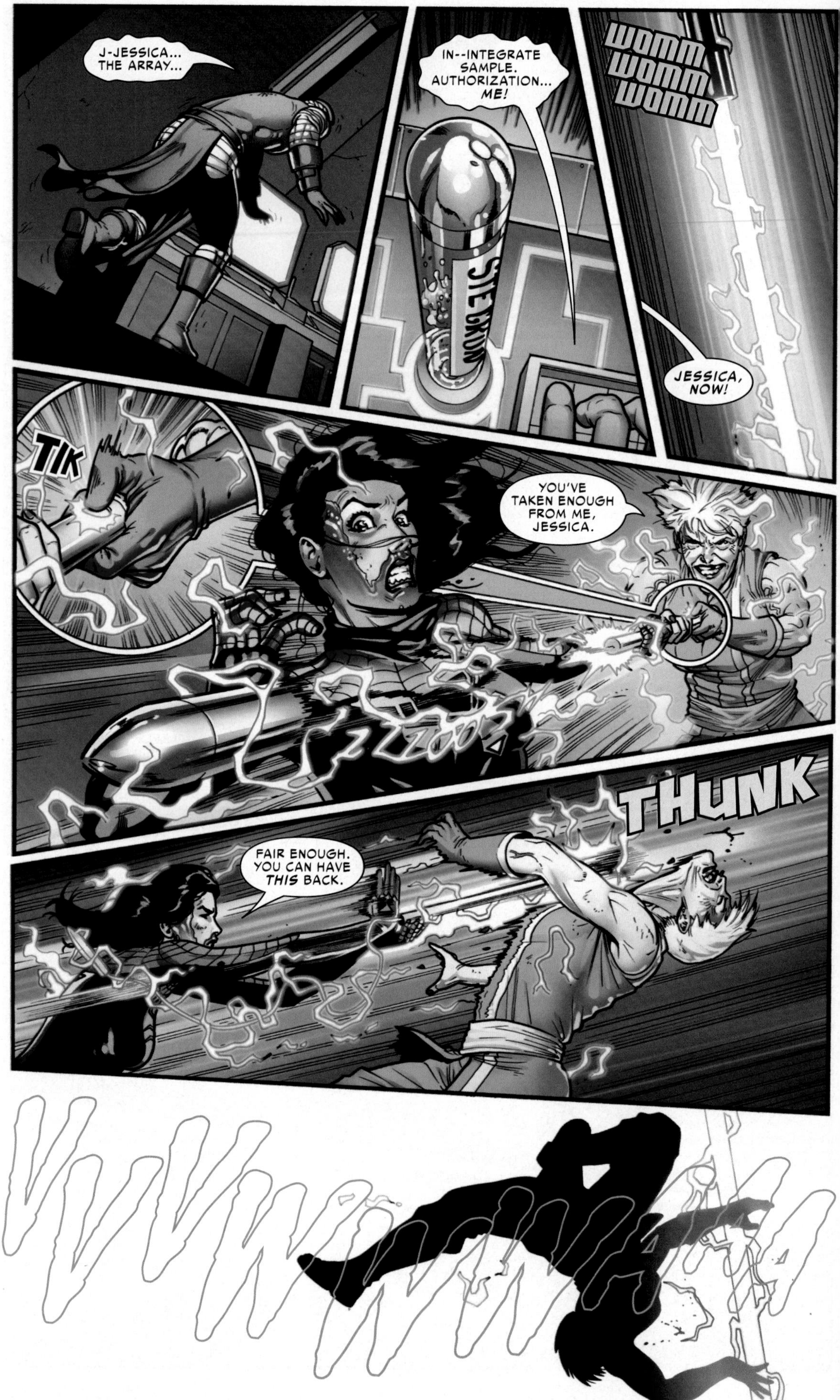
J-JESSICA... THE ARRAY...
IN--INTEGRATE SAMPLE. AUTHORIZATION... *ME!*
STEGRON
WOMM WOMM WOMM
JESSICA, NOW!
TIK
YOU'VE TAKEN ENOUGH FROM ME, JESSICA.
THUNK
FAIR ENOUGH. YOU CAN HAVE *THIS* BACK.

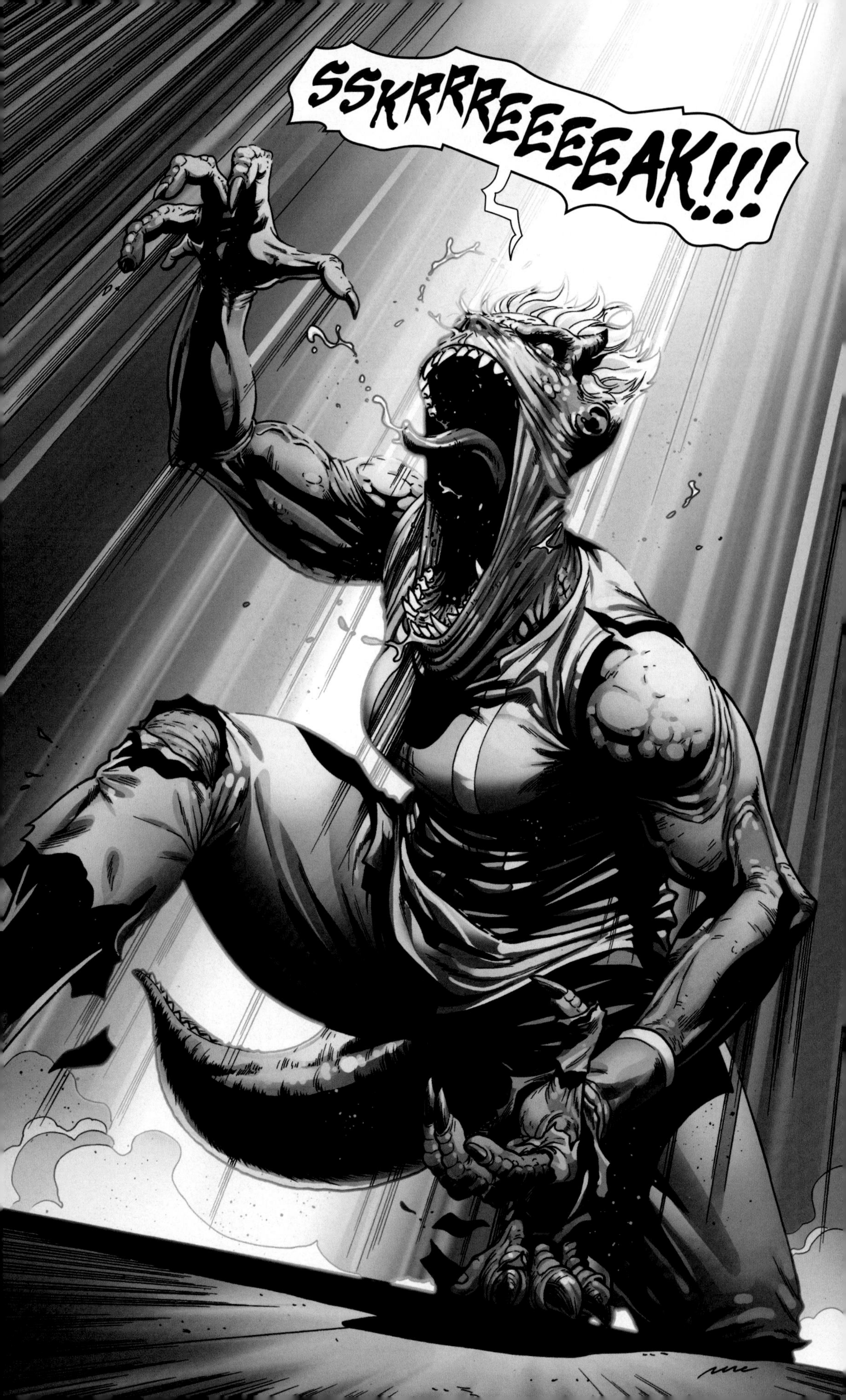
SSKRRREEEEEAK!!!

WILL YOU BE ABLE TO...*FIX* THAT?

OCTAVIA? OR THE ARRAY?

...YES.

YES.

NNNNZZTTT...

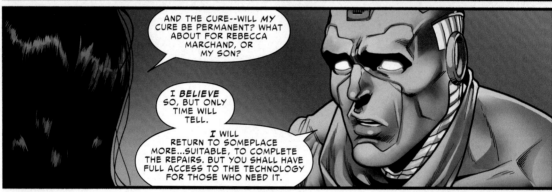

AND THE CURE--WILL *MY* CURE BE PERMANENT? WHAT ABOUT FOR REBECCA MARCHAND, OR MY SON?

I *BELIEVE* SO, BUT ONLY TIME WILL TELL.

I WILL RETURN TO SOMEPLACE MORE...SUITABLE, TO COMPLETE THE REPAIRS. BUT YOU SHALL HAVE FULL ACCESS TO THE TECHNOLOGY FOR THOSE WHO NEED IT.

FOR MY FAMILY.

SHE DID *LOVE* YOU, YOU KNOW.

OCTAVIA???

MIRIAM. IN THE CLONES-- THAT LOVE, HER DRIVE TO PROTECT YOU, IT BECAME TWISTED, *WRONG.* SHE WAS... BROKEN.

THAT MAKES TWO OF US.

THERE ARE MANY THINGS THAT NEED TO BE FIXED. YOU COULD *HELP* ME. CONTINUE YOUR PARENTS' RESEARCH.

WHAT WOULD *YOU* LIKE TO DO, JESSICA?

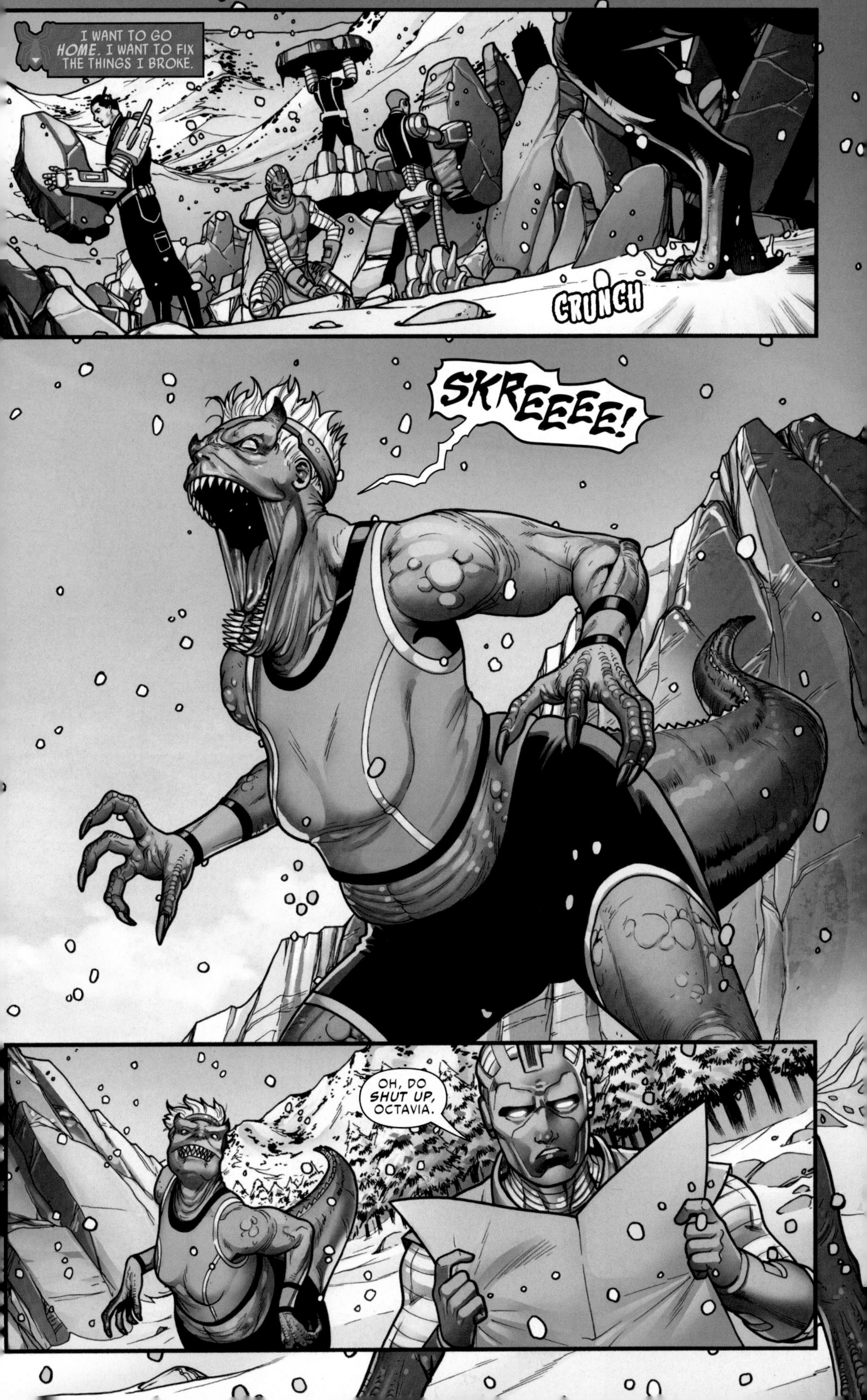
I WANT TO GO HOME. I WANT TO FIX THE THINGS I BROKE.
CRUNCH
SKREEEEE!
OH, DO SHUT UP, OCTAVIA.

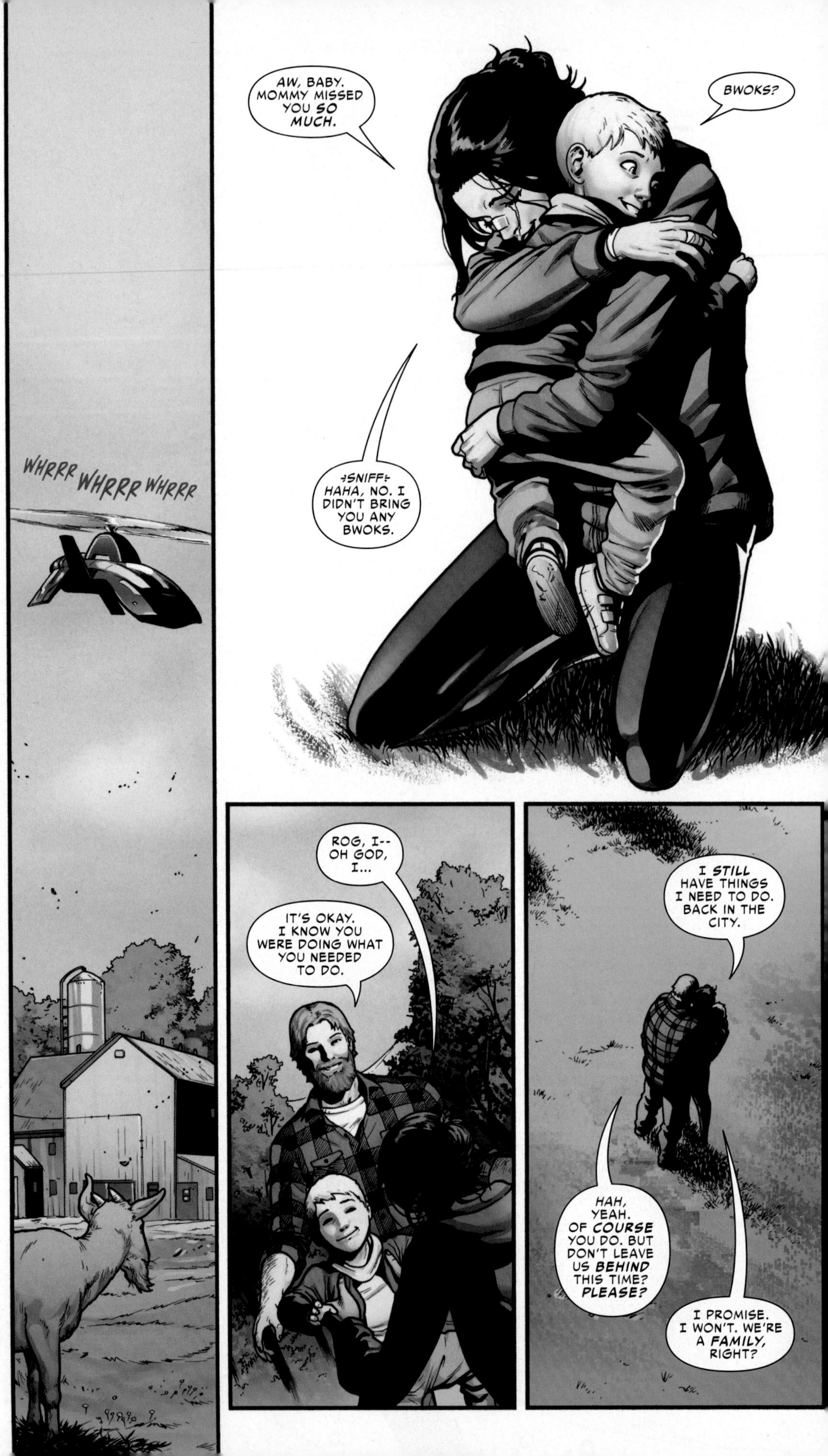
WHRRR WHRRR WHRRR
AW, BABY. MOMMY MISSED YOU SO MUCH.
BWOKS?
SNIFF HAHA, NO. I DIDN'T BRING YOU ANY BWOKS.
ROG, I-- OH GOD, I...
IT'S OKAY. I KNOW YOU WERE DOING WHAT YOU NEEDED TO DO.
I STILL HAVE THINGS I NEED TO DO. BACK IN THE CITY.
HAH, YEAH. OF COURSE YOU DO. BUT DON'T LEAVE US BEHIND THIS TIME? PLEASE?
I PROMISE. I WON'T. WE'RE A FAMILY, RIGHT?

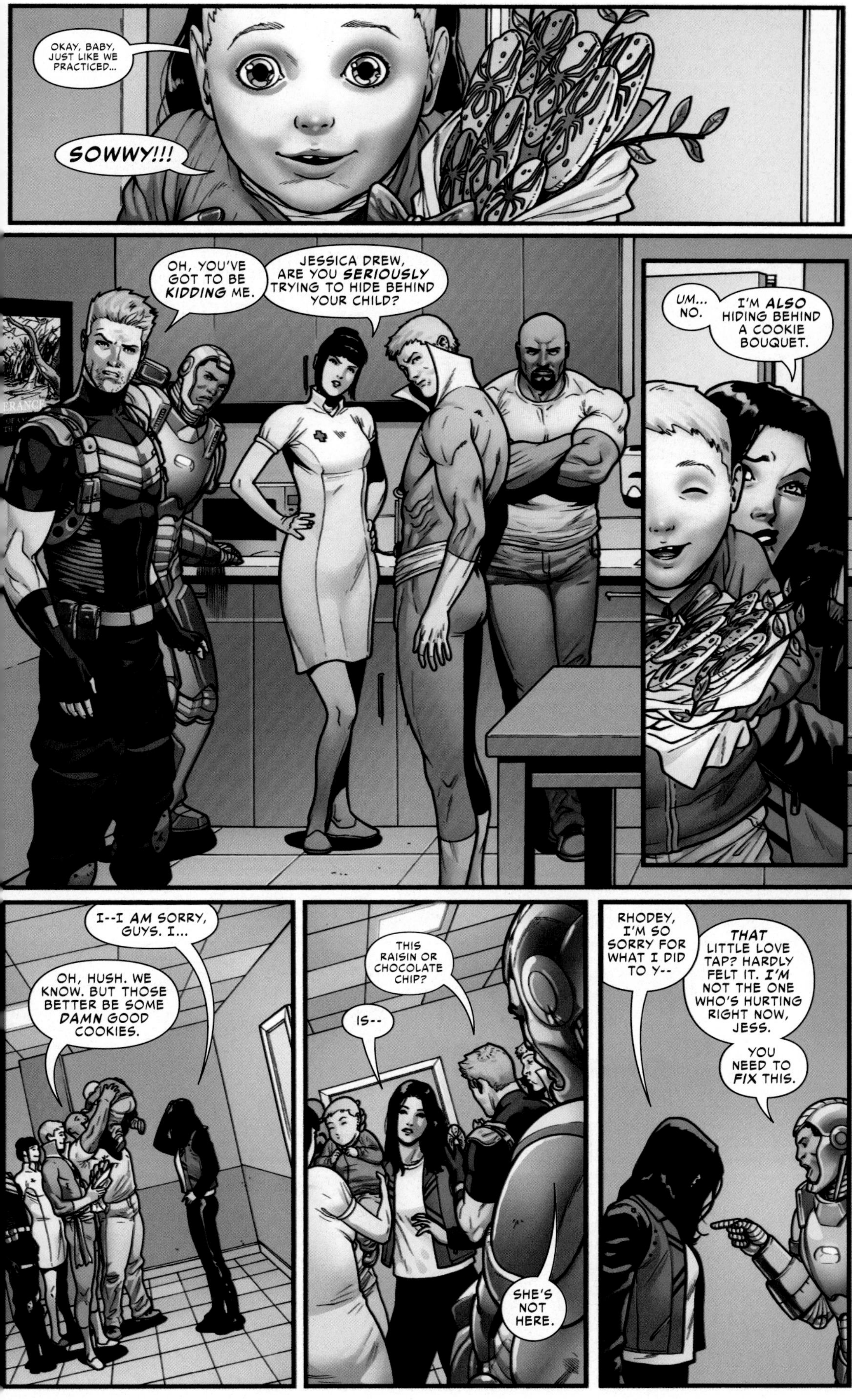
OKAY, BABY, JUST LIKE WE PRACTICED...
SOWWY!!!
OH, YOU'VE GOT TO BE KIDDING ME.
JESSICA DREW, ARE YOU SERIOUSLY TRYING TO HIDE BEHIND YOUR CHILD?
UM... NO.
I'M ALSO HIDING BEHIND A COOKIE BOUQUET.
I--I AM SORRY, GUYS. I...
OH, HUSH. WE KNOW. BUT THOSE BETTER BE SOME DAMN GOOD COOKIES.
IS--
THIS RAISIN OR CHOCOLATE CHIP?
SHE'S NOT HERE.
RHODEY, I'M SO SORRY FOR WHAT I DID TO Y--
THAT LITTLE LOVE TAP? HARDLY FELT IT. I'M NOT THE ONE WHO'S HURTING RIGHT NOW, JESS.
YOU NEED TO FIX THIS.

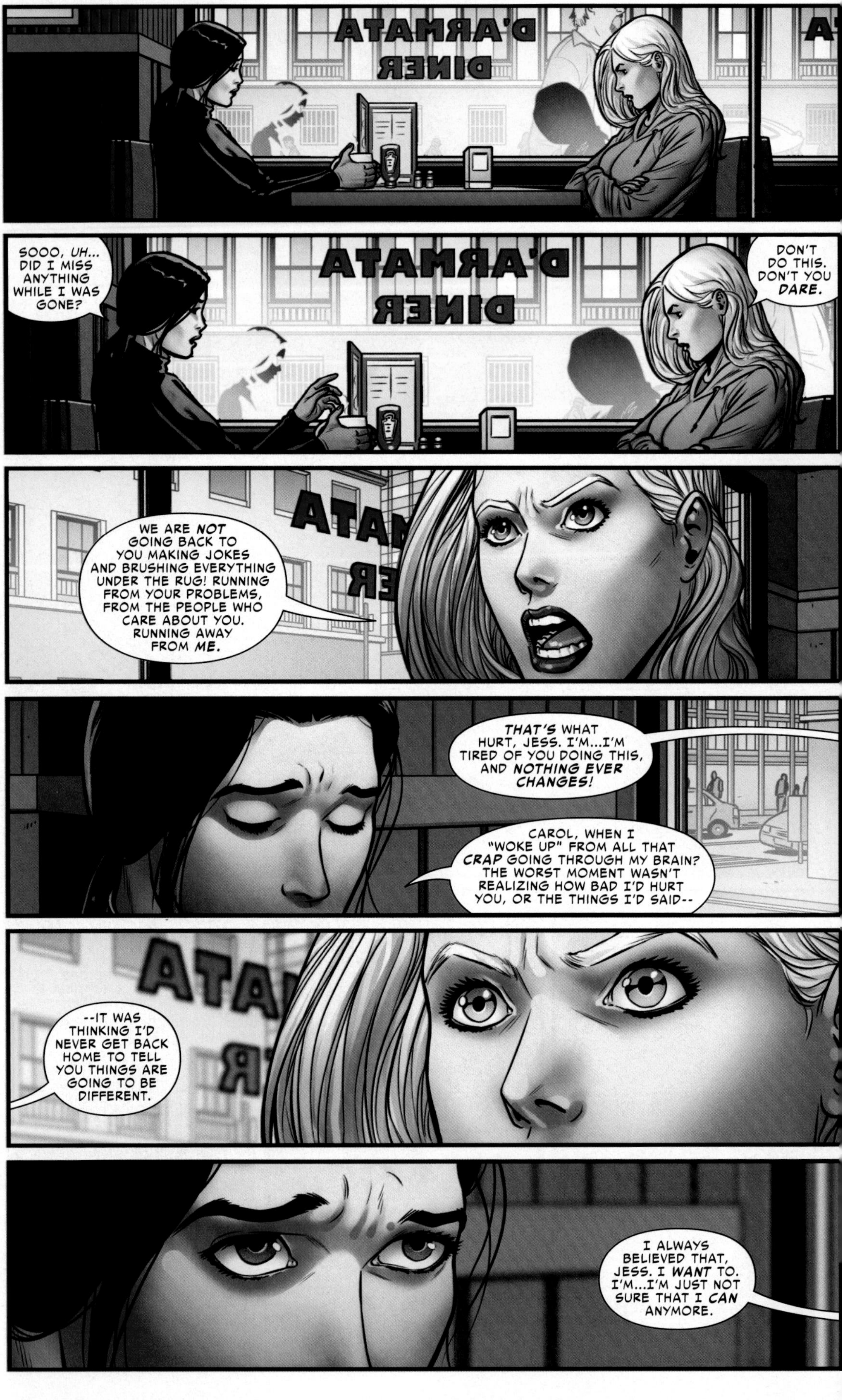
D'ARMATA DINER
SOOO, UH... DID I MISS ANYTHING WHILE I WAS GONE?
DON'T DO THIS. DON'T YOU DARE.
WE ARE NOT GOING BACK TO YOU MAKING JOKES AND BRUSHING EVERYTHING UNDER THE RUG! RUNNING FROM YOUR PROBLEMS, FROM THE PEOPLE WHO CARE ABOUT YOU. RUNNING AWAY FROM ME.
THAT'S WHAT HURT, JESS. I'M...I'M TIRED OF YOU DOING THIS, AND NOTHING EVER CHANGES!
CAROL, WHEN I "WOKE UP" FROM ALL THAT CRAP GOING THROUGH MY BRAIN? THE WORST MOMENT WASN'T REALIZING HOW BAD I'D HURT YOU, OR THE THINGS I'D SAID--
--IT WAS THINKING I'D NEVER GET BACK HOME TO TELL YOU THINGS ARE GOING TO BE DIFFERENT.
I ALWAYS BELIEVED THAT, JESS. I WANT TO. I'M...I'M JUST NOT SURE THAT I CAN ANYMORE.

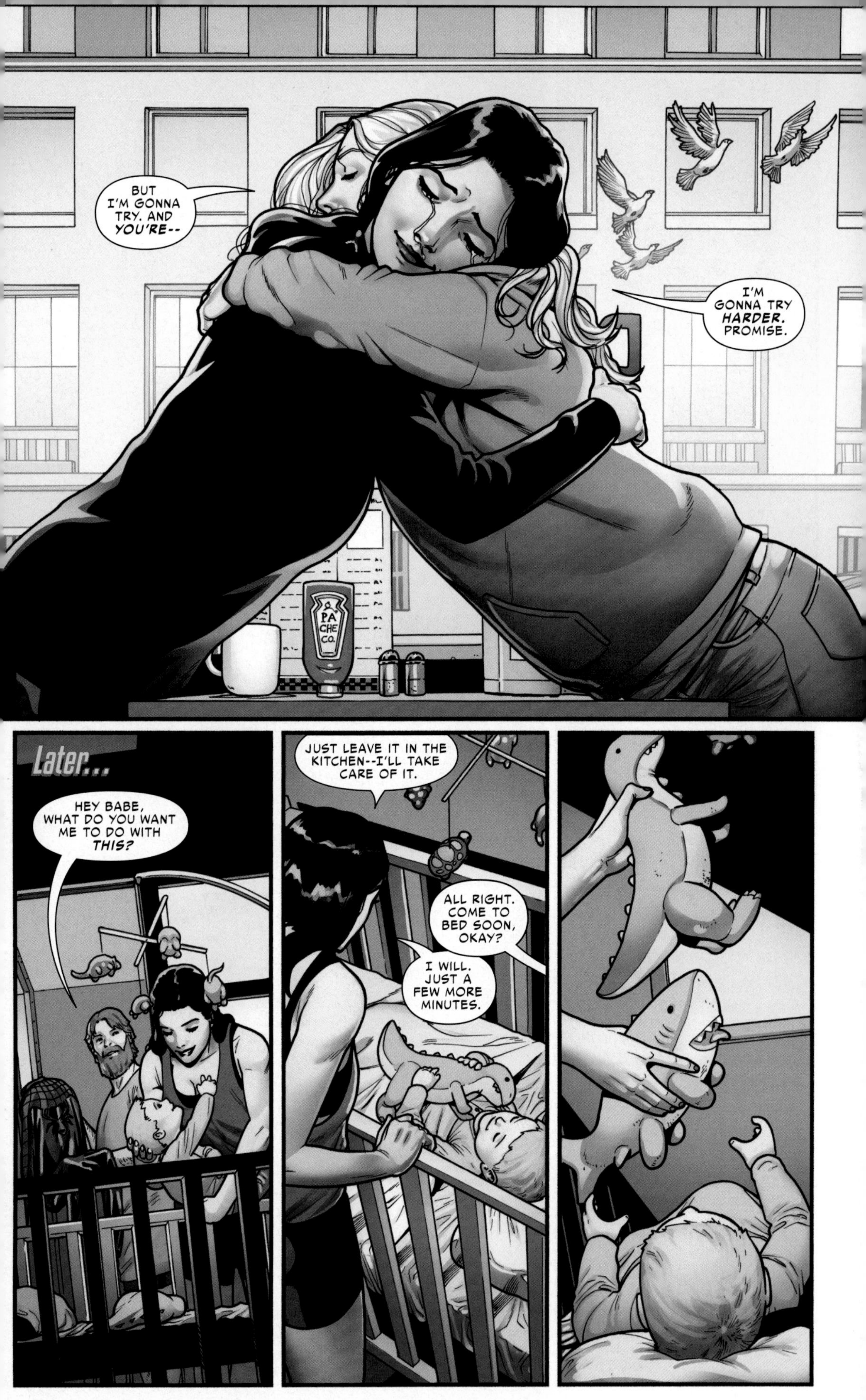

BUT I'M GONNA TRY. AND YOU'RE--
I'M GONNA TRY HARDER. PROMISE.
PA CHE CO.
Later...
HEY BABE, WHAT DO YOU WANT ME TO DO WITH THIS?
JUST LEAVE IT IN THE KITCHEN--I'LL TAKE CARE OF IT.
ALL RIGHT. COME TO BED SOON, OKAY?
I WILL. JUST A FEW MORE MINUTES.

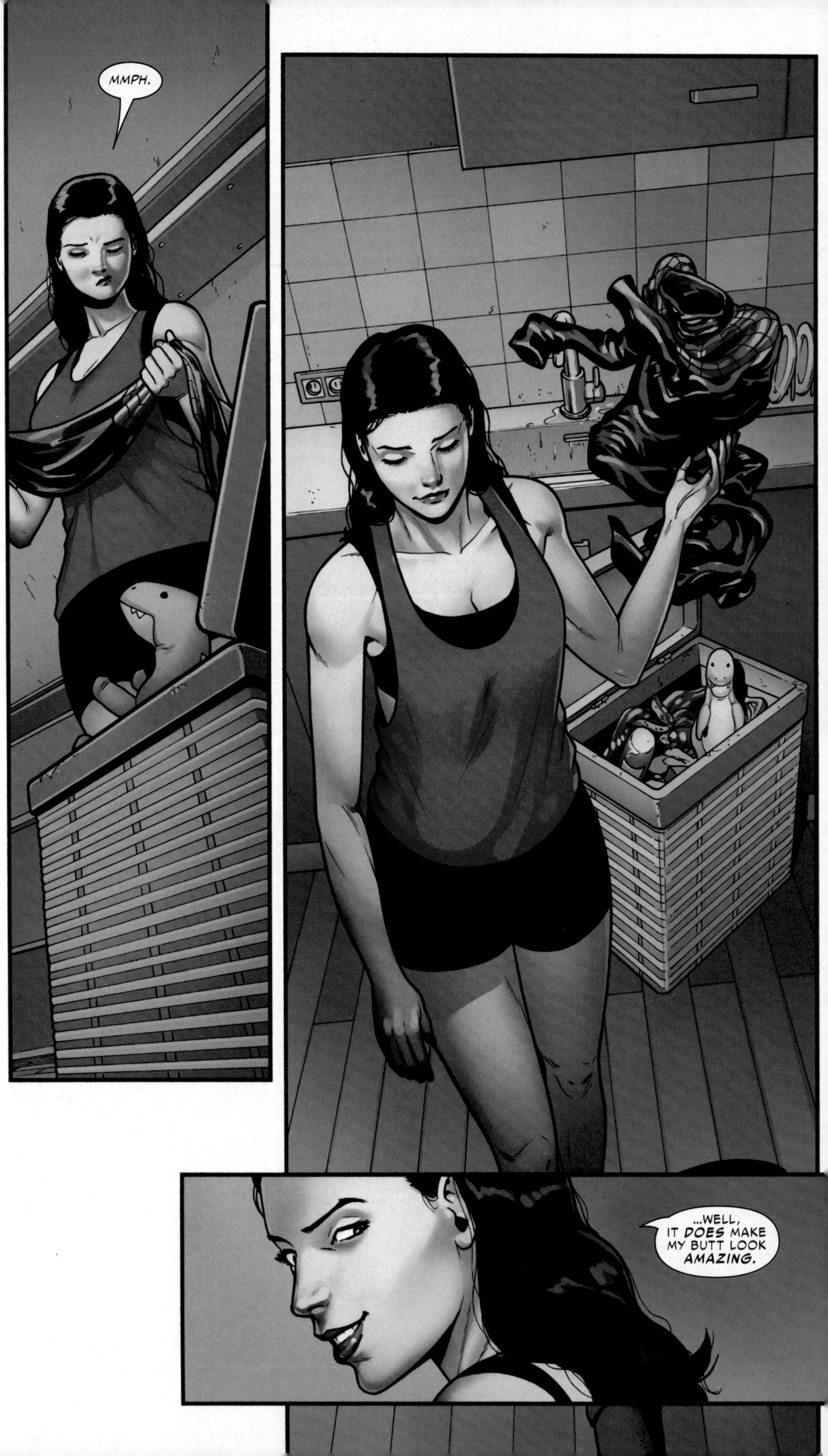
MMPH.
...WELL, IT DOES MAKE MY BUTT LOOK AMAZING.

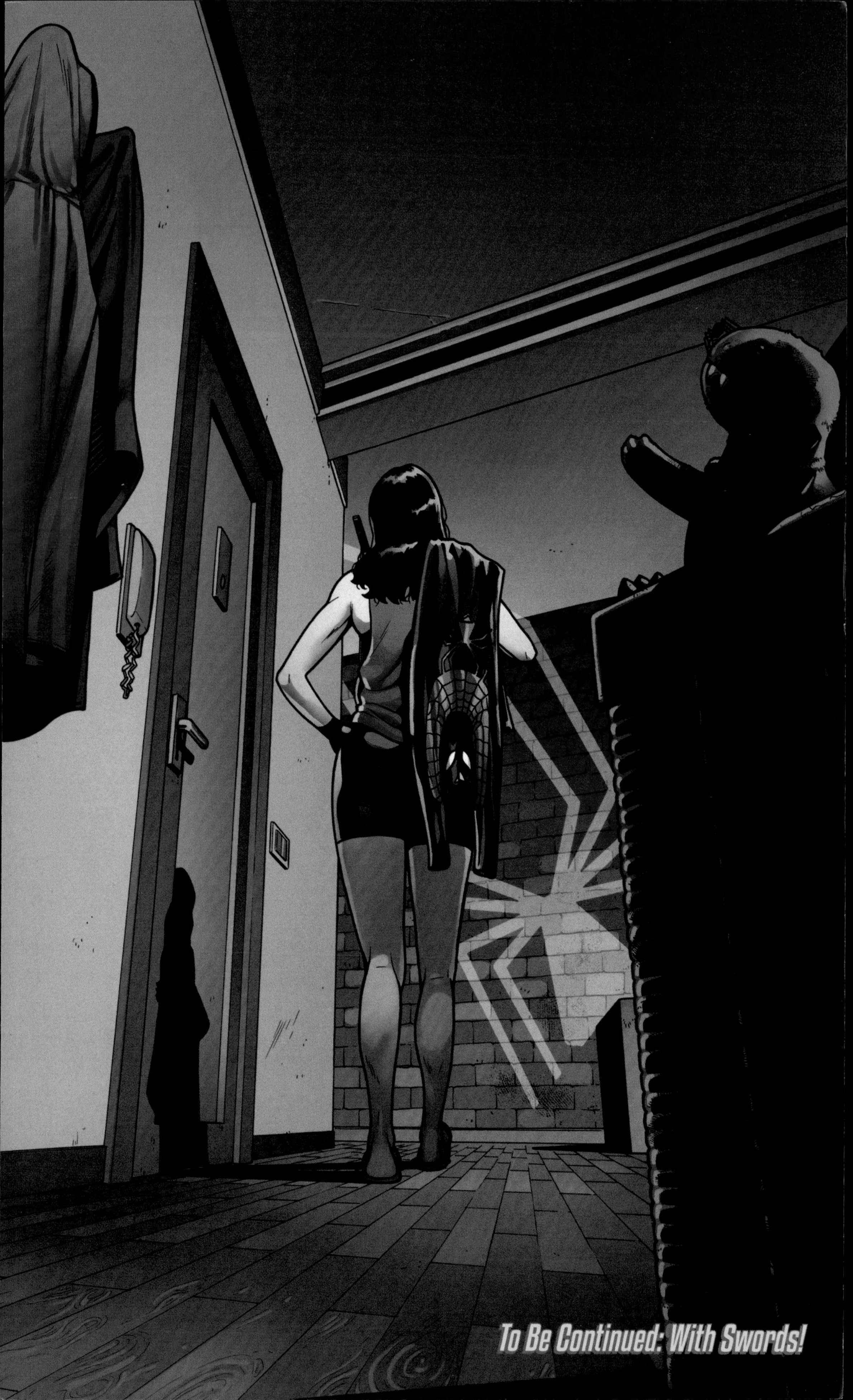
To Be Continued: With Swords!

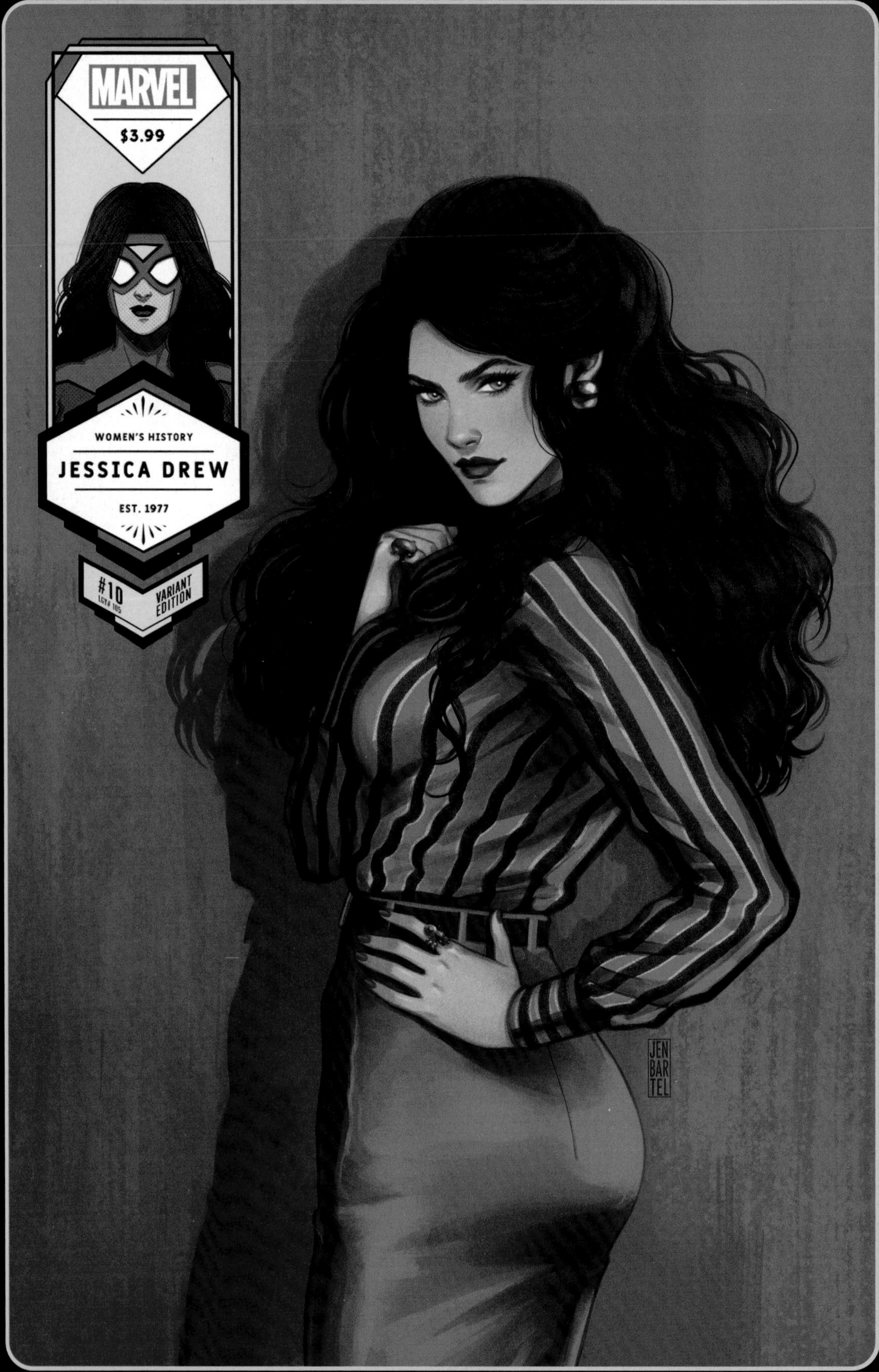
MARVEL
$3.99
WOMEN'S HISTORY
JESSICA DREW
EST. 1977
#10
LGY# 105
VARIANT EDITION
JEN BARTEL

#10 WOMEN'S HISTORY MONTH VARIANT BY
JEN BARTEL